DIGITAL STORYTELLING FOR BRANDS

BRIDGET TOMBLESON & KATHARINA WOLF

DIGITAL STORYTELLING FOR BRANDS

§ Sage

1 Oliver's Yard
55 City Road
London EC1Y 1SP

2455 Teller Road
Thousand Oaks, California 91320

Unit No 323-333, Third Floor, F-Block
International Trade Tower Nehru Place
New Delhi – 110 019

8 Marina View Suite 43-053
Asia Square Tower 1
Singapore 018960

Editor: Matthew Waters
Editorial Assistant: Charlotte Hanson
Production Editor: Gourav Kumar
Copyeditor: Tom Bedford
Proofreader: Sarah Cooke
Indexer: KnowledgeWorks Global Ltd
Marketing Manager: Lucia Sweet
Cover Design: Francis Kenney
Typeset by KnowledgeWorks Global Ltd
Printed in the UK

Library of Congress Control Number: 2022950963

British Library Cataloguing in Publication data

A catalogue record for this book is available from the British Library

ISBN 978-1-5297-4503-0
ISBN 978-1-5297-4502-3 (pbk)

At Sage we take sustainability seriously. Most of our products are printed in the UK using responsibly sourced papers and boards. When we print overseas we ensure sustainable papers are used as measured by the Paper Chain Project grading system. We undertake an annual audit to monitor our sustainability.

Contents

About the Authors

Bridget Tombleson is an academic at Curtin University, Perth, Western Australia with more than 20 years' experience in public relations and the communication industry. She has specialist experience in media relations, issues and crisis management, branding, strategy development and internal communications having worked across government, corporate and consultancy roles. Bridget has a Bachelor of Arts degree in English Literature and it is this undergraduate knowledge she blends with her postgraduate degrees in Business and Public Relations. She has unique knowledge of storytelling from an arts perspective, as well as applied knowledge of working with  organisational brands. She currently teaches transmedia and digital storytelling at Curtin University in the School of Management and Marketing and has been recognised with a number of teaching awards.

Katharina Wolf is an Associate Professor in the School of Management and Marketing at Curtin University in Perth, Western Australia, and Lead of the Faculty of Business and Law's Public Relations programme. Katharina draws on more than 20 years of communication and media experience, as an educator, researcher and industry professional. Her industry experience encompasses communication and research roles in Germany, Spain, the UK and Australia. Originally trained as a publishing manager,  combined with a lifelong passion for libraries and bookshops, Katharina has always been drawn to stories in all kinds of formats. Katharina is an avid explorer – literally and metaphorically – and passionate about student-centred, work-integrated learning; a commitment that has been recognised with a number of local, national and international awards.

Acknowledgements

The authors would like to acknowledge the publishing team at Sage for their patience and guidance on this book, and the students at Curtin University who have helped shape the ideas and research into this book.

INTRODUCTION

No single period or society can do without narratives. And, a good number of contemporary thinkers hasten to add, whatever you say and think about a certain time or place becomes a narrative in its own right. From the oldest myths and legends to postmodern fabulation, narration has always been central. Postmodern philosophers... also contend that everything amounts to a narrative, including the world and the self. If that is correct, then the study of narrative... unveils fundamental culture-specific opinions about reality and humankind, which are narrativized in stories and novels. (Herman and Vervaeck, 2005, p. 1)

Digital storytelling for brands has become a necessity in the 21st century, due to the need to connect and communicate with diverse audiences across multiple channels and platforms. Understanding narrative is a key skill needed by many communication, marketing and public relations students, as well as content creators and journalists. New forms of digital storytelling are changing the traditional narrative and provide a way for audiences to actively participate and create their own narrative. This book teaches essential skills in understanding and deconstructing traditional narratives and adapting them to fit modern platforms and digital communication channels. This book emphasises co-creative methods and provides learners with a strong theoretical underpinning of participatory culture and narrative theory. For the first time ever this book brings together extant arts-based communication models with business theory and discusses how digital storytelling impacts reputation and trust in brands. It provides readers with a clear understanding of the creative and persuasive power of narrative within a digital context, whilst building and positioning a brand. Contemporary case studies from a wide range of backgrounds and contexts are used to highlight best practice and challenges faced in the digital world, including implications for reputation management, challenges associated with mis- and disinformation and the crucial role of the collective narrative.

The premise of this book was motivated by observations by the authors that many business students were struggling with more creative concepts around storytelling, content creation and creative strategy. These business students, while knowledgeable about branding, marketing and public relations in a business context, did not have foundational knowledge of narrative construction, storytelling or cross-platform storytelling. The key aim of this book is to draw together both arts and business theories to form a cross-disciplinary understanding of digital storytelling – one that is applicable for both arts and business students, i.e. tomorrow's well-rounded communication professionals.

This book does not provide a step-by-step approach to digital storytelling – although it does give you the tools. Digital storytelling is not a cookie-cutter exercise; to remain authentic, stories must be creative, adaptive and relevant. In a similar way, this book does not provide an outline of how to manage each individual social media platform. Understanding the principles about why people share, what makes a story authentic, and how timeless narratives can be adapted to digital platforms is a far more important skill in building a lifelong understanding about storytelling – and will ensure you remain relevant despite platforms and algorithms changing. For this reason, we believe this book will remain relevant for many years to come and provide foundational knowledge that bridges business and the arts. A key principle guiding this book is: the more digital we become, the more we crave to feel human and it is this very space/particular need where digital storytelling has the ability to cut through the online noise and provide an authentic connection.

REFERENCES

Herman, L. and Vervaeck, B. (2005). *Handbook of Narrative Analysis*. Lincoln, NE: University of Nebraska Press.

1

NARRATIVE MODELS ACROSS THE AGES

OBJECTIVES

1. Understand how storytelling has been used across the ages
2. Define the concept of digital storytelling and its key elements
3. Introduction to branding theory, convergence culture and audience
4. Understand how marketing, strategic communication and public relations use storytelling to develop brands

This chapter sets the scene, illustrating how storytelling has evolved across the ages. It discusses ancient forms of storytelling, including the role of storytelling among First Nations peoples, prior to the printing press through to digital storytelling. The evolution highlights how technology has shaped narrative, culminating in the convergence culture we have today, observed across films, books, gaming, social media, financial systems and television. Understanding the importance of authenticity, relevancy and resonance in storytelling is key to getting audiences to connect with your story. Small stories create big stories, and when used well, can create a connection with your audience that is both emotional and powerful.

STORYTELLING ACROSS THE AGES

Storytelling is the social and cultural activity of explaining a series of events through narrative. Across time it has existed in many different forms – from visual storytelling in its earliest inception through to spoken, written and digital narrative. The act of storytelling can be conveyed in written or spoken words, sounds, body language and/or images (still and moving). Storytelling is, by design, a co-creative process as it requires a 'storyteller' and someone to 'listen'. Stories or narratives have historically been shared in many cultures, although in different forms. We know visual elements are powerful communication tools in their own right and have a unique ability to influence an audience. However, it is also the act of a narrative that is likely to be remembered more than numbers or facts, due to its ability to encourage the active imagination of the audience (National Storytelling Network, 2022).

The US-based National Storytelling Network (2022) defines five keys ways in which storytelling works to engage with the listener, or audience:

1. **Storytelling is interactive** – there is a 'teller' and 'listener/s'. Stories from the beginning have been a two-way interaction between the storyteller and the 'listeners' or audience. Importantly, audiences do not passively receive or consume stories; rather it is a collaborative process, emerging from the interaction between storyteller and audience. Similar to a game of Chinese whispers, intonation, nuance and cultural understanding can all change the meaning of a story, and this relies on both the teller of the story and the listener.
2. **Storytelling uses words (spoken or written) or images** – spoken or written, stories rely on words, although the shift to digital has seen a heavy reliance on visual content, which signifies a key shift in storytelling in the digital age.
3. **Storytelling uses actions** – vocalisation, physical movement or gesture; at the very basic level of storytelling 'something happens', and the listener or viewer needs to see this through action.
4. **Storytelling presents itself as a story** – humans are hardwired to understand storytelling. We intuitively know a story has a beginning, middle and an end. We also know when we are seeing a micro story (or part of a story), and want to know what happens next. This structure is recognised by all cultures. Different contexts may have their own way of presenting a 'story', but there are common threads all over the world.
5. **Storytelling encourages the active imagination of the listener** – stories rely heavily on storytelling/poetry techniques like metaphors, similes, rhyme, rhythm, repetition, sensory appeal, humour and many

more elements. Humans make sense of stories according to their experience, values and personal worldview and are able to 'picture' it in their minds. This is what makes stories so powerful, the personal engagement with the storyline.

In the digital age, storytelling has seen a resurgence, and represents a way to connect with people online. Understanding the basics of storytelling – from its inception – can help us to understand why humans are hardwired to seek out and want to listen to stories, and how they motivate and influence us to act in ways that can be both valuable and detrimental to the human race. Due to the increased use and prevalence of the internet, there's been a cultural resurgence of storytelling, and understanding the cultural phenomenon helps marketers and communicators become better storytellers for brands, businesses and non-government organisations. This book will discuss how storytelling has evolved from a narrator focus, to a two-way interaction model, and now a truly collective model, in which storytellers can speak to, listen to and engage with many voices at the same time.

First Nations peoples and the role of storytelling

In many cultures, stories are used to pass down traditions and to interpret events. Many cultures share stories as a means of entertainment, education, cultural pres-ervation and also of passing down morals, mores and laws. Australian First Nations culture is one of the oldest – if not the oldest – in the world and has long used storytelling as a way for children to understand the world around them (coun-try) as well as people, spirits and culture (Queensland Curriculum and Assessment Authority, 2018). Aboriginal Dreamtime stories, or creation stories, have been used to explain the history and culture of the land and have been shown to blend 'scientifically verifiable events' from the past, alongside moral tales and life les-sons (Museums Victoria, 2022). These stories have been passed from generation to generation, a practice that continues today. A unique element of Australian First Nations culture is the creation of songlines, also known as dreaming tracks, which can be described as a sacred narrative of creation, linking Aboriginal people to their origins. Songlines are Aboriginal walking routes, often stretching over hundreds if not thousands of kilometres, which cross the Australian continent, linking impor-tant cultural sites and geographical markers, including food sources, safe places to rest and cultural boundaries. Some songlines are believed to have been forged by the great Creator Spirits of the Dreaming and hence have ancestral stories attached to them (Deadly Story, 2022). Also referred to as a 'cultural passport', the path of each individual songline is recorded and recalled using song, stories, dance and art and represents a vital part of connecting Aboriginal people to their land. These songlines are represented and re-told in multiple ways, including in paintings and other artworks.

Oral storytelling by First Nations Australians is an 80,000-year-old oral tradition that is now becoming digital in this modern age (Bracken, 2021). A recent project has seen many of these stories translated into 'sleep stories' for anyone to access on podcast apps (see e.g.: www.dreamysleep.com.au/). Facilitated by new technologies, these stories, which would usually be passed down by elders, are now available for broader audiences to enjoy.

Before the printing press

Storytelling dates back to long before the invention of the printing press in the mid-15th century, to the use of stories by hunter-gatherer societies to relay social behaviours like marriage, food sharing, hunting and taboos (Smith et al., 2017). There is a long history of storytelling being used by the ruling classes to narrate public messages, which can be traced back to ancient Greece, Alexander the Great, the Roman Empire, and also the early Christians, who used storytelling as a way of gathering disciples. Prior to the Industrial Revolution, storytelling primarily conveyed the opinions of the elite (Mendoza, 2015). The oral tradition of town criers, mostly employed by councils, used storytelling and the techniques of argument, persuasion and emotion to engage people and motivate them to spread the word further.

The Victorian age

The invention of the printing press in the mid-15th century by Johannes Gutenberg was hailed as a revolution in communication, and also storytelling. The publication of the 'Gutenberg' bible in 1456 could be considered the first written act of storytelling the world had seen on a large scale (Giles, 1996).

Moving through to the 18th century, magazines started to appear in England and the serial – a reinvention of storytelling – started to appear, with Charles Dickens being the most famous author that used this particular technique in his *Pickwick Papers* (Patten, 2000). A serial is a larger narrative that is broken down into smaller parts. Its use, popularised by Dickens, has become an enduring method of storytelling, and one that has particular relevance in the digital space today. In the true sense of 'everything old is new again', the serial can be seen in podcasts, 'Netflix' style shows and even social media posts, whereby smaller narratives join to form a larger narrative.

The digital age

The terms 'traditional media' and 'new media' are tied up in the history and appreciation of how digital storytelling has evolved. In the last 40 years, these paradigms have shifted and storytelling is no longer purely about understanding the media (platform) alone, but also about how to be adept at translating information across platforms (both social media and traditional). Digital storytellers need an ability to 'think across media platforms' when producing content (Jenkins, 2010a). The biggest shift for marketers, communicators and digital storytelling professionals has been the shift from media that was predominantly focused on channels of mass communication (i.e. television, print and radio) and largely one-directional, to a personalised form of communication in the mode of social media that is

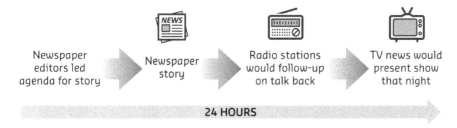

Figure 1.1 Old media cycle, Source: Curtin University/EdX, Reputation Management in a Digital World

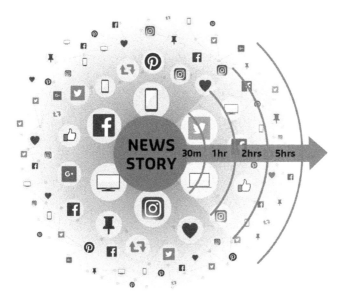

Figure 1.2 New media cycle, Source: Curtin University/EdX, Reputation Management in a Digital World

omni-directional and reliant on peer-to-peer engagement. This has shifted the focus of publishing from the elite few to anyone who has access to an internet connection and a computer or digital device. 'The media', once considered to be journalists, reporters, editors and producers, has now expanded to include bloggers, influencers and indeed anyone who shares or creates content. Challenges arise in that journalists, reporters and editors are governed by a code of ethics in most cases, while the latter group is largely free to publish what they want, even though some

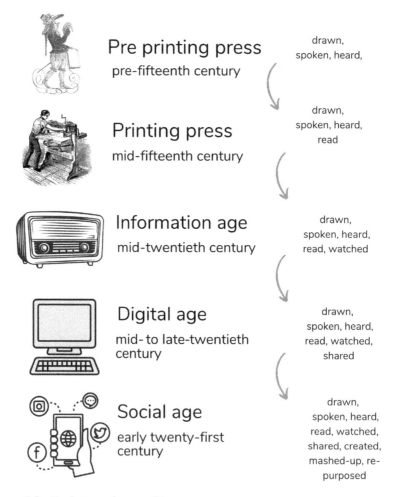

Figure 1.3   Evolution of storytelling

governments are trying to put further controls around online content. Everyone now has the potential to be a publisher and a producer and this has resulted in a power shift in voices, an amplification of minorities and the ability to reach – and engage with – targeted (niche) audiences.

The social age

Traditionally, a story is often considered to be a two-way process, involving both the teller and the listener playing an active role. However, in the digital age, stories have become multi-directional. As they are co-created, shared, re-made, mashed-up and added to, a collective narrative emerges that gives a story varying meaning in different contexts. The #BlackLivesMatter campaign, which we'll explore in this book, personifies this shift. The hashtag has been used in different contexts across the world, although the overarching narrative has a similar thread across continents. The social age has expanded how we tell stories. Historically storytelling started through drawing on rock walls. Now we have augmented reality and virtual worlds that can take us back to those rock walls and further expand the ancient art of storytelling through interactive images and voices.

CASE STUDY
Eva.Stories

www.instagram.com/eva.stories/

    Eva.Stories appeared on Instagram and Snapchat in 2019 and documented the life of 13 year old Eva Heyman during the 1944 German invasion of Hungary (Holmes, 2019), with the aim of teaching young people about genocide. It documented the Jewish girl's life as if she had a smartphone during the time, and quickly gained 1.1 million followers. True to the use of the Instagram platform, the story used hashtags, emojis and 'internet lingo' similar to that of a teenager in the 21st century (Holmes, 2019). The account has a minimal number of posts (images), and mostly used Instagram's stories feature to upload video in a storytelling manner that used actors in a diary storytelling film style. Similar to Charles Dickens' serials, the story was serialised and broken down into a number of moments that were gradually uploaded to watch and unfolded to tell the bigger story. A voice over in the 'voice of Eva' was used, alongside music reflecting the era/time. The first-person point of view was compelling in its use of emotion and sees Eva's experience spiral from the life of a carefree teenager, to being captured and taken to a concentration camp. The last few stories use a black screen with text to document her death. At the time,

Eva.Stories, or rather its use of contemporary social media effects, sparked controversy in Israel, attracting criticism and describing it as a display of bad taste (Holmes, 2019). However, the producers argued the digital representation of Eva's story was told in a way that made it accessible to a new, social media focused generation. The bite-sized story, and serial form of the digital narrative, was key to reaching that generation. It is an example of a traditional narrative form (serial) presented in a modern and compelling way on a new platform. The use of video, music and sound built an emotional connection with the audience and it was made relevant to a younger audience by speaking the language of the 'tribe' (for example, hashtags).

THE DIGITAL STORYTELLING ENVIRONMENT

Stories have a beginning, middle and an end. We know immediately when we are about to hear a story. Stories are not passively received; instead we create our own images and meanings based on our personal experience and beliefs. Stories have been shared as a means of entertainment, education, cultural preservation and to instil moral values. Across the ages, there have been consistent elements of storytelling, and in this section we'll discuss key considerations that make storytelling effective, irrespective of the platforms used.

Social media has arguably had a major impact on storytelling. Social media enhances the way experiences are shared and allows for greater, and easier, co-creation. Digital technologies are presenting communication and marketing professionals with a number of new challenges, as well as unique opportunities to apply those traditional skills in new ways, fostering deeper, more meaningful engagement.

The social media revolution and increased availability of peer-to-peer internet platforms have allowed storytelling to flourish at both a peer-to-peer, but also a multi-audience level. Relatively low entry cost and an increase in participatory culture (and hence stakeholder engagement) makes storytelling more accessible than traditional platforms (magazines, newspapers, television), and much easier to monitor engagement. Storytelling from a personal perspective became popular on the internet with the rise of the blogging community from 1999 through to its peak just prior to 2010 (Highfield, 2017). The emergence of YouTube (from 2005 through to 2013) and then social media saw many bloggers move to these platforms. The idea of the blog was adapted to vlogs and microblogging, spurred on by the rise of the influencer. As Highfield (2017) points out, blogging sat firmly in the participatory culture space and paved the way for the increase of user-generated content, with some blogs shifting into the public arena when they were published as opinion pieces in media outlets like the *Huffington Post* (Polgreen, 2018).

Both technology and social media have increased communication professionals' and marketers' ability to tell a story in an intimate and personal manner. Live streaming and the ability to interact in real time have changed models of stakeholder engagement and issues management (to name a few), as communication responses need to be authentic, less scripted and more thoughtful of environmental trends in order to be meaningful to audiences 'on the go'. In this book we discuss three key theories that have affected digital storytelling – convergence culture, participatory culture and transmedia storytelling. These theories will be discussed throughout the book, but first we need to understand what they mean.

Convergence culture

Media convergence is an ongoing process, occurring at various intersections of media technologies, industries, content and audiences. (Jenkins, 2001)

Jenkins (2006b) defines convergence culture as the bringing together of all media. A general definition of convergence culture is combining old and new media in a single creation, e.g. characters of the video game *Fortnite* hosting a music concert with fans (see https://techcrunch.com/2021/08/09/fortnite-ariana-grande-concert-metaverse/). There are different types of convergence and these include technological, economic, global, social and cultural (Jenkins, 2006b). Some examples may be (Jenkins, 2001):

- Technological convergence – Kindle (reading a book on a screen).
- Economic convergence – Google, who own search engines, advertising platforms, publishing tools, analytics, email systems etc.
- Global convergence – globalisation of media, across countries and cultural contexts.
- Social convergence – multi-tasking – i.e. working on an assignment, whilst simultaneously 'Facebooking' and listening to music.
- Cultural convergence – consumers or the audience can edit and create content, e.g. Wikipedia.

Participatory culture

Participatory culture is a culture where the community can create, share and express themselves through any media channel (Jenkins, 2006a). While participatory culture existed pre-internet, there's no doubt the rise of social media platforms has allowed participatory culture to thrive and grow.

A digital story doesn't serve its true purpose if audiences don't engage with it. In the digital world, storytelling is a multi-directional experience. A story should be developed with a target audience in mind, and in the online space it is important to give consideration as to how that audience may participate in and engage with the story. It is important to consider the attributes of your audience so that meaningful stories can be identified and developed and your audience is more likely to actively participate in the narrative. There are different levels of creating a participatory culture, from comments and likes, to re-shares, hashtag use, user-generated content and the building of online communities. The level of participatory culture built into a story may increase the value and longevity of the story. Stories resonate differently with different audiences, and as a result they'll engage in different ways. How to create an online participatory culture will be discussed further in this book, however Henry Jenkins identifies five key factors that are important in creating an environment in which your audience will engage. These are used as a framework in some of the case studies.

Participatory Culture

| Relatively low barriers to artistic expression and civic engagement | Strong support for creating and sharing one's creations with others | Informal mentorship / what is known by the most experienced is passed along to novices | Members believe that their contributions matter | Members feel some degree of social connection with one another / they care what other people think about what they have created |

Figure 1.4   Participatory culture, Source: Based on Jenkins (2006a)

Audiences as co-creators

Viewing stakeholders and audiences as co-creators of a brand's digital story will build a powerful participatory culture that has far-reaching benefits in terms of reputation management and brand growth. Co-creation also adds to a brand's authenticity and credibility gained by participation and word of mouth.

Today's audiences play various roles, including that of viewer, user, listener, player (gaming) and co-creator of content. Taking concepts from public relations scholars Hunt and Grunig (1994) and transmedia specialist Jenkins (2006a), there are three types of audience in a participatory culture context (see Figure 1.5).

Types of audiences

The 'passive' audience, who are spectators

The 'sharers', who are the ones who help the spreadability of the narrative

The 'prosumers', who don't limit themselves to just sharing, but also contribute to content development

Figure 1.5 Types of audiences

Transmedia storytelling

Transmedia storytelling, in its contemporary form, and as a theory, practice and communication approach, has evolved over the last 15 years. The term 'transmedia' dates back to Kinder (1993) who defined it as a way in which narrative and non-narrative media was communicated across multiple platforms. Jenkins further developed the term in 2006 and defined it as:

> a process where integral elements of a fiction get dispersed systematically across multiple delivery channels for the purpose of creating a unified and coordinated entertainment experience. Ideally, each medium makes its own unique contribution to the unfolding of the story. (Jenkins, 2006b, p. 944)

Jenkins (2010a) cites seven key elements to transmedia storytelling and these will be used as part of this book's framework on how to build a robust digital storytelling strategy. The term 'transmedia storytelling' has been used by many different scholars across multiple disciplines, but notably it is the transmedia specialist Jeff Gomez's (2022) version that has most relevance in the digital storytelling space.

Gomez took Jenkin's original definition and applied it in a communication and marketing context, stating:

> Transmedia storytelling is the process of conveying messages, themes or story lines to a mass audience through the artful and well-planned use of multiple media platforms. It is both a technique and philosophy of communications and brand extension that enriches and broadens the lifecycle of creative content. (Gomez, 2022)

Eleven elements of digital storytelling

Participatory culture and transmedia storytelling are important to gain a holistic understanding of the digital storytelling environment. At a micro level, there are 11 key elements to digital storytelling that can be used as a starting point to develop a digital story based on originally seven elements, as identified by the Centre for Digital Storytelling in Berkeley, California (Lambert, 2003; Storycenter, 2022), expanded by the University of Houston, and the authors to 11, to take digital elements into consideration.

1. **The overall purpose of the story.** Why now? Why this story? What do you hope to achieve?
2. **The narrator's point of view.** Who am I telling the story to? Who is the storyteller?
3. **Dramatic question.** What is the key question that will keep the audience's attention and be answered at the end?
4. **Choice of content and platform.** How does the platform change the style of content? (For example, Instagram stories are often from a first-person point of view.) What is the content?
5. **Clarity of voice.** Who is the voice? Is it the brand voice? Is it an employee or customer? Is it an influencer? Is it consistent? What is the tone?
6. **Pacing of the narrative.** Depending on the platform – Instagram, YouTube, Facebook, Tiktok and more – the pacing may change. Digital stories often work inverse to traditional narratives, with the hook first, then increasingly becoming shorter.
7. **Using audio and soundtrack.** For some audiences, music is a critical part of the language. If the story is in a podcast format, it's all about audio and soundtrack.
8. **Quality of images, video and multimedia.** Create a vision board of who you are trying to be. Glossy? Amateur? Comic? Crowdsourced?
9. **Economy of story detail.** Digital is short and dependent on the platform.
10. **Language.** Speak the language of the tribe, but maintain authenticity.
11. **Authenticity.** How authentic is the voice used? Does it have relevance and resonance?

Source: The above elements are based on the seven elements of digital storytelling (Lambert, 2003; Storycenter, 2022); University of Houston, 2015).

BRANDING THEORY, CONVERGENCE CULTURE AND THE AUDIENCE

Within marketing and communication disciplines, digital storytelling has been a part of brand building since organisations started designing logos. Storytelling has been a crucial part of many professionals' roles for years. Gill (2011, p. 19) states that 'storytelling is a natural, engaging and deeper form of communicating across a diverse audience (often characteristic of organisations) as stories allow listeners to tap into their own personal elements and reach the same conclusion as the desired conclusion of the narrator'.

There are many familiar communication theories that can be applied to how professionals have communicated over the last 50 years. However the internet, and indeed digital storytelling, have changed these entrenched models of communication which no longer fit the new digital space; so we must look to new models. Hutchins and Tindall (2019, p. iii) state 'the established model of one-way communication and message control no longer exists' and while this has been true for a while, even the two-way model of communication developed by Grunig (1992) did not take into account the participatory nature of the digital age and the level of engagement that would be possible with stakeholders and audiences. We now have a multi-directional model of communication with one that is often user generated and crowdsourced. Brands must now evolve and learn to let go of their desire to control the narrative, instead understanding fans, collective stories and how to harness multi-directional conversations, and noise. Hutchins and Tindall (2019) suggest that managing two-way communication has always been important to the communication industry, but 'the importance of community management has expanded on a global scale' (p. 4) and current communication and marketing theory and discourse needs to catch up with these changes.

Branding theory

A brand can be considered as a name, symbol, design or other feature that identifies a business, government or charity as distinct from other entities. The idea of modern branding came into existence during the Industrial Revolution (Roper and Parker, 2006). Branding is a form of identification and has become so powerful in its use of signs and symbols that it can represent the brand promise, as well as the corporation. It is also a way to differentiate your product or service from anyone else offering the same or even a similar item. An example of this is the brand Apple. The logo is now iconic and stands for innovation and simplicity as much as it represents the organisation, Apple. In much of the literature brands have become an asset for an organisation – they exist as a tangible measure of an organisation's value (Manrai, 1995). The brand is linked with a company's value (share price) and also its reputation.

Figure 1.6   Hat with Nike logo, Source: Canva

The brand icon is the visual representation that develops further into what is called a brand narrative. Big name brands like Nike and Apple have used a familiar narrative for many years to build trust with their audiences. Roper and Parker (2006) state that the idea of a brand narrative didn't really come into use until the 1970s with the development of mass produced products (and communication), as well as a growth in the service sector.

Brand narrative

A good brand narrative should have a coherent 'big idea', consistency across branding elements, a cumulative effect (the whole narrative is greater than individual parts) and a transmedia presence, which is responsive to users.

Narratives can be created internally and externally. Internal narratives are those created to target members of the organisation, in particular employees. These can be used to persuade, perpetuate tradition, motivate and inspire. Equally, the brand narrative can increase attraction and recruitment of talent, positioning an organisation as an employer – or even volunteer organisation – of choice, as validated by its existing staff.

With the rise of social media, internal storytelling has gained another important role as employees may act as ambassadors or detractors through social media channels. As humans we engage with individuals, not organisations. It is those personal interactions that shape our perception of an organisation and its brands.

External brand narratives are created with external stakeholders or audiences. With the development of digital technologies, organisations are now publishers and take a lead role in their own content creation, also referred to as 'owned media'.

Audience vs stakeholders

In the world of branding and digital storytelling stakeholders, or audiences, are key groups that will engage with the brand. The terminology around these groups is shifting, however, and as stories become co-created, we must look more broadly at who is engaging with the brand.

In the marketing and communication fields, and indeed business, the term stakeholder has been widely used. A stakeholder can be defined as groups or individuals affected by an organisation's objectives (Freeman, 1984). When developing digital storytelling strategies, stakeholders are important and need to be identified, however, the viral and participatory nature of the online world means they may not be the only groups that engage with your content. In the digital world, and indeed digital storytelling, individuals and groups that engage with your organisation may not be considered a stakeholder in the first place, hence we should recognise these groups as 'publics' or 'audiences'. For example, a group of people which you had not previously identified may call for a boycott of one of your products because it has not been ethically sourced. Likewise, an audience that you have not previously engaged with, or may not even be aware of, may accuse you and your organisation of 'woke' or 'cause washing', i.e. appropriating a contemporary social issue for the purpose of seeking a competitive advantage or marketing benefit, without a genuine interest or track record in the issue. International Women's Day is an example, and brands are increasingly being called out for posting supportive statements on the day, whilst not addressing gender gap issues during the rest of the year (see: www.theguardian.com/world/2020/mar/06/international-womens-day-risks-corporate-mothers-day-feminists-say).

The term 'public' was defined by Dewey as 'a group of people who face a similar problem, recognize the problem, and organize themselves to do something about it' (Rawlins, 2006, p. 3; see Dewey, 1927). While stakeholders and publics are common terms used in communication and public relations disciplines, the digital storytelling definition originates in academic film and television (and transmedia) studies where the terminology is more often 'audiences'. In the business realm, it's likely both stakeholders and audiences/publics would be identified.

In digital storytelling, while stakeholders are relevant, they do not represent the entire environment in which the digital story exists. The term audience is used more often for digital storytelling as it is broader in concept and encompasses people watching or listening to your story who may not be originally part of your target audience and indeed stakeholder mapping. This is important to understand because digital stories do not exist in silos, nor are they 'owned' by organisations. Audiences are listening to, engaging with and co-creating stories, often irrespective of who they were created by. Old communication paradigms, while still important, shouldn't be retro-fitted to the digital space. Instead, we need to visualise new theories that better fit this co-creative, organic and (if done well) authentic space.

CASE STUDY

Storytelling in marketing and public relations: How Burberry took a traditional brand and launched it into a digital space

Figure 1.7   Example of Burberry fashion, Source: Canva

In terms of an exemplary digital storytelling case study, the Burberry example is one that implemented a well researched and executed campaign that was focused on building a sustainable brand narrative. Although Burberry's transition towards digital storytelling started in 2011, the robust approach has seen this brand continue to develop its narrative, all based on the original storytelling approach. It's a testament to spending the time, energy and money to do it right from the beginning. The re-brand commenced with a traditional approach, with a book written to document Burberry's history. This traditional, linear narrative was an ideal platform for Burberry to launch into the digital space - taking a traditional narrative, and understanding the long history of the brand, allowed it to invert the branding approach and take it in a completely new direction.

Target audience: Millennial consumer

While it may appear as if the audience is a little limiting for Burberry, research highlights that Millennials are still the fastest growing consumer group with an expendable income. In the US, Millennials have surpassed Baby Boomers as the 'nation's largest living adult generation' (Fry, 2020). Millennials, also known as Generation Y, were born between 1981 and 1996. They have been increasing their purchasing power and financial security, which makes them a key audience for many luxury brands. Burberry stated their digital storytelling campaign entirely focused on the Millennial consumer. This was the first true 'digital generation' and Burberry was conscious that the campaign needed to have a digital focus (Future of Storytelling, 2013). Storytelling can be used by most brands, but for a fashion brand, it's an ideal platform, as what we wear tells a story about us, and is ultimately a part of our identity.

Watch the video on YouTube: Authentic Branding for a Global Audience: Angela Ahrendts, https://youtu.be/krQG2Hceov4 (Future of StoryTelling 2013).

Strategic approach

In the Future of Storytelling video Angela Ahrendts talks about how Burberry launched products 'digitally first', and thereby flipped the traditional marketing model on its head. Millennials did not need the physical events like fashion shows and formal launches that were so crucial to engaging with older generations, as it was the online space where they were most active and that allowed them to engage, share, repurpose and become a part of the overall brand story. Burberry launched everything online first. This was an extraordinary move at the time when most brands were still focusing on physical events.

Media content as a focus

Brands that understand digital storytelling expand their brand offering to include media-content creation as a part of their core business. While Burberry makes clothes and is considered a luxury fashion retailer, moving into the digital storytelling space also made them a content creator. This placed storytelling at the forefront of the brand and illustrates the link between brand and reputation. Digital storytelling is a strategy, not a technique. Chief Creative Officer Christopher Bailey emphasised this when he stated that 'Burberry is now as much a media-content company as we are a design company' (Indivik, 2011). Underpinning Burberry's success in storytelling was a deep understanding of their brand and history. While not all organisations will have the resources to research their history in such depth, Burberry used anthropologists to document the brand's history, resulting in a dedicated book.

Digital media

Overall the digital media Burberry used in the campaign included:

- YouTube (see: www.youtube.com/user/Burberry)
- Instagram (see: www.instagram.com/burberry/)
- Pinterest (see: www.pinterest.com.au/burberry/)
- RFID chips (mirrors in the physical retail outlets were multi-purposed as giant screens)
- Twitter (see: https://twitter.com/Burberry)

Using what Jenkins (2010a) describes as a 'world building' approach, Burberry aimed to build a Burberry world where the line between the physical and digital are blurred (Rose, 2015). Their approach went beyond a social media or digital strategy, as every element of the brand added a deeper sense to the luxury brand's story.

They also took on a leadership approach to using digital media, and in some cases innovative uses of platforms. As early as in 2012 Burberry organised a #tweetwalk design show. The fashion show appeared first on Twitter and hence customers from all over the world could view the new design range at the same time. This approach built on an already popular use of the platform as Burberry had previously run Twitter Takeovers, using prominent fashion editors to take over the account for question and answer segments (Indivik, 2011).

Music

Understanding the Millennial consumer group through their research, Burberry placed an important element on the music used in the digital space. To own it and make it a part of the brand, Burberry supported up-and-coming British musicians and launched a dedicated music series on YouTube called Burberry Acoustic. This music-focused element displays Burberry's understanding of the transmedia storytelling narrative beyond text and visuals, providing the consumer with an array of deep media as a way to engage and build brand trust. Simultaneously, Burberry modelled advocacy, supporting young and emerging musicians (mostly Millennials) - aligning themselves with the brand values of being British and youthful, and consequently building - as well as further strengthening - its reputation.

Longevity

Digital storytelling is a sustainable branding approach to building a long-term relationship with consumers. Burberry understood this and did not necessarily expect to see an increase in sales in the immediate quarter following the campaign. The building of a brand, and the community around that, is something a brand commits to, similar to building a reputation. Part of the success of the campaign was the longer-term approach and belief that this campaign would evolve and develop, much like the digital space it sits in.

The outcome

While Burberry's digital storytelling approach was unique at the time and certainly turned a traditional marketing approach on its head, the proof in determining the success of the digital pivot is shown by what they achieved.

For Burberry, the campaign improved the brand and brought it back to its British roots. In addition to this, it also developed the luxury narrative around the brand, and one that resonated with its core audience.

Key points in the Burberry storytelling approach included:

- Re-focusing their marketing from 'everyone' to one consumer group: Millennials.
- Re-focusing their product to a core (iconic) item: the trench coat.
- Understanding who their audience was: a shift from local UK buyers to overseas.
- Telling the Burberry story that was authentic to the brand, including its 'Britishness'.
- Focusing on platforms where Millennials were: social media.
- Digitally launching products first, further building and connecting with their core audience.
- Maintaining the digital storytelling approach over the years, evolving from short films about British musicians to Burberry Kisses, a short film story about the Tale of Thomas Burberry. This approach was consistent with the brand narrative of being British, exclusive and digital.

In terms of their reputation, this approach has paid off for Burberry with the brand now considered a 'leading digital luxury brand' and a leader in the immersive customer experience space (du Preez, 2020). Revenue is a trickier element to analyse as profits have fluctuated, especially as the impact of COVID-19 has affected many luxury brands. In terms of reputation, however, Burberry was successful in bringing back the 'luxury' and exclusive element to the brand and it continues to adapt to the market, maintaining relevance with each up-and-coming demographic.

CHAPTER SUMMARY

This chapter provides an overall understanding of some of the key terminology and elements surrounding digital storytelling. It sets up the broad level elements that need to be considered in the digital storytelling environment.

History

The history of storytelling is important to understand to see how time and culture have shaped how stories are being told. Storytelling is one of the oldest forms of communication and has existed in visual, spoken, written and digital forms.

It is a co-creative process that requires both a teller and listener. The National Storytelling Network (2022) defines five key ways storytelling is used to engage with the listener:

1. Storytelling is interactive between the 'teller' and 'listener/s'.
2. Storytelling uses words and is spoken or written; stories rely on words.
3. Storytelling uses actions and the listener or viewer needs to see this through action – vocalisation, physical movement or gesture.
4. Storytelling presents itself as a story and humans are hardwired to understand storytelling.
5. Storytelling encourages the active imagination of the listener and relies heavily on storytelling/poetry techniques like metaphors, similes, poetry, rhythm, repetition, sensory appeal, humour and many more.

The digital age has experienced a resurgence of the way in which stories are told with the rise of the serial, podcasts and short films. Co-creation elements mean that there are often many voices involved in a single story.

Key elements in digital storytelling

Convergence culture is a key element in digital storytelling as it brings together all media channels and platforms. Convergence culture has facilitated the formation of digital storytelling as we understand it today. It shapes and changes storytelling as technology becomes more embedded within each platform.

Participatory culture in the digital sense has emerged out of online communities since the introduction of the internet. Social media platforms encourage participatory culture – both positive and negative. This has changed the way audiences interact with brands.

Transmedia storytelling is a theory, practice and strategy to communication that defines how to tell a story across platforms to create a unified narrative. Transmedia storytelling allows for a deep and rich experience of a brand with each element contributing to a bigger narrative.

ELEVEN ELEMENTS OF DIGITAL STORYTELLING

At a micro level, there are 11 key elements to digital storytelling (originally 7 but expanded by the University of Houston and the authors for digital storytelling):

1. The overall purpose of the story.
2. The narrator's point of view.

3. Dramatic question.
4. Choice of content and platform.
5. Clarity of voice.
6. Pacing of the narrative.
7. Using audio and soundtrack.
8. Quality of images, video and multimedia.
9. Economy of story detail.
10. Language.
11. Authenticity.

Source: The above elements are based on the seven elements of digital storytelling (Storycenter, 2022; University of Houston, 2015).

Branding theory

Branding is a way to identify your service or product and differentiate it from others. A strong brand can protect the reputation of an organisation. It is both a tangible asset in terms of logos and design elements, and an abstract one in terms of value and reputation. Brand narrative extends the idea of what a brand is and creates a key idea around the brand in which all elements contribute to the broader narrative. Online platforms have encouraged brands to take on a content creator role in terms of digital content, as well as their core business, making digital storytelling for many organisations a necessity.

In the following chapters, we will take these concepts and continue to develop and expand them in the context of case studies and examples. These elements are critical to a solid understanding of digital storytelling and how it can be applied to brands.

DISCUSSION QUESTIONS

1. In your own words, define storytelling and transmedia storytelling.
2. Can you think of any good examples of brands using storytelling as part of their communication and marketing efforts? What makes these efforts stand out from others?
3. In groups, use the following reading and create an infographic on how each organisation used digital storytelling for their purpose. Choose one of the four case studies per group.
4. Investigate the types of digital stories you are aware of and create a list. Note down if there are different styles on different platforms.

READINGS

Allagui, I. and Breslow, H. (2016). Social media for public relations: Lessons from four effective cases. *Public Relations Review*, 42(1), 20–30.

This reading is useful to understand how four different brands use storytelling in different ways. Breaking students into groups in class and looking at different cases, students can compare and contrast their findings.

REFERENCES

Bracken, C. (2021). Sleep stories by First Nations storytellers to help you get snoozy. [online] *Triple j*. Available at: www.abc.net.au/triplej/programs/triplej-break-fast/dreamy-stories-first-nations-storytellers-help-you-get-to-sleep/13536842? [Accessed 18 October 2022].

Deadly Story (2022). Songlines. [online] *Deadlystory.com*. Available at: www.dead-lystory.com/page/culture/Life_Lore/Songlines [Accessed 18 October 2022].

Dewey, J. (1927). *The Public and Its Problems*. Athens, OH: Swallow.

du Preez, D. (2020). COVID-19 hits Burberry's profits, but digital channels continue to soar. [online] *diginomica*. Available at: https://diginomica.com/covid-19-hits-burberrys-profits-digital-channels-continue-soar [Accessed 19 October 2022].

Freeman, R.E. (1984). *Strategic Management: A Stakeholder Approach*. Cambridge: Cambridge University Press.

Fry, R. (2020). Millennials overtake Baby Boomers as America's largest generation. [online] *Pew Research Center*. Available at: www.pewresearch.org/fact-tank/2020/04/28/millennials-overtake-baby-boomers-as-americas-largest-generation/ [Accessed 19 October 2022].

Future of StoryTelling (2013). Authentic Branding for a Global Audience: Angela Ahrendts (Future of StoryTelling 2013). *YouTube*. Available at: www.youtube.com/watch?v=krQG2Hceov4 [Accessed 20 October 2022].

Giles, M. (1996). From Gutenberg to gigabytes: Scholarly communication in the age of cyberspace. *The Journal of Politics*, 58(3), 613–626.

Gill, R. (2011). Corporate storytelling as an effective internal public relations strategy. *International Business and Management*, 3(1), 17–25. doi:10.3968/j.ibm. 1923842820110301.107.

Gomez, J. (2022). Who we are. [online] *Starlight Runner*. Available at: https://starlight-runner.com/about [Accessed 19 October 2022].

Grunig, J.E. (1992). Excellence in public relations and communication management. Hillsdale, Nj: Lawrence Erlbaum.

Highfield, T. (2017). Histories of blogging. In: G. Goggin and M. McLelland (eds.), *The Routledge Companion to Global Internet Histories*. Abingdon: Routledge, pp. 331–342.

Holmes, O. (2019). Instagram Holocaust diary Eva.Stories sparks debate in Israel. [online] *The Guardian*. Available at: www.theguardian.com/world/2019/may/08/

instagram-holocaust-diary-evastories-sparks-debate-in-israel [Accessed 18 October 2022].

Hunt, T. and Grunig, J.E. (1994). *Public Relations Techniques*. Fort Worth, TX: Harcourt Brace College Publishers.

Hutchins, A. and Tindall, N.T.J. (2019). Public Relations and Participatory Culture: Fandom, Social Media and Community Engagement. London: Routledge.

Indivik, L. (2011). Burberry's evolving role as a media company. [online] *Mashable*. Available at: https://mashable.com/archive/burberry-media-fashion-company [Accessed 19 October 2022].

Jenkins, H. (2001). Convergence? I diverge. [online] *MIT Technology Review*. Available at: www.technologyreview.com/2001/06/01/235791/convergence-i-diverge/ [Accessed 19 October 2022].

Jenkins, H. (2006a). Confronting the challenges of participatory culture: Media education for the 21st century (part one). [online] *Henry Jenkins*. Available at: http://henryjenkins.org/blog/2006/10/confronting_the_challenges_of.html [Accessed 19 October 2022].

Jenkins, H. (2006b). *Convergence Culture*. New York: New York University Press.

Jenkins, H. (2010a). Transmedia education: The 7 principles revisited. [online] *Henry Jenkins*. Available at: http://henryjenkins.org/blog/2010/06/transmedia_education_the_7_pri.html [Accessed 19 October 2022].

Jenkins, H. (2010b). Transmedia storytelling and entertainment: An annotated syllabus. *Continuum*, 24(6), 943–958. www.tandfonline.com/doi/abs/10.1080/10304312.2010.510599.

Kinder, M. (1993). Playing with Power in Movies, Television, and Video Games: From Muppet Babies to Teenage Mutant Ninja Turtles. Berkeley, CA: University of California Press.

Manrai, A.K. (1995). Mathematical models of brand choice behavior. *European Journal of Operational Research*, 82(1), 1–17. doi:10.1016/0377-2217(94)00236-6.

Lambert, J. (2002). Digital Storytelling Cookbook. Berkeley, CA: Digital Diner Press.

Mendoza, M. (2015). Reporter. [online] Rit.edu. Available at: https://reporter.rit.edu/tech/evolution-storytelling.

Museums Victoria (2022). Creation stories. [online] *Museums Victoria*. Available at: https://museumsvictoria.com.au/bunjilaka/about-us/creation-stories/ [Accessed 18 October 2022].

National Storytelling Network (2022). What is storytelling? [online] *Storynet.org*. Available at: https://storynet.org/what-is-storytelling/ [Accessed 18 October 2022].

Patten, R. (2000). Dickens as serial author: A case of multiple identities. In: L. Brake, B. Bell and D. Finkelstein (eds.), *Nineteenth-Century Media and the Construction of Identities*. [online] London: Palgrave Macmillan. Available at: https://link.springer.com/chapter/10.1007/978-1-349-62885-8_10 [Accessed 18 October 2022].

Polgreen, L. (2018). Introducing HuffPost Opinion and HuffPost Personal. [online] *HuffPost UK*. Available at: www.huffpost.com/entry/huffpost-opinion-huffpost-personal_n_5a5f6a29e4b096ecfca98edb [Accessed 19 October 2022].

Queensland Curriculum and Assessment Authority (2018). Storytelling in Aboriginal and Torres Strait Islander cultures. [online] *Qcaa.qld.edu.au.* Available at: www. qcaa.qld.edu.au/about/k-12-policies/aboriginal-torres-strait-islander-perspectives/ resources/storytelling [Accessed 18 October 2022].

Rawlins, B. (2006). Prioritizing stakeholders for public relations. [online] *Institute for Public Relations.* Available at: www.instituteforpr.org/wp-content/uploads/2006_ Stakeholders_1.pdf [Accessed 18 October 2022].

Roper, S. and Parker, C. (2006). Evolution of branding theory and its relevance to the independent retail sector. *The Marketing Review,* 6(1), 55–71. doi:10.1362/146934706776861555.

Rose, F. (2015). Deep media. [online] *Deep Media.* Available at: www.deepmediaonline.com/deepmedia/2015/04/burberry-how-a-luxury-brand-turned-itself-around. html [Accessed 19 October 2022].

Smith, D., Schlaepfer, P., Major, K., Dyble, M., Page, A., Thompson, J., Chaudhary, N., Salali, G., Mace, R., Astete, L., Ngales, M., Vinicius, L. and Migliano, A. (2017). Cooperation and the evolution of hunter-gatherer storytelling. *Nature Communications,* 8(1), 1853.

Storycenter (2022). National Storytelling Network. [online] *Storycenter.* Available at: https://storynet.org [Accessed 19 October 2022].

University of Houston (2015). Educational Uses of Digital Storytelling. [online] University of Houston, Education. Available at: https://digitalstorytelling.coe. uh.edu/ [Accessed 2023].

2

SEMIOTICS IN A DIGITAL WORLD

OBJECTIVES

1. Understand signs, symbols and semiotics theory and key terms
2. Apply semiotics theory to visual storytelling
3. Understand how semiotics relates to telling a digital story
4. Identify the role of multimodal visual stories in content creation

Understanding semiotics can help shape digital stories and make them more powerful. This chapter looks at meanings of visual communication and how to construct meaning for different audiences. It considers how visual communication might be used for behaviour change or reinforcement campaigns and explores the key principles related to visual storytelling. The role of the visual in content branding is discussed, including how content marketing fits into the broader digital storytelling strategy.

THE LANGUAGE OF SEMIOTICS: SIGNS, SYMBOLS AND SEMIOTICS THEORY

Our world is a composite of signs that have literal and non-literal meanings, including street and warning signs, brands and emojis. Semiotics is the study of these signs and symbols and how we interpret them. The Italian philosopher, novelist and social commentator Umberto Eco underlined the importance of semiotics, as he believed 'everything can be taken as a sign' (Eco, 1976, p. 7). Semiotics is deeply tied up in the understanding of digital storytelling and how audiences understand visual images. The study of semiotics has existed since Hippocrates (460–377 BCE) and it is a theoretical study used to look at the production of meaning (Chandler, 2007). Key scholars of semiotics include Ferdinand de Saussure and Charles Sanders Peirce, who are considered the founders of the discipline (Chandler, 2007). de Saussure was a linguist and suggested semiotics as the study of signs in relation to society (O'Sullivan et al., 1994). His work is still relevant today, and is broad enough that it can be used in relation to internet culture, despite the science being devised more than 100 years prior to the emergence of the World Wide Web. Communicators can use semiotics to apply purposeful meaning to digital stories, but also to understand what meaning may be created by the audience. It's a critical part of digital storytelling where the visual takes on its own meaning independent of words, and at times, becomes more important and powerful than written communication. The visual nature of social media and video content has re-invigorated the use of semiotics and understanding of how digital stories can inspire, motivate and engage with the use of images.

According to the underlying theories of semiotics developed by de Saussure (de Saussure, Harris and Bloomsbury Publishing, 2016), there are three key elements in semiotics; the sign, and as a part of this, the signifier (the physical form) and the signified (its meaning or personal interpretation). In simple terms, semiotics is often known as 'the science of signs', and indeed the term 'sign' is important to understand the field. A 'sign' can refer to something that is used to communicate. In the world of digital storytelling this could be a meme, a video, a photo, text or an image. The signifier is the physical sign and can be understood as anything that gives meaning – i.e. words, letters, costume or dress, a facial expression, or the image style, choice and composition. The signified can be understood as how the signifier is interpreted, i.e. the personal interpretation of the sign. Chandler (2007) refers to the difference between the signifier and the signified as the difference between form and content. Both are needed to understand the sign in its full context. For example, you might see smoke rising in the distance (signifier) and automatically assume that there is fire (signified) – or indeed interpret this as a warning sign that it is time for you to leave the area and call for help.

Semiotics theory

Semiotics is considered in terms of value for its theoretical and practical application. Social semiotics is a framework within the study of semiotics and is used to make sense of cultural meanings. It's closely aligned to cultural studies and is often used as a fundamental theory by language, literature, film, television and communication students to make sense of novel and media texts. Social semiotics expands de Saussure's meaning of semiotics to understand how 'codes' are used as part of the communication process (Halliday, 1979). As codes are understood in relation to culture, language and other social systems this may alter the meaning of the code. This critical theory is relevant to digital storytelling whereby language and cultural understanding may change how a particular audience interprets and perceives an image or narrative. We've seen examples of cross-cultural campaigns that haven't taken into account different audiences' understandings of signs and symbols and hence have caused controversy and sometimes embarrassment.

For example, Tourism Australia came under scrutiny in 2006 when it launched an international tourism campaign with the tagline 'Where the bloody hell are you?' In an Australian context this is a commonly understood, colloquial expression, and not considered rude; however other cultural contexts did not hold the same view. The UK banned the advertisement based on the inclusion of a swear word, stating that it did not meet its advertising standards. In Canada the campaign was also banned due to a comment in the advertisement that mentioned 'we've poured you a beer', which is considered a form of 'unbranded alcohol consumption' and hence considered promotion of alcohol. Both countries are regarded as key markets for Australia's tourism industry. In addition the use of the word 'hell' was deemed to be an expletive (Wikipedia, 2022). In this particular case the signs in question are the words and the particular use of the language. A basic semiotic analysis of this advertisement would have indicated other cultures may find the language offensive. However, while it is true that the ad was banned in some countries, in the digital space there was much chatter about the promotional campaign. The attention drawn to the advertisement created a lot of media coverage, and indeed, free of charge airing of the advertisement. The campaign may be considered a failure by some, and perhaps a clever marketing strategy by others, depending on who you are seeking to target in the first place.

SO WHERE
THE BLOODY HELL
ARE YOU?

Figure 2.1 Headline similar to Tourism Australia's campaign, Where the bloody hell are you?

APPLYING SEMIOTICS TO VISUAL STORYTELLING

Understanding how audiences respond to visual and written content is a critical component of digital and visual storytelling. The ubiquitous nature of social media has resulted in the visual aspects of content being now at least as important as verbal or written communication.

Visual elements in storytelling form a part of identity construction in terms of corporate branding, but also personal branding. For the Millennial and Gen Z generations images and memes are a way of communicating and defining yourself. Participatory culture plays a key role in the popularity of memes, as the act of co-creation, collaboration and mashups allows the audience to be a part of a brand, and the process of communication.

To apply semiotics to digital storytelling we need to understand the four key modes of social semiotics, which are:

1. Representation
2. Interaction
3. Composition
4. Modality

These four modes were developed by Kress and van Leeuwen (2017). Their semiotic framework was originally designed to understand photography, which often uses a multimode approach to meaning. Multimodality is the understanding of semiotics beyond one channel. For example, where once semiotics was applied in a linguistic sense to a novel, convergence culture and mass media have resulted in communication including images, film, text and voice. This has given rise to multiple channels of meaning to be created. Kress and van Leeuwen (2017) call this a multimodal approach, thereby expanding the theoretical framework of the study of semiotics. Multimodality in semiotics pertains to the use of different modes (for example visual and language) to help the audience understand meaning. Digital storytelling, in its own form, is multimodal in nature. Both images and language are often used in digital stories, and copy; sound and the story itself may also be composed across different platforms.

Kress and van Leeuwen's four modes are relevant for digital storytelling, and in particular how storytelling is used on social media, due to the highly visual manner of communication. They are most relevant for analysing a digital storytelling approach – either in terms of planning, or understanding campaigns.

Representation

Representation refers to 'the ability of semiotic systems to represent objects and their relations in a world outside the representational system or in the semiotic systems of a culture' (Kress and van Leeuwen, 2017, p. 47). In a simple sense, this means a symbol or object is universal and widely recognised and understood. This comes back to the question of 'how is the subject being represented?' The universal 'danger' or 'warning' sign is an example of this.

Figure 2.2 Danger symbol, Source: Canva

In the digital context this can be how people are represented through their clothes, body language or the image background (anything that may show representation of something, for example a cityscape). Graffiti artist Shamsia Hassani uses representation in her artwork to portray women in Afghan society. See: www.shamsiahassani.net/

While the viewer may not have a background understanding about Afghanistan and the role of women in Afghan society, each artwork uses strong representation to give meaning that requires no use of words. In her images (see: www.shamsiahassani.net/prestige-exhibition) she often displays a woman alone or juxtaposed against a city. The use of the colour blue, often seen as calming, is another way to represent the woman, along with a thin veil across her face, which indicates her religion. The use of a keyboard or digital piano is often used and suggests she is protective of music, or the arts, in her country.

Interaction

No sign can exist without the meaning that the interpreter or audience attributes to it. Interaction is about the relationship between the image and the audience (the producer and the receiver of the sign). Within an image certain elements may change the interaction between the sign and the receiver, for example visual cues, eye contact, power relations (high camera angles), social distance (close up, distance), if the subject is looking at the camera and any photographic element that may change the way the viewer perceives the image (Durrani, 2020). The image in Figure 2.3 invites the viewer to look up at the light because the subject is looking up. The illumination of the subject's face invites the viewer to look first at their face, and also their feet and the light.

Figure 2.3   Person looking up at light, interaction, Photo by Javier Molina on Unsplash

Composition

Composition is a term often used in graphic design and seen in newspapers, magazines and webpages. It is the arrangement of graphic elements on a page. Depending on graphical layout choices, this can affect how the viewer interprets the image and can give particular focus to certain elements. It does not just pertain to graphic design however; a photographer can 'compose' a photo in a certain way that will change how the viewer interacts with the photo, e.g. where their eyes may be drawn first, encouraging certain assumptions prior to taking in other elements of the image. This affects how someone may process the information and hence is a key element in understanding how semiotics can change how we view a sign. In the digital age, flat lays are an example of composition.

Modality

Modality is a way in which information is presented to us as true and real (or indeed not true and real) (Chandler, 2007). In the age of social media this takes

Figure 2.4   Example of flat lay composition, Photo by Sincerely Media on Unsplash

on a particular meaning with regards to images in terms of colour saturation, differentiation, filters, black and white, hand drawn, digital graphics, cartoon or photography. The modality of an image or digital story can give credibility to the sign, in terms of authenticity. Social media has changed our idea of modality, however, as the prevalence of hundreds of images that present the same or very similar image, with the same filters and almost identical captions, takes away the authenticity and creates a sense of inauthenticity (see: www.boredpanda.com/instagram-identical-photos/).

The example in Figure 2.5 is an illuminated tent with a night sky. Prior to social media, this image would have been unique, but the prolific nature of handheld

Figure 2.5   Lit up tent in front of night sky, Photo by Sincerely Media on Unsplash

phones and digital cameras now makes the image almost a cliché. No doubt you can think of plenty of other examples.

MEMES

Memes have become so much a part of digital storytelling online they are now used by brands, governments and not for profits as a way to engage with (often) a younger audience. The Oxford English Dictionary defines a meme as a 'cultural element or behavioural trait whose transmission and consequent persistence in a population, although occurring by non-genetic means (esp. imitation), is considered as analogous to the inheritance of a gene' (Oxford English Dictionary, 2022). The term originated from evolutionary biologist Richard Dawkins and the 'word "meme" is an abbreviation, modelled upon the word "gene", of "mimeme", from the Ancient Greek μίμημα ("imitation, copy"; whence "mimetic" and "mimicry")' (Marino, 2015, p. 43). Milner's definition of a meme is perhaps the most relevant to internet culture, with a meme being described as an 'amateur media artefact, extensively remixed and recirculated by different participants on social media networks' (Milner, 2018, p. iii). Cannizzaro (2016) echoes this, stating new media artefacts have similar characteristics such as 'participation, self-organisation, free labour, amateur culture, networks and even virality' (p. 562). The particular focus on the participatory nature of memes is an important aspect of digital storytelling, and in this sense Kress and van Leeuwen's (2017) four modes of semiotics come into relevance when analysing memes.

Memes have become a legitimate mode of communication in their own right and have been used in the political campaign space (see e.g. the 2019 Australian Federal election, as discussed below). The visual elements of memes can distil very complex policy, portray nuance and provide audiences with an understanding of multi-faceted issues in a very short space of time. The terms relevance and resonance are important in relation to memes as they must be timely and they must relate to current affairs or social events. Some brands are starting to see the value of memes in addition to, or ahead of, advertising. Memes can portray a feeling and authenticity in a way advertising finds hard to replicate. In the luxury branding space, Gucci (see Gucci's TFW campaign: www.thedrum.com/news/2017/03/22/gucci-takes-dip-the-ever-dangerous-world-memes-promote-its-watches) used memes to promote its line of watches, using the hashtag #tfwgucci. Embracing key principles of participatory culture, this was considered a collaborative project that sits in the realm of user-generated content and invites the online community to be a part of the campaign's creative process. The move to memes by Gucci garnered a mixed response – some saw it as an attempt to be 'hip' and hence inauthentic, and yet many praised the move as a clever marketing ploy – aimed directly at Millennials

(Thompson, 2017). Regardless of the controversy, Gucci had people talking about their brand, and perhaps that was their only goal.

Memes for campaigns

While some brands embrace the participatory element, not all meme campaigns are user generated, although once a meme is 'public' the participatory nature of the campaign comes into effect. The Australian 2019 Federal Election saw the Liberal party use memes as a strategy and a coordinated way of reaching different demographics on Facebook (in particular). The average Facebook user does not spend a lot of time reading material (average 1.7 seconds per post), hence memes were considered the ideal way to convey an idea in a short space of time (Workman and Hutcheon, 2019). Content that was both relevant and resonated with the audience was key to gaining 'likes' and ensuring shares on the platform, in a bid for authenticity. Notably, campaign content was not slick, or designed via professional graphic programs, but consisted of memes that were developed for their ability to feed into popular culture, with the aim of being re-shared widely. Here, speed of distribution was prioritised ahead of proofreading and attention to detail.

Memes rely on cultural context and are very much reflective of any given particular moment in time. An example of a meme being used in different contexts is the image of Kabosu, a Shiba Inu dog, apparently engaged in some kind of internal monologue, deliberately written in a form of broken English. Also known as the Doge meme, it became widely popular in 2013 and was then used in the Dogecoin (cryptocurrency) logo in the same year.

Figure 2.6 Image of Dogecoin, Photo by Crystal Mapes on Unsplash

Often memes are used as a simple signifier to a bigger political issue or philosophical statement, and in this way they have an added layer of ideological power, as a person can communicate their identity through the sharing of certain memes. In the case of Dogecoin, an open-source cryptocurrency, the use of the meme was an ode to the satirical nature of the foundation of the cryptocurrency. Yet, despite relying on cultural context, a meme can also be used out of context, as shown by the Bernie Sanders meme used in Ikea advertising. See: www.thedrum.com/news/2021/01/25/ikea-muscles-the-bernie-sanders-meme-with-get-the-look-ad

Memes are not exclusively used for humorous reasons and can take on a serious meaning. In 2015 the South African Salvation Army tapped into an existing widespread online debate by effectively transforming the discussion over the colour of the dress a Scottish mother intended to wear to her daughter's wedding into a powerful domestic violence campaign. The photograph of 'The Dress' became a viral phenomenon, as audiences vocally disagreed on whether the depicted garment was coloured black and blue, or white and gold. The Salvation Army recognised the viral nature of the image, and the resulting memes, and developed a domestic violence awareness campaign featuring a version of the iconic dress, with the tagline 'Why is it so hard to see black and blue?', thereby showing the relevance and resonance of what was being discussed online at the time. Notably, the original dress was eventually confirmed to be coloured black and blue, to the dismay of the #whiteandgold 'camp'. See: www.salvationarmy.org/ihq/news/inf060315

Memes and semiotics

While memes have been around for a while, the study of memes from a semiotic perspective has been minimal. While they represent a certain cultural 'zeitgeist' in terms of internet culture, they also reflect power, and hence become a sign in their own right, and have their own relationship with the viewer and the real world (Marino, 2015). The Salvation Army tapped into this zeitgeist and contemporary debate, which required agility from the organisation, and were able to see their campaign featured across the globe, in media they did not have to pay for (earned media). More importantly, their fast-thinking action brought attention to domestic violence beyond their local efforts.

In using the principles of participatory culture (Jenkins, 2006) memes have low barriers to artistic expression and engagement as social media allows for ease of creation and sharing. They also facilitate co-creation and sharing with others. In the political space, this is where memes have become a way to distil more complex ideas and political narratives, and hence be easily digested into something that engages and can be easily understood – particularly by young generations. Understanding the nuance and terms like relevance and resonance allows us to see the cultural power in memes. They can sum up a feeling, emotion and affiliation in a way that is much more effective than traditional advertising (and much faster). They may oversimplify issues, however in an era of reduced attention spans they can have a major impact on political debate and voter opinion.

Authenticity and memes

The ability for memes to be shared and further adapted by any audience, at any time, adds to their authenticity, and hence more trust is placed in a meme than in traditional communication messages placed via conventional channels. In terms of modality, there are many different forms of the meme. They may 'entail an epistemic set of messages about truthfulness, authenticity, and ways of knowing' and also can be used for social or political purposes (Shifman, 2018, p. 173). Some memes have specific intent and are used by brands for campaigns, while others exist purely for entertainment reasons. However these categories are not mutually exclusive, with many brands utilising existing memes as a way to build on existing momentum and strengthen engagement with their audience, such as Gucci in our earlier example.

Some scholars argue it is authenticity, not truthfulness that drives social media engagement (Shifman, 2018). Indeed, the success of some campaigns point to the accuracy of this, as the ability to connect in an authentic manner is the driving force behind the campaign. For example #shotoniphone, a Cannes Lions Grand Prix-winning campaign by Apple and its dedicated agency that encouraged ordinary iPhone users to share their photos taken via the device, was consequently featured on big billboards and other paid media channels. The importance of authenticity within the context of memes is their ability to express an individual or brand's 'essence'. Official, slick and well-produced content is almost seen as inauthentic, as it has been crafted too carefully to represent reality. It looks staged. Digital storytelling audiences can be very forgiving if something is perceived as authentic, and yet it may not be professionally produced. Spelling errors, basic graphics and unfinished content are forgiven if the meme is relevant, humorous and resonates with its audience. This is a rather important shift in storytelling – the emotion of the viewer will overrule the effort that has gone into the production.

CASE STUDY:

Childish Gambino, 'This Is America', a semiotic analysis

Putting together the key elements in semiotics can help us understand how we can design an effective digital story. It also allows for the embedding of concepts, and an understanding of how they might work on a digital artefact that isn't a photograph, but instead a video. To illustrate this, we explore the four modes of semiotics and apply them to Childish Gambino's (Donald Glover's) music video, 'This Is America' which uses highly stylised imagery to represent African American culture (echoed by the lyrics).

Figure 2.7   Donald Glover, Childish Gambino, Source: Screenshot from YouTube – This Is America (Official Video)

'This Is America' came out in 2018 to highlight gun violence amongst African Americans and has relevance to the #BlackLivesMatter campaign as the song was later used on TikTok during the 2020 George Floyd / #BlackLivesMatter protests. The video embraces digital storytelling concepts such as the collective narrative (which we discuss in Chapter 4), relevance and resonance, as well as transmedia narratives.

A semiotic reading of this video breaks down the importance of imagery to convey culture, and context, which the audience is already familiar with through film, television and popular culture. Much of this context extends beyond the US. Throughout the video Glover uses exaggerated body movements, similar to African dancing, to symbolise his African American roots. Yates (2018) discusses Glover's deliberate use of the 'Jim Crow' pose, which is a reference to a minstrel character in the US in the 1800s. Usually played by a white man in blackface, the Crow pose is indicative of how non-African Americans viewed African-Americans; this representation is now considered racist and offensive. In terms of **representation**, the use of the Crow pose is instrumental in conveying that this is how some parts of America continue to view African Americans. The iconography is littered throughout the video, with many references to African American culture, including a gospel choir and gun violence.

Glover has filmed the video to ensure the viewer is aware they are watching a re-enactment of what they have already seen on television/film/internet and in music videos. This is a way of using both **composition** and **modality** in terms of semiotics. In this Brechtian style video the audience understands they are interacting from an aware voyeur perspective as Glover looks directly at the camera. He films each new scene by 'walking into it', almost as if the audience is watching a play. 'Breaking the fourth wall' is often used to ensure the audience doesn't remain passive and 'gets lost in the story'. It is this deliberate **modal** choice that captivates the viewer. This form of **interaction** highlights Glover's (producer of the sign) use of deliberately reminding the audience (receiver of the sign) they are watching a music video unfold. This production style immediately distances the audience, and hence lessens (to some extent) the impact of the brutal actions unfolding in the scenes. The entire video consists of a series of montages and they juxtapose against each other to build a bigger narrative.

The iconography in the 'This Is America' video is critical in understanding the video and also makes the message powerful. Semiotics is a useful framework to help build this impact and ensure the desired understanding with the audience. Tapping into elements of cultural relevance and resonance has given this video new significance within the context of the long-running #BlackLivesMatter campaign. The video now exists outside its original form and has been used in recent campaigns in another mode on TikTok. Much like the original #BlackLivesMatter hashtag, the music has become a part of co-creative efforts which in turn are re-shaping the song's meaning and lyrics.

VISUAL STORIES IN CONTENT MARKETING

There's a reason for the saying 'a picture is worth a thousand words'. Audiences pay attention to images over words and information may be easier to retain with the use of images, simply because a viewer's/reader's eye is drawn to an image more than it is drawn to text. There have been numerous eye tracking studies that have shown how people's eyes are drawn to images first (Beymer, Orton and Russell, 2007). Hence, visual content is now a major consideration for all brands. As this chapter has discussed, semiotics is a way to give the viewer visual cues so they understand what an image is trying to convey. In the last decade, technology has also allowed us to tell complex stories with the aid of data visualisation (see: www.abc.net.au/news/2022-06-29/census-australia-as-100-people/101181614), which allows the breaking down of complex numbers, presenting them in a digestible format.

As generations have adapted to social media, audiences' brains are changing how they view, consume and make sense of complex data. It has hence become a necessity to present information visually, as well as in written form. The online team working for Australia's national broadcaster, ABC Australia, are adapting to changing audience needs. Its internationally recognised Digital Story Innovations team is breaking down news stories, complex issues and big data sets into shorter, more visual content, whilst maintaining long-form journalism, so readers have an option to delve deeper into stories (see: www.abc.net.au/news/2021-09-17/wonnerup-minninup-massacre-the-ghosts-are-not-silent/100458938). The articles use a mix of images and video to add to the dynamic nature of the story.

Key elements in visual storytelling

As social media platforms become the dominant platform for digital stories, content must adapt in a way that engages the audience and forms a real connection. While the elements of semiotics are critical in developing a meaningful digital story, there are four key elements that will make a digital image powerful; these are:

1. Authenticity
2. Sensory
3. Archetype
4. Relevancy

These concepts, while not new in their own terms, have been highlighted by NewsCred and Getty Images (2022) as key in ensuring content is powerful and connects with the audience. The science behind storytelling in this sense is important as our brains are hardwired to want to 'listen' to stories. Furthermore, our bodies like to use all our senses (not just hearing) to understand and immerse ourselves in the story.

Authenticity

We've discussed authenticity in relation to memes, but it also holds importance in a visual sense. The rise of 'deep fakes' (images, videos and digital material that are highly produced to look real, but are not) (see e.g. www.abc.net.au/news/2021-06-24/tom-cruise-deepfake-chris-ume-security-washington-dc/100234772) leads to people seeking out more authenticity from brands. This comes back to the term 'resonate': an image must resonate with the audience, and in our hyper-connected, cynical world, the real and candid resonates with audiences, and in turn, the content holds more relevance. If we can recognise ourselves in a photo or sketch, we are much more likely to connect with that image. Authenticity, at its very core, strikes at the emotional heart of the viewer.

Creating authentic content for a brand comes back to what the brand represents and what it stands for. While digital storytelling and social media are important for many brands, it is important to know that digital storytelling doesn't always need to be brand led. In this context, the brand Apple is an interesting case that illustrates this point. As of November 2021, Apple's social media accounts looked as follows:

Facebook

Apple 13.5M+ Likes, 13.0M Followers; Apple TV 28.6M+ Likes, 28.7M Followers; App Store 14.1M+ Likes, 14.1M Followers; Apple Music 3.9M+ Likes, 4M+ Followers; Apple Books 100k+ Likes, 122k+ Followers; Apple Podcasts 31,300+ Likes, 38,900+ Followers

Twitter

@Apple 7.2M Followers; @AppleMusic 9.9M Followers; @AppleTV 1.3M Followers; @AppleBooks 679.4k Followers; @AppleArcade 79.8k Followers; @AppleNews 319.5k Followers; @ApplePodcasts 623.6k Followers

Instagram

@Apple 26.9M Followers; @applemusic 4.5M Followers; @appletv 2.6M Followers; @applebooks 368k Followers; @applefitnessplus 116k Followers; @AppleTVPlus 141k Followers; @AppleNews 105k Followers

YouTube

Apple 15.4M Subscribers; Apple Support 1.07M Subscribers; Apple TV 1M Subscribers

LinkedIn

Apple 15M+ Followers

A quick search across their brand-owned platforms illustrates limited corporate-driven social media engagement. On their Facebook page, updates consist purely of banners promoting new products. Their Instagram page features exclusively user-generated content that has been re-posted with credits. Apple is unusual in its approach, as it does not have a brand-led digital storytelling strategy. With 26.9 million followers on Instagram, Apple is proactively creating a participatory space where co-creation is not only encouraged, but a core part of the brand's 'passive' approach to digital storytelling. The participatory approach follows all of Jenkins' (2006) principles of participatory culture, as there is:

- a low barrier to artistic expression (it's easy to share and tag a photo or video taken on an Apple product – see #shotoniphone)
- strong support for creating and sharing creations (Apple is giving the ordinary user a chance to feature on their social media, and even on major billboards – see the award-winning #shotoniphone campaign)

- informal mentorship by the most experienced is passed along (Apple commissions videos and images created by its community to feature in major campaigns)
- a belief among members that their contributions matter (the user-generated model encourages this by creating engagement, further exaggerated by Apple sharing user-generated content via official channels and platforms, including paid advertising on e.g. billboards)
- a feeling among members of some degree of social connection (a sense of community is created through the use of hashtags).

This is a strategy in itself and one that is achievable for a brand that is considered one of the strongest in the world. Apple is known for innovation, simplicity and reliability. Their digital storytelling approach is consistent with this value set. User-generated content has a long history of being seen to be authentic and for many technology companies, see for example GoPro, it is a successful approach to ensure content remains relevant and authentic. In the case of #shotoniphone, Apple has successfully developed a sustainable campaign that has a life of its own. With more than 23.2 million posts, and climbing, this is a user-generated campaign that now costs Apple nothing, yet helps build and strengthen their community, by fostering fan engagement and a sense of belonging.

Sensory

While engaging the senses in imagery is not new, sensory visuals are experiencing popularity on social media with an explosion of autonomous sensory meridian response (ASMR) videos. In particular platforms like YouTube, Instagram and TikTok are where the hashtag #asmr has grown in popularity. It is the third most popular hashtag searched on YouTube (Hardwick, 2020) and often involves videos of whispering, touching, crisp sounds and delicate movements (Poerio, 2020) that cause a 'triggering' of calming emotions in the brain. The growth of this phenomenon has led to videos featuring hashtags like #strangelysatisfying and #oddlysatisfying, which accompany sensory images that seem to create satisfaction in the viewer watching. The trend has not gone unnoticed by brands. For example, McDonald's tapped into the trend for the creation of its Egg McMuffin (Watson, 2019). McDonald's advertising agency TBWA created looped animations to promote the Egg McMuffin in an animated form that focused on soothing ASMR principals. The campaign was aimed at Millennials and designed to be 'soothing and hypnotising' to watch (Ravenscroft, 2019). In true transmedia form this is where creation and the creative meets brand awareness and audience relevance and resonance.

Images can also be sensory and harness our 'known experience' to create a feeling similar to the one shown in the image in Figure 2.8. In the image, our mind fills in the sensation of milk running over a hand because most people have personally

Figure 2.8 Example of ASMR image, Photo by Ian Dooley on Unsplash

experienced the phenomenon with either milk, water or another cool liquid. In this way the image uses more than our sense of vision, as audiences inadvertently engage the feeling of touch. Creating sensory images may ensure a brand's image is more likely to be seen and recalled. Using trends like #strangelysatisfying, if relevant, could enhance and intensify the way in which audiences engage with the brand.

Archetype

An archetype can be defined as a collective conscious idea of a person or character that embodies a persona humans have (unconsciously) known for hundreds or thousands of years. Archetypes are defined and replicated in stories and folklore. The simplest known archetype is the understanding of a good vs evil character. Archetypes can be useful to help define brands as something we are all familiar with and easily recognise. An archetype facilitates the use of symbolism to relate to something, or someone. The concept, meaning original pattern in ancient Greek, was coined by the psychologist Carl Jung during the first half of the 20th century, when he identified 12 universal, mythic characters that reside within our collective consciousness. Hence, archetypes are types of personalities that we are all familiar with through the process of storytelling. The creator, the joker, the hero and the outlaw are just some examples of archetypes used in (digital) storytelling. Archetypes allow you to tell your story in a format that is familiar to most people, allowing them to connect with your content at a subconscious level (see: https://brandsbyovo.com/expertise/brand-archetypes/).

The sports brand Nike, for example, uses the hero archetype in much of their advertising. They have adapted and expanded their understanding of the hero across time and present a contemporary and often re-defining view of the hero. Nike's approach follows a well understood archetype – someone who leads the way, is strong and overcomes challenges – and yet breaks from the traditional model of the hero archetype (which is often considered to be a Caucasian male). This is seen in their advertising using both Colin Kaepernick and Serena Williams.

The reason that archetypes are still used today is that they connect with our unconscious brain, enabling audiences to understand an image (and what it represents) almost immediately. Brands like Nike are using archetypes in an innovative way, by not embracing outdated stereotypes, but instead empowering voices often less heard, thereby challenging, shaping and redefining our collective understanding of long-held roles and characters.

Relevancy

The 24 hour news cycle and the fast-paced nature of social media and trending hashtags have resulted in relevancy becoming critical in digital storytelling. Brands that tap into trending hashtags or viral memes can instantly gain recognition and engagement – if done well. At their core, the disciplines of marketing and public relations have traditionally recognised relevance as a key element of business success. If messages, products and services aren't relevant to their customers and audiences, they are unlikely to be used. However, the digital age has seen the meaning of relevancy shift, making it fluid, creative and, at times, unpredictable. Platforms like TikTok, Twitter and Instagram place relevancy firmly at the front of their algorithm strategies, by rewarding content that attracts engagement. Brands like Oreo understand the nuance of relevancy and have used it in a timely manner for campaigns that show both significance and resonance with their audience. An example of this is Oreo's 'You Can Still Dunk in the Dark' tweet that was posted on 4 February 2013, immediately after the power went out during the much televised Super Bowl event at the Mercedes-Benz Superdome in New Orleans. Oreo is an American brand, famous for its Oreo cookies, made up of two chocolate wafers with a sweet cream filling. The tweet essentially features just this: an image of the cookie, juxtaposed against a dark background, introduced by 'Power out? No problem', building on decades-long claims that the best way to eat and savour the taste of the iconic cookie is by 'dunking' – or dipping – it in a glass of milk. The tweet showed relevance as in one of the biggest games in America, without power, many people took to their phones and Twitter to see what was happening. At the time the tweet resulted in 13,600 retweets and 20,000 likes on Facebook. In addition Oreo's Twitter followers increased by 8,000 and its Instagram followers went from 2,000 to 36,000, with 16,000 photos uploaded from personal accounts immediately after the event (Yu, 2020). This type of response requires a social media team that is adaptive, agile and quick to respond to contemporary events and conversations. For the brand, it shows relevancy, which builds trust amongits followers, and also keeps the brand top of mind. As a product-based brand, this connection is particularly valuable for Oreo.

CHAPTER SUMMARY

This chapter builds on Chapter 1, exploring how semiotics and visual elements affect digital storytelling. Semiotics is the study of signs and symbols and how we interpret them. It provides a framework for how we make sense of cultural meanings. Using semiotics, visual storytellers can craft meaning and strengthen the depth of their storytelling.

The key elements of visual semiotics can offer a basic understanding of how to construct images that have purpose and meaning as part of a digital story. Kress and van Leeuwen (2017) developed four modes to understand photography which often uses a multimode approach to meaning. These are representation, interaction, composition and modality.

- **Representation** refers to 'the ability of semiotic systems to represent objects and their relations in a world outside the representational system or in the semiotic systems of a culture' (Kress and van Leeuwen, 2017, p. 47).
- **Interaction** is about the relationship between the image and the audience (producer and receiver of the sign).
- **Composition** is how an image (graphic design) or photo is composed. For example focusing on something in the foreground of a photo is placing this in focus and is a part of how the photo is composed.
- **Modality** is the way information is presented to us in a way that is true and real (or not true and real) (Chandler, 2007).

Memes have become an important part of digital storytelling and a key storytelling strategy for some brands. A meme is an 'amateur media artefact, extensively remixed and recirculated by different participants on social media networks' (Milner, 2018, p. iii). Memes represent a part of the quest for authenticity, by brands but also by audiences.

This chapter uses Childish Gambino's music video 'This Is America' to highlight how to apply semiotic constructs to a storytelling style video and why particular images and composition have been used.

As a part of why visual images are so important in digital storytelling, this chapter highlights the visual in terms of what makes a powerful image, including authenticity, sensory, archetype and relevancy.

DISCUSSION QUESTIONS

1. How has a platform like Instagram changed how audiences engage with brands, places and products? (See: www.boredpanda.com/instagram-identical-photos/). Can you think of and share other examples?
2. What are the implications of 'everything looking the same'? Consider this for audiences and for brands.
3. Find a set of images that represent a brand/organisation/campaign (given by your instructor) and use Pinterest to create a 'vision board'. This can be used as the first step in creating a digital story. Consider semiotic elements in the vision board and how the brand is using them. Create a version that is the brand 'now' and then create an 'aspirational' vision.

READINGS

Marino, G. (2015). Semiotics of spreadability: A systematic approach to internet memes and virality. Punctum. *International Journal of Semiotics*, 1(1), 43–66. doi:10.18680/hss.2015.0004.

This reading is useful to understand the prolific nature of memes and how they are being used to distil complex information in an image. It discusses memes from a semiotic perspective broadening the student's understanding of semiotics and its application in a modern context.

REFERENCES

Beymer, D., Orton, P.Z. and Russell, D.M. (2007). An eye tracking study of how pictures influence online reading. [online] *springerprofessional.de*. Available at: www.springerprofessional.de/en/an-eye-tracking-study-of-how-pictures-influence-online-reading/2873910 [Accessed 25 October 2022].

Cannizzaro, S. (2016). Internet memes as internet signs: A semiotic view of digital culture. *Sign Systems Studies*, 44(4), 562. doi:10.12697/sss.2016.44.4.05.

Chandler, D. (2007). *Semiotics: The Basics*. Abingdon: Routledge.

de Saussure, F., Harris, R. and Bloomsbury Publishing (2016). *Course in General Linguistics*. London: Bloomsbury.

Durrani, S. (2020). What makes an image worth a thousand words? Teaching strategic visual analysis and synthesis via semiotics. *Communication Teacher*, 35(2), 135–141. https://doi.org/10.1080/17404622.2020.1862269.

Eco, U. (1976). *A Theory of Semiotics*. Bloomington, IN: Indiana University Press.

Halliday, M.A.K. (1979). *Language as Social Semiotic*. London: Edward Arnold.

Hardwick, J. (2020). Top YouTube searches. [online] *SEO Blog by Ahrefs*. Available at: https://ahrefs.com/blog/top-youtube-searches/#top-youtube-searches-globally [Accessed 25 October 2022].

Jenkins, H. (2006). Confronting the challenges of participatory culture: Media education for the 21st century (part one). [online] *Henry Jenkins*. Available at: http://henryjenkins.org/blog/2006/10/confronting_the_challenges_of.html [Accessed 19 October 2022].

Kress, G.R. and Van Leeuwen, T. (2017). *Multimodal Discourse: The Modes and Media of Contemporary Communication*. London, Oxford, New York, New Delhi, Sydney: Bloomsbury Academic.

Marino, G. (2015). Semiotics of spreadability: A systematic approach to internet memes and virality. Punctum. *International Journal of Semiotics*, 1(1), 43–66. doi:10.18680/hss.2015.0004.

Milner, R.M. (2018). *The World Made Meme: Public Conversations and Participatory Media*. Cambridge, MA: The MIT Press.

NewsCred and Getty Images (2022). The power of visual storytelling – 4 principles from Newscred & Getty Images. [online] *visualstorytelling.newscred.com*. Available at: http://visualstorytelling.newscred.com/p/1 [Accessed 25 October 2022].

O'Sullivan, T., Hartley, J., Saunders, D., Montgomery, M. and Fiske, J. (1994). *Key Concepts in Communication and Cultural Studies*. London, New York: Routledge.

Oxford English Dictionary (2022). [online] Available at: www.oed.com/view/Entry/239909?redirectedFrom=meme#eid [Accessed 25 October 2022].

Poerio, G. (2020). ASMR: What we know so far about this unique brain phenomenon – and what we don't. [online] *The Conversation*. Available at: https://theconversation.com/asmr-what-we-know-so-far-about-this-unique-brain-phenomenon-and-what-we-dont-135106 [Accessed 25 October 2022].

Ravenscroft, T. (2019). TBWA creates 'soothing and hypnotising' animations of McDonald's Egg McMuffins. [online] *Dezeen*. Available at: www.dezeen.com/2019/09/13/egg-mcmuffin-mcdonalds-tbwa-animation-design/ [Accessed 25 October 2022].

Shifman, L. (2018). Testimonial rallies and the construction of memetic authenticity. *European Journal of Communication*, 33(2), 172–184. doi:10.1177/0267323118760320.

Thompson, R. (2017). Gucci posted a load of weird memes and the internet is cringing hard. [online] *Mashable*. Available at: https://mashable.com/article/gucci-meme-ad-campaign [Accessed 25 October 2022].

Watson, I. (2019). McDonald's finds oddly satisfying way to convey deconstructed McMuffin ingredients. [online] *The Drum*. Available at: www.thedrum.com/news/2019/09/09/mcdonalds-finds-oddly-satisfying-way-convey-deconstructed-mcmuffin-ingredients [Accessed 25 October 2022].

Wikipedia (2022). So where the bloody hell are you? [online] *Wikipedia*. Available at: https://en.wikipedia.org/wiki/So_where_the_bloody_hell_are_you? [Accessed 24 October 2022].

Workman, M. and Hutcheon, S. (2019). How the boomer meme-industrial complex helped shred Bill Shorten's campaign. [online] *ABC News*, 7 November. Available at: www.abc.net.au/news/2019-11-08/topham-guerins-boomer-meme-industrial-complex/11682116 [Accessed 25 October 2022].

Yates, C. (2018). Childish Gambino's 'This Is America' video is a beautiful nightmare. [online] *Andscape*. Available at: https://andscape.com/features/childish-gambinos-this-is-america-video-is-a-beautiful-nightmare/ [Accessed 25 October 2022].

Yu, K. (2020). 'Dunk in the Dark': A single tweet is all this brand needed to win the Big Game! [Fridays: Gorillas of Guerrilla Marketing]. [online] *Valens Research*. Available at: www.valens-research.com/dynamic-marketing-communique/dunk-in-the-dark-a-single-tweet-is-all-this-brand-needed-to-win-the-big-game-fridays-gorillas-of-guerrilla-marketing [Accessed 25 October 2022].

3

PARTICIPATORY CULTURE AND TRANSMEDIA STORYTELLING

OBJECTIVES

1. Understand the key elements of participatory culture, transmedia storytelling and why they are important in digital storytelling
2. Explore the role of audiences as co-creators of stories and brands
3. Recognise ways to foster a strong participatory culture

Digital storytelling relies heavily on participatory culture and transmedia storytelling. This chapter explores how the rise of social media platforms has increased audience involvement. The theory of participatory culture and its key elements are discussed, as well as the role of the audience and how to proactively build a digital community. The definition of transmedia storytelling is explored and further illustrated by two case studies, which look at ways in which digital storytelling can use transmedia strategies to build digital communities.

THE PARTICIPATORY LANDSCAPE FOR DIGITAL STORYTELLING

[We] need to become cultural curators, who are equipped to construct meaning from audiences, who have now become content creators in their own right, and encourage a true participatory environment that sees cultural values shared as an organic exchange, rather than a manufactured one. (Tombleson and Wolf, 2017, p. 15)

The online landscape must be understood in order to grasp how storytelling operates in the digital environment. The speed, scale and scope of the internet and the 24/7 news cycle have changed how information is shared and consumed, how messages are amplified, and given rise to viral content. Simultaneously, this presents a number of challenges, including the risk and increasing prevalence of mis- and disinformation. Participatory culture plays an enormous role in digital storytelling and also shapes how brands understand their audiences. Both the internet and social media have enabled audiences to perform a larger, more active part in brand development, in particular in relation to reputation and growth. Some brands (like the Australian brand BlackMilk Clothing, which is further explored as a case study in this chapter) have used the power of participatory culture to grow their brand, purely through the power of the fan. Building a strong participatory culture that supports a brand's objectives can have enormous benefits in terms of financial gain, but also reputation management. The concept as not only a theory, but also a framework, is intrinsically linked to the emergence of the internet. Understanding the process of how to build a strong participatory culture can set brands apart from their competitors and indeed other content creators, in terms of success and robust brand development.

THE MEDIA IN DIGITAL STORYTELLING

When discussing the term media, it is important to define what we mean by 'media'. Traditional media is a label for pre-internet media, used typically as a channel of mass communication – that is, newspapers, magazines, radio and television. This kind of media is still used today and continues to represent an important part of the brand marketing and communication mix.

New media (devices, software and platforms) is a term that has arisen post the arrival of the internet (around 1989). This includes parts of traditional, or established, media like films, images, music, spoken and written word and combines them with the interactive element of computers and technology. Essentially, new media represents a means of mass communication, using digital technologies enabled via the internet.

As participatory culture increased, so too did news outlets' use of – and in some cases reliance on – content creators. In 2014 the *Chicago Sun-Times* laid off their

Figure 3.1 Traditional media and new media, Source: Curtin University/EdX, Reputation Management in a Digital World

entire photography staff, shifting the focus to require news reporters to source their own images to accompany their stories (DPReview, 2013). This led to a basic form of citizen journalism, whereby members of the public supplied images and video to the news outlets – a practice that is now commonplace.

Society has shifted from a model where information was created and owned by a small number of people and distributed to audiences, to one where individuals seek out information on demand. The traditional push model of marketing was predominantly led by advertising and used persuasive methods to motivate customers to purchase a particular product or service. Today, we see consumers wanting choice – in how they engage, how they buy and how they curate the brands they love. This is a fundamental shift in how information and communication is obtained and consumed. As a result, brands have less control over how information is presented. There are advantages and disadvantages in the way new technology is taking away control from traditional media companies and organisations. In addition, because audiences can consume content any time they want, they will seek out the content they find most engaging. If brands aren't supplying information in the desired formats and style, audiences will simply seek out alternative content.

Understanding the 24/7 media cycle and digital storytelling's participatory environment allows communicators and marketers to build better content that is more likely to be engaged with and shared. It is important to note that moments of

Figure 3.2 Push vs pull media, Source: Curtin University/EdX, Reputation Management in a Digital World

connection build a community with your audience – not the platforms. Platforms are a means to an end. They enable the connection, but essentially content is key – and it is the connection with a brand, individual or organisational, that makes people stay, or more importantly, come back again.

THE PESO MODEL

Participatory culture is an important part of digital storytelling. Given the increase in audience participation, there has been a shift in basic principles of the traditional owned, earned and shared media model. In a participatory environment, no single person or entity owns the content. This represents a major shift for many organisations and businesses who have traditionally been accustomed to at least some level of control over what is being communicated about them, and their associated brands.

The PESO model, as defined in Figure 3.3, has long been used by marketers and communicators to differentiate between different forms of media. It offers a way to define how media is produced, owned and distributed and provides a useful framework for brands to break down their communication 'assets' and measure their effectiveness in terms of reputation and brand development. A breakdown is as follows:

- **Paid media:** Media that involves payment for distribution of owned creative concepts or content (for example advertisements, paid influencer content, sponsored social media content).
- **Earned media:** Media that is published on its own merit or 'newsworthiness' as a result of proactive outreach, without any payment (for example a media/ press release provides the basis for editorial content in a newspaper, or a blogger writes about a destination or trip he/she has been invited on. This has traditionally been the domain of public relations).
- **Owned media:** Brand or organisational media that is controlled by the organisation (for example electronic direct mail, an organisation's website, Facebook page or blog)
- **Shared media:** An unprompted conversation about a product, brand, organisation or related experience, shared in a public or social space and not explicitly prompted (for example an Instagram or Twitter post, sharing a service experience or detailing the usefulness of a product that was NOT provided (free of charge) by the organisation nor is linked to some kind of incentive programme.

The PESO model is useful for brands to define their assets and divide their resources between particular content and platforms. While the model still has

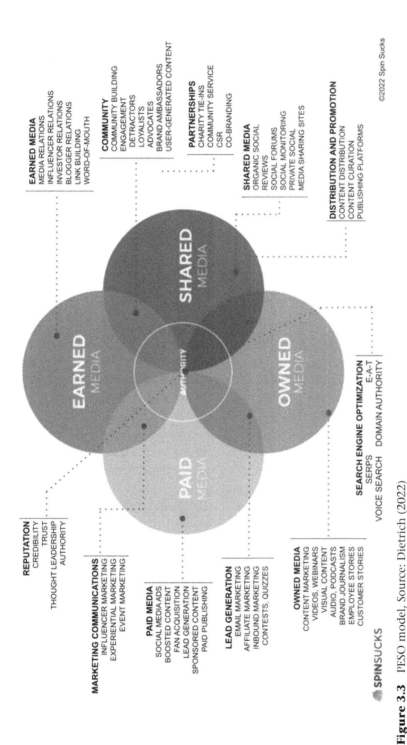

Figure 3.3 PESO model, Source: Dietrich (2022)

Printed with permission of Spin Sucks under Creative Commons

relevance from a theoretical perspective, a Global Communications Report by the USC Annenberg Center for Public Relations (2019) showed that the channels are becoming more and more enmeshed – something that has been reflected in the evolution of the PESO model itself. Consequently, many communication professionals predict that consumers will soon no longer be able to distinguish between paid, earned, owned or shared content. This has implications for professions that focus on 'earned' media (i.e. public relations), but also for all organisations in terms of the value placed on different channels. It further gives rise to the impact of mis- and disinformation on reputation, which will be further explored in Chapter 11.

The digital landscape is endlessly evolving, new platforms and tools are continuously emerging and technology changes the use of participatory tools. The interactive nature of participatory tools is increasing as artificial intelligence, virtual reality and augmented reality become more widely available. These are key growth areas for marketers and communicators, who need to continually develop their skills in these areas.

PARTICIPATORY CULTURE

As mentioned in Chapter 1, participatory culture is a culture with relatively low barriers, where the community can create, share and express itself through any media channels (Jenkins, 2006). Scholar Henry Jenkins has shaped the thinking in how participatory culture shapes influence and communication across different areas of society, including media, activism, fan culture and film and television, to name a few. Jenkins defines participatory culture as 'a world in which anyone can create and share media and anyone can have an opinion and reuse organisational material' (2013). In his video on Edutopia, Henry Jenkins (2013) states that participatory culture can be traced back to the middle of the 19th century through the introduction of the Amateur Press Association in the US, which gave way to locally produced printed material that was created for the purpose of sharing ideas. In digital storytelling, participatory culture is a key element of understanding why stories resonate, how they are shared and why people engage with content. Understanding the key elements may mean a digital story is more likely to be relevant to your audience and encourage people to share your content.

YouTube

One of the first digital channels that harnessed participatory culture in its truest sense was YouTube. YouTube was founded in 2005 and provided a way for people to share videos. While YouTube has evolved into a platform that pays and rewards content creators, it started out as a sharing platform. It wasn't until 2006 that YouTube moved from its key focus of sharing videos to a 'broadcast yourself' model.

Prior to social media (e.g. Facebook), YouTube was one of the few channels content creators could post videos of themselves doing activities *they* wanted to share.

Casey Neistat was just one content creator on the platform who created a brand for himself and became a fulltime YouTube content creator, earning millions in the process. His 2011 video entitled 'Bike Lanes' was listed as *Time Magazine*'s 8th Top 10 Creative Video of 2011. If we view the video through the lens of today's standards, it may appear to be poorly made with handheld shaky footage, simple editing and garish red and yellow text over the top of images and amateur audio (most likely produced through a handheld phone). Despite this, the video has amassed 29 million views as of December 2022, with more than 30,000 comments. Neistat's video was successful because it used storytelling, humour and irony to highlight the very real issue of obstructions in bike lanes in New York. Bicycle advocacy groups all around the world have issued media releases and lobbied politicians to get media coverage on similar issues, and yet this video went viral (around the world) and resulted in global media coverage in *The Guardian*, *The New York Times*, the *BBC* and many radio stations. Notably, Neistat was a filmmaker prior to this video, but it was this video that launched his career as he tapped into the participatory element of the YouTube platform and was able to create content that resonated with his audience on an issue that was relevant and authentic. More importantly, beyond the entertainment factor, the video brought about a policy change in relation to obstructions in bike lanes in New York. Digital storytelling has the power to be shared, gain momentum and have political ramifications. It can be powerful, and as Neistat pointed out, this video cost him $30 to make. This highlights that bigger budgets don't guarantee that something will go viral; instead, relevance and resonance will. The video also heralded the rise of YouTube as a powerful participatory platform with media power akin to well-known news outlets.

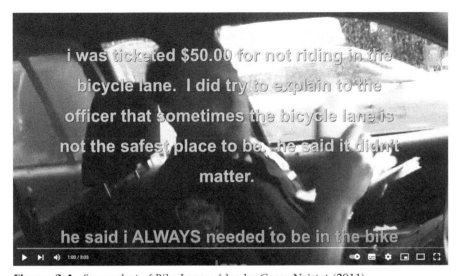

Figure 3.4 Screenshot of Bike Lanes video by Casey Neistat (2011)

Jenkins' five key elements of participatory culture in action

In Chapter 1 we discussed the five key elements that are needed to create a strong participatory culture (Jenkins, 2006). As a refresher, these are:

• There must be low barriers of entry for the community for engagement and artistic expression.
• There must be a strong culture for creation and sharing.
• There should be informal mentorship, so experience is passed on.
• Members should believe their contributions matter.
• Members should feel a social connection with each other.

The elements can be used in isolation or in conjunction to strengthen a brand. A community built from participatory culture may be online or offline, or both, but a strategic approach is required to build these communities. While traditional (linear) storytelling is powerful, in the digital world, it does not deliver a deep enough narrative to meet the audience's needs and to develop communities – not to mention to keep them engaged. Rather than just communicating with audiences, participatory culture may deliver a richer and more effective brand experience for customers. Enabling your audience to become a part of your story (and tell your story) facilitates a more powerful experience that is fully immersive and participatory – and keeps it engaged over time.

CASE STUDY
Australia's BlackMilk Clothing

To highlight how a brand has used participatory culture, and the tools that can encourage participatory elements, we are going to analyse the Australian clothing brand BlackMilk. BlackMilk was founded by James Lillis in 2009. As of mid-2022 the brand has more than 700,000 followers on Facebook and 1.1 million on Instagram. It differentiates itself from more traditional brands by not using any direct advertising. Instead, BlackMilk Clothing has relied solely on social media campaigns to build their following. In addition to this, BlackMilk Clothing has focused heavily on building a community of fans, engaging with them (across the years) on Facebook, Instagram, Pinterest, Twitter, YouTube, Vimeo, Google+, Myspace, Snapchat, Tumblr, TikTok and Vine. Although no money was spent on advertising, BlackMilk Clothing has spent money on marketing through its professional website, copywriting, photography and presence at events. The company has encouraged and proactively built a participatory culture and today has more than 80 private Facebook groups in different geographical locations. These groups often lead to physical catch-up events (often led by the fans) and a local hashtag #blackmilksharkie. The business was built on word of mouth, authenticity, storytelling and accessibility. The infographic in Figure 3.5 highlights how BlackMilk has used the five elements of participatory culture.

While BlackMilk Clothing is a successful brand, it has also faced challenges when it did not stand by some of the key elements of participatory culture that it founded its business on. In 2014 the brand posted what was intended to be a 'fun' May the Fourth (Star Wars 'May the Force') meme on its Facebook page. Some followers thought it was critical

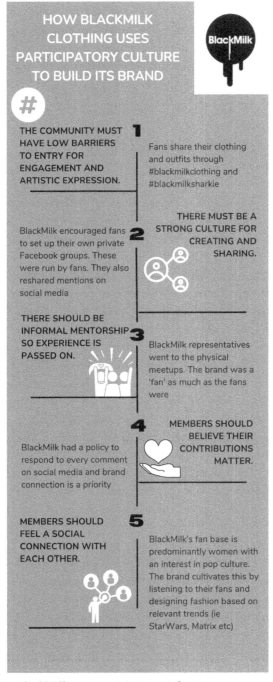

HOW BLACKMILK CLOTHING USES PARTICIPATORY CULTURE TO BUILD ITS BRAND

BlackMilk

#

1 THE COMMUNITY MUST HAVE LOW BARRIERS TO ENTRY FOR ENGAGEMENT AND ARTISTIC EXPRESSION.

Fans share their clothing and outfits through #blackmilkclothing and #blackmilksharkie

2 THERE MUST BE A STRONG CULTURE FOR CREATING AND SHARING.

BlackMilk encouraged fans to set up their own private Facebook groups. These were run by fans. They also reshared mentions on social media

3 THERE SHOULD BE INFORMAL MENTORSHIP SO EXPERIENCE IS PASSED ON.

BlackMilk representatives went to the physical meetups. The brand was a 'fan' as much as the fans were

4 MEMBERS SHOULD BELIEVE THEIR CONTRIBUTIONS MATTER.

BlackMilk had a policy to respond to every comment on social media and brand connection is a priority

5 MEMBERS SHOULD FEEL A SOCIAL CONNECTION WITH EACH OTHER.

BlackMilk's fan base is predominantly women with an interest in pop culture. The brand cultivates this by listening to their fans and designing fashion based on relevant trends (ie StarWars, Matrix etc)

Figure 3.5   How BlackMilk uses participatory culture

of women's bodies (Do, 2014). Despite the controversial nature of the meme, the real issue was the brand's social media response when they defended the post, deleted comments and blocked fans. When you have a strong fan community, dismissing, or blocking them, is not best practice particularly when the brand uses social media so heavily for brand growth and sales. It was a learning point for BlackMilk who re-assessed their social media policy as a result. Had BlackMilk acknowledged the concerns and apologised, the meme would have been a minor issue. Brands can make mistakes; as long as they are perceived to be honest and transparent about how they have learned from these, fan communities tend to be more forgiving, especially when they are as strong as in the case of BlackMilk Clothing.

AUDIENCE AND FAN THEORY

Audiences and fans form a critical part of digital storytelling. For some brands, they are crucial for keeping the story alive. If the definition of a fan is an enthusiastic devotee, then how do we define a fan as opposed to a stakeholder? A supportive stakeholder can be considered a fan and previously in communication fields the term 'advocate' has been used as a label. The term fan is a distinctive transmedia narrative term but can be interchanged with advocate. Transmedia and social media have changed the traditional model of stakeholder communication and 'the emergence of supportive audiences represents a significant shift from the types of stakeholder publics identified in existing public relations and relevant literature' (Dodd and Kinnally, 2015, p. 1). Previous stakeholder models in communication haven't considered the importance of the fan, or highlighted the significant role they can play in contrast to less involved and passionate stakeholders, particularly in the realm of co-creation and influencers. Undoubtedly, there is further development needed in this area. Dodd and Kinnally (2015) take on the idea of 'supportive stakeholders' in an attempt to define stakeholders in the role of the 'fan'.

We introduced the idea of the audience as co-creators in Chapter 1. Fans and storytelling are intertwined as audiences consume content, if they are interested in it. However, to motivate them to create content and distribute your messages, you need to have established an emotional connection with the audience. Building a fan base and a community is a sustainable approach to digital storytelling. Storytelling, especially on/via social media, is a personal experience, contrary to mass produced content. Over the years there's been a noticeable shift towards authentic and personalised content and experiences. For this reason, co-creation has become the norm in many marketing and communication campaigns. In addition to this, we've seen the rise of civic media; and as discussed in this book, the collective control over meaning and circulation of content has given more power to audiences.

For the average user on social media there are powerful ways to participate, and yet we need to check the quality of information we share. For brands, this is very much the case too, and brands should:

- check the quality of information they share
- be clear where they have received the information they are sharing from
- think twice before sharing material a brand hasn't evaluated.

(Jenkins, Ford and Green, 2013)

User-generated campaigns

User-generated content is a participatory approach to digital storytelling that has been used by brands all over the world. For some brands, user-generated content is a critical part of the branding (see e.g. GoPro). In the PESO model, user-generated content sits in the shared content space, and adds authenticity to the brand. While there can be negatives to user-generated content, the authenticity and credibility gained by greater participation and word of mouth adds more value than a controlled message or marketing campaign.

The *Just Another Day in WA* campaign, or #justanotherdayinwa, is a perfect example of an organisation (WA Tourism) using its audience as co-creators of content – and specifically user-generated content. Audiences involved in the campaign shared their stories about what it means to live and travel in Western Australia across multiple online platforms, using the hashtag. Consequently, Tourism WA saw the campaign take on a life of its own as the audience truly 'owned' the hashtag. The hashtag is still in use years after the official campaign and a quick search on Instagram will highlight the longevity of the hashtag and how much (mostly) West Australian, and Australian, tourists have owned the hashtag. Despite some criticism and arguably some low-level brand hijacking to voice criticism predominantly related to costs of living, content shared has shifted to an array of overwhelmingly beautiful, positive and most importantly authentic images that have been shared by residents and travellers.

In creating a campaign that will encourage user participation, you need to make it immersive, engaging or collaborative. The *Just Another Day in WA* campaign was both engaging and collaborative.

User-generated campaigns require a few considerations:

- Make sure to promote the campaign over the organisation – or in other words, be authentic.
- There needs to be a prize, or pay-off – if you think back to Jenkins' elements for participatory culture, this is a crucial part of members feeling their contributions are valued.

- Match the campaign to your audience – in terms of language, focus and platform used.
- Match the concept to something you can use in your organisation.

User-generated campaigns that take on a life of their own become the ultimate transmedia storytelling approach to digital storytelling. They are sustainable, after the initial campaign require little funding, and present an authentic and credible view of the brand.

How to build a strong participatory culture with fans

Studies of fans and fandom are prolific, and while not a key focus of this book, fans do play an important role in building participatory communities. The BlackMilk Clothing example is a great introduction to the role fans can play in building a strong participatory culture. While the internet and social media provide spaces to be participative, brands need to be strategic about how they encourage audiences to participate. Fans play a unique role in helping build participatory culture as they act as advocates for the brand, and in time can minimise the resources needed by brands to run online communities. We discussed authenticity in Chapter 1 as a key concept of digital storytelling, and the reason for this is that it plays a key role in participatory culture and is one of the drivers for why audiences will engage (and participate) with a brand. Reilly et al. (2012) take Jenkins' idea of participatory culture and break it down into the four Cs – how does a brand create, circulate, connect and collaborate with its audiences. The study of fans or fandom can be described as the social and cultural ways of how people interact with their passions (Reilly, 2016). Fandom becomes important in participatory culture as if brands want to really connect with their audiences they need to understand what motivates people (or in particular, the fans of their brand). Reilly's study on what motivates fans (from the perspective of soccer fans) can be used by brands to understand how and why a fan may engage with them. Reilly groups fans into different categories, which include:

- The follower – passionate and participatory
- The patriot – dutiful but not necessarily passionate
- The explorer – fiercely loyal
- Connoisseurs – it's all about the game
- Observer – invested but not a part of their lives
- Guardians – high-energy fans

Knowing what kind of fans you have will change how you interact with them. It's a very similar model to segmenting stakeholders, but this group is much broader than your traditional stakeholder segments.

The challenge of working with the concept of fandom is the absence of a hierarchical ranking into which we can slot various fan groups. The entertainment and media industry widely believes that 80 percent of its revenue comes from the 20 percent of its audience who are frequently referred to as 'superfans'. Some might not consider Followers to be true fans; in contrast, Connoisseurs could be classified as superfans. But this sort of taxonomy papers over the opportunities that each mind-set offers in an engagement strategy. And when we look at fans through the lens of our two core questions of motivations and triggers, we discover multiple points of entry into a fan community, with multiple versions of meaningful engagement. (Reilly, 2016)

The key motivators of fan behaviour according to Reilly's study are:

1. **Entertainment** – the enjoyment of the activity and following a passion.
2. **Social connection** – creating and building relationships with other fans.
3. **Mastery** – learning more about their passion and developing knowledge.
4. **Immersion** – being involved deeply in their passion, away from their everyday lives.
5. **Identification** – defining themselves as a fan, and deeply identifying with their passion.
6. **Pride** – showing they are fans both privately and publicly.
7. **Advocacy** – taking on the role as advocate for the passion/brand.
8. **Play** – participating in activities, both online and offline, to be involved.
9. **Creation** – wanting to know about the history of their passion, and being involved in future creations relating to their passion.
10. **Exploration** – seeking out new areas of interest in relation to the passion.
11. **Collection** – deeply committed to collecting things involved with their passion.

(Reilly, 2016)

Using this model, BlackMilk Clothing fans had a number of motivators, including social connection, identification, pride and creation, to become and remain engaged. Chin (2016) discusses how social media can be used to mobilise fans into action for social and charitable causes. This has been seen in campaigns run by environmental organisations like Greenpeace, and even more so in viral campaigns like the ALS Ice Bucket Challenge. Fans represent a different audience than 'stakeholders', and need to be considered as a broader part of the branding mix. Previous stakeholder models in communication don't usually take into consideration the idea of a 'fan', as 'passion' is frequently underestimated in the context of lack of perceived power or influence. However, we now see that audiences (whether they are stakeholders or not) have more power. The implication for brands are that what was once a mass-produced experience has now become personal; audiences consume and create content, if they are interested in it. Building an emotional connection (through storytelling) is now more important than ever.

Fans, while powerful in their own right, can also undermine and damage brands. The rise of the anti-fan, or troll (as often referred to in the media), is amplified in the digital space where algorithms reward engagement volume, irrespective of whether positive or negative. Indeed, controversial content typically attracts a greater volume of attention, e.g. shares and even comments. An anti-fan is very different from an uninterested bystander. They are passionate in their dislikes of something, which could be a fictional character, a creative work or a person, but also a brand, and devote time to mocking or criticising it. Just think of the US President Donald Trump, who attracted a large following of both fans and anti-fans, both groups of which invested similar amounts of resources and energy into creating artefacts, seeking to contribute to the conversation both on- and offline. According to anti-fan scholars, 'disownership' is being recognised as a form of self-identification (Hind, 2007) and can lead to strong anti-fan communities in their own right, connected via a mutual sense of loathing. We discuss the role of the anti-fan and mis- and disinformation in Chapter 11.

TRANSMEDIA STORYTELLING

Transmedia storytelling in its current form was first defined by Henry Jenkins as representing 'a process as part of which integral elements of a fiction get dispersed systematically across multiple delivery channels for the purpose of creating a unified and coordinated entertainment experience. Ideally, each medium makes its own unique contribution to the unfolding of the story' (Jenkins, 2007).

The term transmedia was first mentioned as a concept by Marsha Kinder (1991) who defined transmedia as a narrative or non-narrative that could be communicated across multiple platforms. The term has since been further developed in industry and by academics. Jeff Gomez from Starlight Runner, a transmedia marketing organisation, defines transmedia storytelling as 'the process of telling stories across multiple platforms' (Escobedo, 2017). Gomez stresses that the importance of transmedia storytelling lies in the ability to break a story apart and understand how the story themes and characters work best on each platform (Escobedo, 2017).

For transmedia storytelling to thrive, participatory culture must play an important role, and using the two constructs in digital storytelling creates a powerful strategy that is robust and considered. In a sense, transmedia storytelling can't exist without a participatory environment, and for this, the internet and social media have been key in its development. Jenkins (2010) discusses seven core concepts for transmedia storytelling. These are the foundation for how to distribute content and can be used as the basis for a strategic approach for brands.

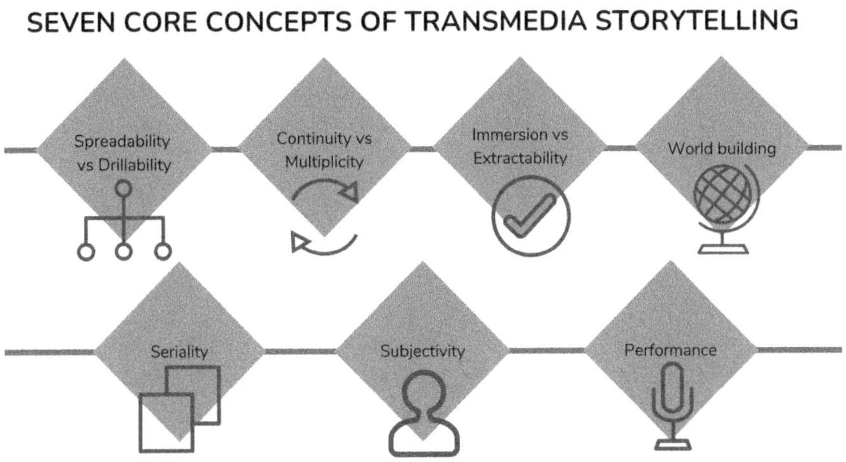

SEVEN CORE CONCEPTS OF TRANSMEDIA STORYTELLING

Figure 3.6 Seven core concepts of transmedia storytelling, Source: Jenkins (2010)

1. **Spreadability vs Drillability:** The degree to which content is shareable, and what motivates someone to share it. Spreadability reflects how many platforms your content is spread across, drillability is the depth of information you provide.
2. **Continuity vs Multiplicity:** Does the content show plausibility across all extensions (continuity)? Or is it acceptable that the content may adapt, i.e. there are alternate versions (multiplicity)? Continuity is the ability to continue a narrative that extends beyond the original campaign. In the case of #BlackLivesMatter the hashtag has been used across the world for many different (but similar) causes. Multiplicity is the ability to multiply a narrative but in different versions or formats. If we look at the traditional story of *Pride and Prejudice*, it has been adapted to a traditional film and television series, followed by mashup movies like *Pride and Prejudice and Zombies*.
3. **Immersion vs Extractability:** In immersion, the consumer enters into the world of the story, e.g. immersion in the Burberry case study was the ability to walk into their flagship stores and experience digital elements similar to the website. Extractability is the ability to take something away from the brand/campaign. This may be physical, e.g. a hat with the logo/concept, or digital, e.g. a logo/badge or something you can share on your own platform.
4. **World Building:** How does the story give a richer depiction of the world in which the narrative plays out? Franchises like e.g. Disney or Marvel may use both real-world and digital experiences (think: amusement parks, merchandise, video games etc. building on and extending the original narrative).

5. **Seriality:** Transmedia storytelling breaks up the narrative arc into discrete instalments, but rather than show this through a single medium it spreads this across multiple platforms. Eva.Stories is an example of a serial – the story was broken up into separate short narratives that formed a bigger story.

6. **Subjectivity:** Transmedia storytelling explores the narrative through new eyes, such as secondary characters or third parties. This may be the audience. The audience can add to the story and change it. It embraces diversity of perspective. A great example in this context is fanfiction, which has been made popular by platforms like Wattpad.

7. **Performance:** Transmedia storytelling activates the audience – on- or even offline – by giving it something to do. A great example in this context is PokemonGo, which motivates participants to engage with key characters and the narrative beyond their home, on the go, and frequently in collaboration with others.

Source: Based on Henry Jenkins' seven elements of transmedia storytelling (Jenkins, 2010)

An important concept of transmedia storytelling is that it is not about replicating content across multiple or even every platform available, as was frequently the approach in the early days of social media. The focus should be on using every platform most effectively, ensuring that each platform makes a unique contribution to the unfolding of the story, based on its strength and (engagement) style. Frank Rose (2012) uses the term 'deep media' to describe the creation of a deeper level of content on different platforms that lets the audience drill deeper. The approach also assumes that at any time, the audience may come across your content at a different entry point or level, which needs to be factored into your strategy.

CASE STUDY

RAC, The Elephant in the Wheatbelt

Information Provided by the RAC, Western Australia

The Royal Automobile Club (RAC) in Western Australia launched a road safety campaign in 2014 with the aim to highlight unacceptable road deaths in regional areas. The aim of the campaign was to encourage residents in the rural Wheatbelt region, an area singled out for its high per head rate of car crashes, to take ownership of the issue and change attitudes - with the ultimate goal of reducing road fatalities and serious injuries. The RAC wanted to use hard facts, such as that locals were statistically 11 times more likely to die on Wheatbelt roads than if they lived in the metropolitan region. The membership organisation invested significant funding and resources into the five year campaign and worked with the community, road safety organisations and all levels of government on this project. Below is a breakdown of how the campaign used participatory elements and transmedia storytelling principles to engage the community in the issue.

Figure 3.7 The Elephant in the Wheatbelt, Western Australia

Figure 3.8 RAC advertising campaign for road deaths

Key elements of the campaign

The Elephant in the Wheatbelt used storytelling as the key hook to gain interest. It started off with a large metal statue in the shape of an elephant, publicly appearing in the Wheatbelt town of Narrogin. The elephant in itself was a metaphor to 'start the conversation' - i.e. the elephant in the room, addressing an issue most residents would be very aware of, but often fail to acknowledge or publicly mention. The elephant, made from the metal of cars that had crashed, was placed across a number of Wheatbelt towns, unbranded and unannounced. Using Jenkins' key transmedia storytelling concepts the campaign utilised the following elements:

1 **Spreadability** - Content was used on YouTube, mainstream media, Facebook, Instagram, Twitter and the web. The campaign targeted multiple levels of stakeholders, from locals (small business owners, community leaders, school children, etc.), to journalists and policy makers (politicians).
2 **Continuity** - The campaign evolved and deepened over time, with each platform adding depth to the campaign.
3 **Immersion** - The campaign offered physical and digital experiences, with live events, music and art. Overall, there was a strong focus on the visual element (shareability).
4 **Subjectivity** - The concept of 'it's my elephant' encouraged local residents to talk from their perspective and share stories (most regional locals know someone who has died on the roads).
5 **Performance** - Content creation from local artists was commissioned, but community participation was also encouraged, including photos, sharing of story aspects and even classroom-based activities.

A strategic transmedia storytelling approach doesn't require all elements to be covered, only the ones most useful to a campaign. Instead, it is more impactful to focus on the key concepts that will best serve the campaign and its intentions. True to transmedia storytelling and behaviour change campaigns, this campaign showed longevity and spanned across five years.

> **2015:** 'Start the conversation' (story of intrigue). The elephant was placed at a number of Wheatbelt towns, unbranded and unannounced, and also visited events, shows and Western Australian landmarks, including Parliament House.

> **2016:** Second phase, 'it's my elephant' (story of ownership). This phase encouraged residents to take ownership of road safety issues in their community by featuring a number of local residents in stories, who were inspired to take action in their community. This approach championed community members doing their part to keep themselves and others safe on the road. The RAC featured these locals on billboards, radio advertisements, printed media and social media to encourage others to do their bit.

> **2017/18:** The RAC released a new children's storybook, written and designed by Perth teacher and artist, Sean Avery, titled *My Family, The Elephant and Me*. The book follows a Wheatbelt family on a road trip and has a central message at its heart: 'we travel safe or not at all'. The book was delivered free of charge to all primary school students across the Wheatbelt. RAC also commissioned six artists to paint unique elephant murals in towns across the region to encourage the continuation of the conversation beyond the official campaign lifespan. The original elephant statute now resides in the RAC Head Office in West Perth, Western Australia as a permanent road safety reminder.

Figure 3.9   The book written by Sean Avery, *My Family, The Elephant and Me*

Figure 3.10   Example of community ownership

The main outcome of the campaign was to promote ownership (facilitated through transmedia elements that encouraged participatory and co-creation) and the start of a community discussion around road safety myths. The release of the book highlights a longer-term sustainable approach to road safety, targeting younger generations as potential change agents, understanding they will eventually become road users. There were multiple levels of audiences targeted in the campaign, from children, to the broader community, to politicians and the media. This multi-level approach ensured the message was delivered in multiple formats, to multiple stakeholders.

CHAPTER SUMMARY

This chapter describes two important concepts in digital storytelling: participatory culture and transmedia storytelling. This chapter outlines how participatory culture has changed the media landscape, and in turn, digital storytelling. The prolific nature of the internet and the 24/7 news cycle have increased the need for outsourced content creation and citizen journalism. The pull (i.e. audiences seeking out content when and if needed or desired) model of information has led to increased depth and understanding of what kind of content engages audiences. Brands need to consider depth as well as the strategic dispersion of content across platforms.

Participatory culture

Participatory culture in the digital sense has emerged out of online communities since the introduction of the internet. Social media platforms encourage participatory culture – both positive and negative – and have changed the way in which audiences interact with brands.

Based on the BlackMilk Clothing case study, this chapter illustrates how participatory culture can be used to build engagement, and how participatory culture in practice can develop fans and curate a culture of co-creation and sharing. This particular case study highlights the power of participatory culture, as the organisation has not used traditional models like advertising to promote its clothing and instead relies on the power of its growing fan community.

Transmedia storytelling

Transmedia storytelling is a theory, practice and approach to communication that defines how to tell a story across platforms to create a unified narrative. Transmedia storytelling allows for a deep and rich experience of a brand with each element contributing to a bigger narrative. The term transmedia storytelling refers to a 'process where integral elements of a fiction get dispersed systematically across multiple delivery channels for the purpose of creating a unified and coordinated entertainment experience. Ideally, each medium makes its own unique contribution to the unfolding of the story' (Jenkins, 2007).

The case study of the RAC WA's Elephant in the Wheatbelt provides an example of a behaviour change campaign, aimed at reducing the number of road deaths in regional Western Australia. It's an ideal campaign to highlight how transmedia storytelling can be used to reach multiple stakeholders and audiences across many different platforms, including offline, to encourage deep conversations and the continuation of the storyline based on personal experiences.

DISCUSSION QUESTIONS

1. Using a specified brand, search online and try to find examples of different audiences – passive, followers and prosumer – and how they are interacting with the brand/organisation. Use Erin Reilly's idea of a fan and break down the audience further to identify the types of fans, and how they interact with the brand.
2. Find an example of a co-creation/user-generated content/campaign for a brand. Note down the participatory and transmedia elements and analyse if it was effective or not. Develop an infographic to display the information and share with the class (similar to the BlackMilk example).
3. Identify an example of a brand or organisation that has effectively integrated both online and offline channels for their transmedia storytelling approach, encouraging engagement and deep conversations among its target audience (similar to the Elephant in the Wheatbelt example).

READINGS

Mcerlean, K. (2018). The business of transmedia storytelling. In: *Interactive Narratives and Transmedia Storytelling: Creating Immersive Stories across New Media Platforms.* [online] New York, London: Routledge. Available at: https://ebookcentral.proquest. com/lib/curtin/detail.action?docID=5323303 [Accessed 26 October 2022].

This chapter outlines different transmedia campaigns and how they were executed across social media platforms. There's a discussion on the role of transmedia storytelling in virtual reality.

Johnston, J. and Rowney, K. (2018). Transmedia storytelling. In: *Media Strategies: Managing Content, Platforms and Relationships.* Sydney: Allen & Unwin.

This chapter outlines the brief history of storytelling and discusses ways to find good stories. It discusses how brand narrative fits into transmedia storytelling and the platforms that may be used. An introductory read into transmedia storytelling.

Dionisio, M. and Nisi, V. (2021). Leveraging transmedia storytelling to engage tourists in the understanding of the destination's local heritage. *Multimedia Tools and Applications*, 80. doi:10.1007/s11042-021-10949-2.

This journal article discusses the role of transmedia storytelling in destination tourism in terms of raising awareness about sustainable tourism.

REFERENCES

Chin, B. (2016). Social media, promotional culture and participatory fandom. In: A. Hutchins and N. Tindall (eds.), *Public Relations and Participatory Culture: Fandom, Social Media and Community Engagement.* New York: Routledge.

Dietrich, G. (2022). *Spin Sucks: Communication and Reputation Management in the Digital Age*. Indianapolis, IN: Que, Cop.

Do, E. (2014). BlackMilk's dream social media run plunges off a cliff (and how it should have handled the issue). [online] *Marketing Mag*. Available at: www.marketingmag. com.au/news-c/black-milks-dream-social-media-run-plunges-off-a-cliff-and-how-it-should-have-handled-the-issue/ [Accessed 26 October 2022].

Dodd, M.D. and Kinnally, W. (2015). 'Fan publics': An interdisciplinary conceptualisation of external supportive stakeholders. *PRism*, 12(1). www.prismjournal.org/uploads/1/2/5/6/125661607/v12-no1-a1.pdf

DPReview (2013). *Chicago Sun-Times* lays off entire photo staff: Switches to freelancers. [online] *DPReview*. Available at: www.dpreview.com/articles/6745486958/chicago-sun-times-lays-off-photo-staff [Accessed 26 October 2022].

Escobedo, J. (2017). Transmedia will shape the future of Hollywood and Fortune 500 firms. [online] *Forbes*. Available at: www.forbes.com/sites/joeescobedo/2017/07/01/meet-the-man-behind-hollywood-and-fortune-500-firms-transmedia-success/?sh=6138872333da [Accessed 26 October 2022].

Hind, J. (2007). This modern life: The rise of the anti-fan. [online] *The Guardian*. Available at: www.theguardian.com/theobserver/2007/apr/22/features.magazine47 [Accessed 31 October 2022].

Jenkins, H. (2006). *Convergence Culture*. New York: New York University Press.

Jenkins, H. (2007). Transmedia storytelling 101: Confessions of an aca-fan. [online] *Henry Jenkins*. Available at: http://henryjenkins.org/blog/2007/03/transmedia_storytelling_101.html [Accessed 26 October 2022].

Jenkins, H. (2010). Transmedia education: The 7 principles revisited. [online] *Henry Jenkins*. Available at: http://henryjenkins.org/blog/2010/06/transmedia_education_the_7_pri.html [Accessed 26 October 2022].

Jenkins, H. (2013). Henry Jenkins on Participatory Culture: Big Thinkers. *YouTube*. Available at: www.youtube.com/watch?v=1gPm-c1wRsQ&t=36s. [Accessed 26 October 2022].

Jenkins, H., Ford, S. and Green, J. (2013). *Spreadable Media: Creating Value and Meaning in a Networked Culture*. New York: New York University Press.

Kinder, M. (1991). *Playing with Power in Movies, Television, and Video Games: From Muppet Babies to Teenage Mutant Ninja Turtles*. Berkeley, CA: University of California Press.

Reilly, E. (2016). Fan favorites. [online] *strategy+business*. Available at: www.strategy-business.com/article/Fan-Favorites [Accessed 26 October 2022].

Reilly, E., Jenkins, H., Felt, L.J. and Vartabedian, V. (2012). Shall we play. [online] *Slide Share*. Available at: www.slideshare.net/ebreilly1/play-doc-01-15613677 [Accessed 26 October 2022].

Rose, F. (2012). *The Art of Immersion: How the Digital Generation Is Remaking Hollywood, Madison Avenue, and the Way We Tell Stories*. New York: W.W. Norton & Co.

Tombleson, B. and Wolf, K. (2017). Rethinking the circuit of culture: How participatory culture has transformed cross-cultural communication. *Public Relations Review*, 43(1), 14–25. doi:10.1016/j.pubrev.2016.10.017.

USC Annenberg Center for Public Relations (2019). *PR:Tech, The Future of Technology in Communication*. [online] Available at: https://assets.uscannenberg.org/docs/2019-global-communications-report.pdf [Accessed 26 October 2022].

4

THE TRADITIONAL NARRATIVE AND THE COLLECTIVE NARRATIVE

OBJECTIVES

1. Understand how to structure narrative
2. Define the hero's narrative vs the collective narrative
3. Understand how the key elements of the collective narrative apply to a modern case study

In a story, you do not only weave a lot of information into the telling but you also arouse your listener's emotions and energy. Persuading with a story is hard. Any intelligent person can sit down and make lists (e.g. for use in a lecture, such as writing 'reason-why-to-buy advertising copy'). It takes rationality but little creativity to design an argument using conventional rhetoric. But it demands vivid insight and storytelling skill to present an idea that packs enough power to be memorable. If you can harness imagination and the principles of a well-told story, then you get people rising to their feet amid thunderous applause instead of yawning and ignoring you (McKee, 2003, p. 52).

This chapter explores narrative theory, and how it has evolved. The chapter delves into the traditional story arc, and seeks to understand common plots used in brand narrative. It also takes a deeper look at the hero's journey and how this traditionally dominant storytelling model has only recently been disrupted by user-generated content and the collective narrative. The chapter examines how the traditional narrative has changed in the digital context and explains the main constructs of the collective narrative. The authors draw on industry-led knowledge to explore key brands using the collective narrative. Story formula and structure are discussed in a brand context.

THE NARRATIVE STRUCTURE

Narrative structure, in its simplest form, is the/'how to' of a story. Narratives have a natural shape that our brains automatically recognise as we've been hearing stories from the moment we were born. Some may even argue that stories are part of our DNA. In their simplest form, narratives have a beginning, a middle and an end, and these act as signposts or 'acts' that allow our mind to understand that the story will have a resolution. Each act builds on the one that precedes it. This structure is used across all forms of media, including film, television, novels, comic books and much more.

At the highest level, narrative structure can be broken down into:

- **Linear plot structure:** A narrative where events are presented in a chronological order. For many brands, a linear brand narrative is used.
- **Non-linear plot structure**: This is a narrative where several plots may be used and introduced at different intervals. A transmedia narrative may be thought of as a non-linear plot structure, where the audience can enter at any point.
- **Parallel plot structure**: A narrative where there are two different plots (or points of view) delivered at the same time. Some brands may use this plot for micro narratives.
- **Circular plot structure:** This is a narrative where the story ends where it begins; there may be transformation along the way but the characters end up back where the story started.
- **Interactive plot structure:** This is a 'choose your own adventure' style plot where the audience can decide where the story will take them. Some brands adopt this style of branding, letting audiences decide where they will go and what information they will receive.

Although this is not an exhaustive list of storytelling structures, specific examples of plot styles are shown in the following six narratives:

Monomyth (hero's journey), circular plot

The hero's journey has been a popular mode of storytelling for thousands of years. It's a narrative model that many people are familiar with and has been used in popular novels ranging from Homer's *Odyssey* and *Anne of Green Gables* to *Dune* and the *Harry Potter* series. In films the narrative can be seen in *Star Wars*, *The Matrix*, most Marvel movies (i.e. *Spiderman*) and of course, *The Lord of the Rings* (novel and movie). In the hero's journey, the hero sets out, encounters a difficulty or challenge, has pressure applied (the ordeal), but ultimately overcomes any challenges. Joseph Campbell wrote about the hero's journey in his book *The Hero with a Thousand Faces* (2012) and defined story structure through the protagonist's journey.

The hero's journey has 12 main steps (Campbell, 2012):

1. **Hero's world is revealed:** Here we learn about the hero and their view on life.
2. **Call to adventure:** Something happens to upset the hero's normal existence.
3. **Refusal**: The hero's rejects the initial call through fears that need overcoming.
4. **Meeting the mentor:** Someone arrives in the hero's life who gives them guidance.

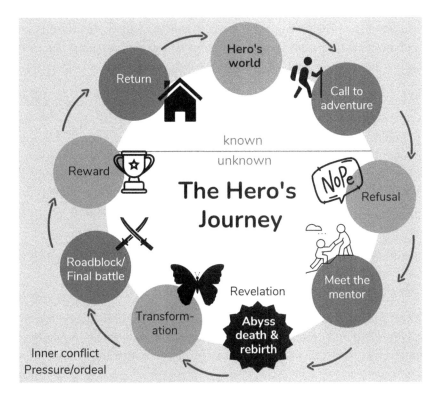

Figure 4.1 Hero's Journey, Source: Based on Campbell (2012)

5. **Revelation:** The hero is ready to act and does so despite the unknown.
6. **Transformation:** The hero encounters challenges in the way of enemies or difficulties and obstacles are thrown in their path.
7. **Inner conflict:** The hero comes across great conflict and sometimes physical danger. There is a great leap into the unknown.
8. **Ordeal:** Pressure is applied by means of an event that does not go to plan and the hero again struggles with how to respond.
9. **Reward:** The hero 'takes up the sword' and is surprised by their abilities and overcomes their fears.
10. **The road block**: More pressure is applied to the hero in terms of something not going to plan. The hero must adjust their approach in order to complete their journey.
11. **Resurrection**: The final battle and the most dangerous point of the journey happens with the hero finally winning the battle.
12. **Return**: The hero returns… a hero and is known to all to have saved the day.

From a brand perspective, many organisations use the hero's journey as a narrative, including Coke, Apple, Amazon and Nike. Kent (2015) identified 20 key narratives that organisations use frequently. Further, he identified five plots that stand out within a marketing and communication context: quest, adventure, rivalry, underdog and wretched excess. Most of these plots fall within the hero's narrative definition (with the exception of wretched excess) and are used in a brand context to persuade, communicate and create compelling stories. A breakdown of the key plots is shown.

In using core narratives for brands, multiple versions may exist at one time. For example a brand like Extinction Rebellion is using the 'wretched excess' narrative to promote action on climate change. At the same time, however, it is drawing on the collective narrative to progress its brand and build a community of climate change advocates. This example illustrates that the different types of narratives are not mutually exclusive; sophisticated brands are building on the common hero narrative to develop a more inclusive and expansive brand narrative.

Bartlett (2022) defines the hero's journey as good for:

- taking the audience on a journey
- showing the benefit of taking risks
- demonstrating how you learned some new wisdom.

Through a contemporary lens, the hero's journey is all about resilience; it requires courage to face uncertainty, embrace challenges, and to adapt to unforeseen circumstances – even if in some cases only reluctantly at first (just think of Frodo Baggins in *Lord of the Rings*).

Figure 4.2 Kent's Five Key Master Plots in Brand Storytelling, Source: Kent (2015)
Printed with permission of Elsevier

Dramatic arc (three-act structure), linear plot (also known as the mountain)

A narrative arc is considered an arc due to the rise and fall of conflict or tension. There are a number of ways to break down a narrative arc; different authors have defined this in slightly different ways, however most models follow a similar pattern.

The dramatic arc was considered by Gustav Freytag in the 19th century and is one of the best known narratives. The dramatic arc is one where the main character faces a dilemma at the beginning of the story, the story is driven forward by conflict and/or action until the climax of the story is reached, leading to the resolution at the tail end (Freytag, 1894). The simplest version of this is a three-part structure and although generalised and simplistic, it has endured as one of the most straightforward forms of narrative arc across time. Boyd, Blackburn and Pennebaker (2020) identify Aristotle as the first scholar to apply the three-part narrative structure. Freytag furthered this in his book, defining five main elements of the narrative dramatic arc. These five elements include:

1. **Exposition**: Background and introduction to the story. Here, the audience learns about the main character, setting and time, and often is introduced to the problem or main issue facing the character.
2. **Rising action**: Many scholars argue that the story is driven by conflict, and in this part of the narrative the first sign of conflict is shown. This is often called the 'inciting incident' and is the event that propels the story forward.
3. **Climax**: The pinnacle of the story and essentially what everything is leading to. This is the highest point in terms of conflict.
4. **Falling action**: Action that comes after a main decision by the key character at the climax.
5. **Resolution**: How the story ends. Traditionally in the narrative arc, this may be a 'happy' or 'sad' ending.

A recent study looked at 40,000 traditional narratives (e.g. novels) and 20,000 non-traditional narratives (e.g. TED talks, science reporting etc.) between 1989 and 2017 using computer-based language analysis methods (Boyd, Blackburn and Pennebaker, 2020). The study sought to understand if narratives shared similar arcs to Freytag's dramatic arc and compared and contrasted traditional narratives to see if they were similar to non-traditional narratives. The study found that across this period of time narratives still follow a three-part format in their structure with an introduction, rise in plot progression and fall towards resolution at the end. This is a common technique used in podcasting and can be seen in podcast series like *This American Life*. The study's findings are important as they illustrate that common narrative structures have stood the test of time and are now being applied within the context of non-traditional narratives. For digital storytelling, the dramatic arc

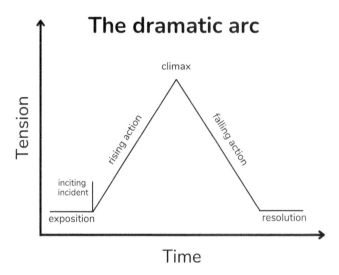

Figure 4.3 Five elements to the narrative arc, Source: Based on Freytag (1894)

has maintained its relevance and is now used in unique and deconstructed ways, as will be discussed in this chapter.

There are a few different names for this style of storytelling, such as the mountain narrative, but they are similar in their approach. In the mountain narrative events build on each other to eventually reach a peak, in which the narrative is resolved. The resolution represents the 'way down the mountain'. Bartlett (2022) defines the mountain narrative as suitable for:

- showing how you overcame a challenge
- slowly building tension
- delivering a satisfying conclusion.

Nested loops

Nested loops are a circular way of telling a story with the key story being at the centre. Other stories may form around this story (without replicating the original story). Nested loops apply the layering of three or more narratives within each other and are usually stories within stories. You can use this storyline to:

- provide a first-person perspective for the main story
- gain different perspectives of the story from others
- develop a main story with loops expanding on key themes.

(Bartlett, 2022)

Nested loops are often used in keynote talks, to pitch ideas, explain a concept or to convince and inspire others.

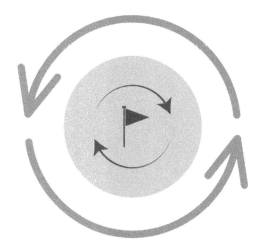

Figure 4.4   Nested loops, a circular way of storytelling

Sparklines

Sparklines, designed by Nancy Duarte, are used to juxtapose a narrative and show what is 'now' and what the future or the 'aspirational' narrative may be (Solomon, 2014). These types of narratives may be used to highlight issues and can be useful in speeches to 'paint a picture' and emotionally engage the audience. Bartlett (2022) defines sparklines as good for:

- inspiring action in the audience
- creating hope and excitement
- building a following by resonating with the audience.

Figure 4.5   Sparklines juxtapose 'now' and aspirational narrative

Reverse or middle narrative

Reverse or middle narrative provides a way to grab attention quickly, followed by placing the audience in the centre of the action. The narrative then moves

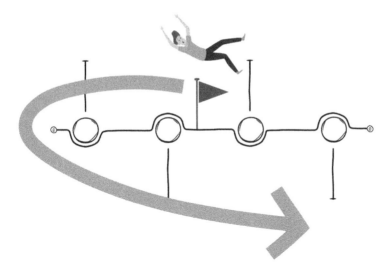

Figure 4.6 Reverse narrative places the audience in the centre of the action

back to the beginning to explain how you got there. This type of narrative can work very well for digital storytelling where there is less time to engage the audience, and slow burn narratives are less likely to work, i.e. you want to commence with an attention-grabbing element. Bartlett (2022) defines reverse narrative as good for:

- grabbing attention quickly
- keeping the audience's attention, as it seeks to find out more
- focusing on an important part of the narrative.

Petal structure

The petal structure is a way to organise multiple narratives (or speakers) around a central message. This structure works well in a transmedia storytelling approach as the smaller stories help to develop a bigger, overall narrative. The narratives may not initially seem to be connected, but as each narrative links back to the main story, it becomes apparent that they are. Bartlett (2022) defines the petal structure as good for:

- showing how strands of a story or process are interconnected
- showing how several scenarios relate back to one idea
- letting multiple speakers talk around a central theme.

Figure 4.7 Petal structure organises multiple narratives around a central message

ARCHETYPES

Archetypes are important to understand in digital storytelling as they are recognised innately by humans, and now can be presented in ways that empower different cultures and beliefs. Many branding personas can be defined as having one or two archetype personalities. The reason archetypes are used in both storytelling and branding is that they draw upon our unconscious understanding of characters and storylines, based on archetypes that we have become familiar with throughout our lives. Indeed, it is argued that archetypes draw not only on our own, but on the accumulated experiences of past generations that influence who we are today. Imagine a deposit of memories that enable us to recognise symbols quickly, thereby acting as a type of shortcut, helping us to make sense of the world around us. In the digital era, characterised by shortened attention spans and information overload, archetypes can be particularly valuable in 'hooking' an audience. A good story often begins with the listener or audience immediately understanding the context. Archetypes offer one way to ensure this. Just like Kent (2015) described the 20 most common plots used in public relations branding and campaigns, archetypes offer a signpost as a way of understanding who is in the story and how we might relate to them (i.e. the hero or the villain).

> An archetype is an unconscious primary form, an original pattern or prototype in the human mind; archetypes are not learned or acquired – they are with us from birth and are as natural and embedded in us as our own DNA;

archetypes are collective unconscious forces affecting beliefs, attitudes, and behavior implicitly and/or explicitly. (Jung, 1969, cited in Woodside, 2010, p. 533)

As visuals are often less intrusive – and more easily digestible – than words, they can alter an audience's perception in powerful ways, i.e. they require less cognitive load (Rodrigues and Dimitova, 2016). This means audiences tend to accept archetypes in a visual form more readily, as they allow the creation of an immediate response and evoke an emotional reaction (Holiday et al., 2016). According to Jung (1969) there are 12 main archetypes and they embody the following traits:

Archetype	Trait	Storytelling narratives	Brand examples
The Innocent	A brand that follows the rules and does the right thing. Optimistic, happy and a great team player. Sometimes utopian	Nostalgia Morals	Disney Dove Coca-Cola
The Everyman (person)	Everyone's friend. Successful and open yet down to earth. Known to be respected and relatable. Great team player	Humour to connect ordinary, everyday values Casual	GAP Uniqlo Ikea
The Hero	Takes the lead and gets the best outcomes. Will do hard work and is comfortable in the spotlight. Will always solve the problem. A journey and a transformation	A journey that overcomes a challenge A sense of achievement	Nike BMW Duracell
The Nurturer	Compassionate and kind. Often selfless and linked to a mother-type figure. Valued for being caring and trustworthy	Finding a cure/ solution Concern for the larger world	Red Cross Panadol United Nations
The Explorer	Adventure is key here; not afraid to go out and explore. Innovation and risk are key components here	Being independent and taking a risk Seeking out freedom	Tesla Jeep Patagonia
The Rebel	Not one to play by the rules and keen to break them. A quest for freedom, against conformity	Breaking traditional moulds Rebelling against what is 'normal'	Uber XR Rebellion Virgin
The Lover	Relationships are a key focus and values include small detail and looking for quality in people	Self-acceptance and care Indulgence	Pandora Lindt Chanel
The Creator	Imagination and spontaneity are key here. Creativity through something different and looking at things in a different light	Finding solutions in creativity Self-expression	Lego Ikea Crayola

(Continued)

Archetype	Trait	Storytelling narratives	Brand examples
The Jester	Humour, doesn't conform and likes to have fun. Things aren't taken too seriously and charisma and joy are important	Breaking the rules and having fun Self-deprecating humour	M&Ms Skittles Old Spice
The Thinker	Research, discussion, analysis and planning are important. Everything is considered	Seeking the truth Seeking wisdom	Google Harvard University IBM
The Magician	Big dreams and big thinking. An archetype to inspire and use wonder and awe	New innovations A sense of renewal	General Electric Dyson Apple
The Leader	Goal oriented; people look to this brand for guidance and direction. Trustworthy yet an ability to motivate	Precision and control Bringing order	Rolex Microsoft British Airways

THE COLLECTIVE NARRATIVE

> Collective journey stories are an evolved version of traditional hero's jour-
> ney tales, and showcase the importance of listening and negotiating to drive
> systemic, collective action. Such stories have increased capacity to improve
> the civic imagination and provide symbols that individuals can draw from
> to manifest meaningful change. (Webster, 2020, p. 60)

Current shifts in the origin of storytelling (i.e. the narrative being increasingly
driven by audiences, as opposed to traditionally being told by brands and organisations) point to a greater need for practitioners to understand how collective narratives are built. The hero's journey is an enduring story model that has existed for
many years and still has great relevance. However, over the last 20 years there's
been a shift occurring that has seen a new, collectively driven form of narrative
emerging. Scholars recognise its relevance and importance in terms of impact for
brands, organisations and individuals. Jenkins (2008) discussed the idea of collective intelligence from an educational perspective, and Gomez (2017) applies it to
brands and social activist groups.

Gomez argues the hero's journey (the classic storytelling model that has existed
for hundreds of years) is no longer as valid in a participatory culture. The key shift
has to do with the audience, who are now part of the story. Due to technological
advances the audience can create, change and guide the story. This means brands
no longer own their own narrative, and with the rise of consumer activism, this has

never been truer. This is a novel and emerging area that offers much potential for scholarly investigation, as well as for communication and marketing professionals. Understanding this shift is critical as we see both innovative and dangerous precedents set in online movements (Gomez, 2017).

To date, storytelling frameworks have failed to adapt to the evolution of digital storytelling and many brands still work on the premise that they 'control' their brand and its narrative. The mindset of ownership is important to understand as it is impossible to embrace the collective narrative if you don't appreciate the power and changes occurring outside the traditional brand models. Some brands, like Nike and Extinction Rebellion (as discussed in the case study) have embraced the collective narrative model – to much controversy, and also great success. A key shift from the hero's narrative to the collective narrative indicate that the voiceless now have a voice; 'the participative, non-linear narratives of collective journey are a response to how pervasive communication has supremely impacted classic linear storytelling, giving rise to remarkable – some say unexplainable and even frightening – developments in consumer behaviours, media, politics, and world events' (Gomez, 2022).

The collective narrative builds on transmedia storytelling. As narratives are non-linear and include many perspectives, audience members can participate at any time via multiple channels and platforms. Likewise, the narrative may change at any time. In Gomez's (2017) collective narrative, brands need to identify:

- how the audience participates in the story
- how the brand tells the story (it's not one-directional)
- how brands interconnect on multiple platforms
- how brands deal with disruptive communication.

A key difference between the hero's and the collective narrative is the shift away from a narrative with conflict at its core (Gomez, 2017). The collective narrative seeks systemic change (see #MeToo, #BlackLivesMatter, #ExtinctionRebellion) and understands that 'hero' isn't coming to save you; instead society needs to save itself. In some ways this can explain the increasing number of brands that are aligning themselves with particular social movements (i.e. Nike and #BlackLivesMatter). The branding alone is no longer enough. 'What the brand stands for, what it is contributing to the world, and how it engages people have become even more important than its advertising stories, because these are the elements of meaningful and lasting dialog' (Gomez, 2017).

A great recent example of the collective narrative, which has signalled both a continuation of a brand journey and a departure from the traditional hero's journey, is Nike's 'Play New' campaign. Rather than inviting audiences to look up to inspiring athletes and trend setters, 'Play New' embraces everyday life and the fact that most of us – indeed the vast majority of Nike's customers – are not athletic superstars. Featuring regular people, the campaign invites Nike's global audience to embrace the #fails, to celebrate the flops and to laugh at themselves. The original campaign video attracted 92 million views on YouTube (Muntasir, 2022). However, the real strength of this campaign is that everyone has a place, can identify, belong and contribute to the overall story. Although elite athlete sponsorship is a core component of sports marketing, the reality is that Nike apparel is worn by a large number of people who will never win the Olympics, nor their local Parkrun. Campaigns like this create an inclusive community that draws on the audience's collective storytelling abilities. As you read through the next section, try to apply 'Play New' to Gomez' six areas of interest for digital storytelling.

Applying the collective narrative

Currently, there is no established academic framework for the collective narrative, and while transmedia storytelling can address some elements, it doesn't fully articulate the key reasons behind a collective approach to storytelling. That in itself changes the way we understand storytelling. This is a fundamental shift for marketing and communication professionals as it changes the way in which we understand how content is produced and – ultimately – who 'owns' a brand. Collective narratives are entwined with cultural events and hence also entwined with the brand story and evolution. Collective narratives are porous and suitable for building sustainable brands. It has never been more important to understand how to approach the collective narrative. Gomez (2017) identifies six areas of interest for digital storytelling – resonance, regenerative listening, super positioning, social self-organisation, narrative reversal and change making – which will be explored here.

Resonance

Resonance, and indeed relevance, have been discussed in marketing and communication literature for many years. Resonance can be defined as the ability of a brand or campaign to tap into a cultural trend, or zeitgeist, and connect the brand in a meaningful way. These are key elements when it comes to content creation and ensuring your brand can 'cut through' the ever increasing noise and competing messages in a digital world. Resonance and relevance are often referred to as if they may be minor players, but the reality is, in the social media age, communication and storytelling that resonates with your audience (and hence has relevance) may be more effective than a well-executed strategy without the resonance. The reason for this has equally to do with human emotion as it has to do with the digital algorithms. Gomez (2017) points to a common desire of people to be connected to something bigger than themselves and in part this could explain the success of movements such as #BlackLivesMatter and #MeToo. In addition, the affiliation of particular hashtags and/or campaigns builds a sense of brand or personal identity in the digital world and hence increases the resonance of relevant campaigns. Authenticity and alignment with brand values and actions is key though, as otherwise brands who seek to tap into cultural trends can easily be accused of woke washing, i.e. the desire by profit-driven brands to cash in on an audience's idealism by promoting social issues without taking meaningful action.

Regenerative listening

Regenerative listening is a way to reinforce our beliefs and the fundamental core of our moral system. Gomez (2017) defines regenerative listening as 'a process where the storyteller listens so intently to the audience that the audience's language, attitudes and concerns start to show up in the story itself'. This is very true of brands that follow a participatory approach to social media, brands like BlackMilk and campaigns like #BlackLivesMatter. Much like the idea of the collective narrative, this approach requires a rethink of brand 'management' and allows for social listening to develop and build a brand, rather than pushing predetermined brand ideals onto the audience. It's not for every brand to do this, but brands like Nike, Black-Milk and Apple are examples of allowing their audience to lead and guide how the brand evolves across time.

Super positioning

Super positioning can be defined as the way in which a brand/campaign/organisation/person uses both the viral nature of social media and current trends to position themselves. Super positioning means even the smallest voices can be amplified well beyond their original size, and the collective nature of this takes it even further (Gomez, 2017). There are multiple factors at play that allow this super positioning and they include:

- The ease and speed at which material can be shared.
- Hashtags that allow information to be targeted and shared to people following what is trending.
- The algorithms that elevate /promote information that is being engaged with to be seen first.
- The 'pile on' nature of the internet where users are keen to share and be a part of what is trending (beware: there are positives and negatives to this; you don't want to be trending for the wrong reasons).
- The low barrier to entry in creating shareable material (i.e. memes, images, reinterpretations, videos).

- The ability for anyone to contribute to and create a crowdsourced campaign to raise awareness, funds, demand change and tag influential politicians, governments etc.

Memes are an example of super positioning and as seen in the Salvation Army domestic violence advertisement mentioned in Chapter 2, they provide a powerful way to highlight a campaign goal, while using a trending meme. The skill for a digital storyteller is to actively follow trends and be able to relate them in a meaningful (and relevant) way to the brand. When the two collide, as seen in the Salvation Army campaign, it creates a powerful way to reach and connect with an audience.

Social self-organisation

The nature of social media and GPS location sharing makes it easy for individuals to organise campaigns and demonstrations, as seen by the #BlackLivesMatter and also #freedomconvoy2022. In what Gomez (2017) refers to as a level of self-determination, audiences can very quickly mobilise online campaigns and evolve into a physical/in-person protest in a short space of time. Both the #BlackLivesMatter and #MeToo campaigns led to real-life demonstrations in a show of solidarity and belief in the online campaigns. This adds further pressure for governments to act. 'Nonlinear, resonant, networked stories – the rivers and tributaries of communal narrative – are the life force of social self-organization' (Gomez, 2017). Social self-organisation can explain how Extinction Rebellion can organise a worldwide protest in the space of a few months, as discussed in this chapter's case study.

Narrative reversal

Narrative reversal is not a new idea and brands have been using a form of narrative reversal for many years by addressing potential issues, challenges and misconceptions. The key difference with narrative reversal in the collective model is understanding that the brand won't be able to control the message. Stories are shaped by the audience and hence are no longer one-sided. User-generated campaigns may enhance reputation, but can also damage it, depending on the context of the image/content shared. Recognition that a narrative may change over time is the first step in using the collective narrative as a framework for your brand's digital storytelling. 'Embracing the narrative reversal is the strategy of designing your story to acknowledge and address criticism, counter-narratives, and misperceptions while validating your audience's participation' (Gomez, 2017).

Change making

In an ideal collective narrative, the final step is that lasting change is made. This may be in the way of behavioural change, policy changes, government changes or as simple as a brand re-focus (smaller scale). Change making is the powerful culmination of all the elements of the collective narrative colliding and making long-lasting impacts on the world. Hashtag campaigns reach audiences without the traditional media gatekeepers. This means they have an ability to span geographical borders and time zones and allow grassroots organisations to leverage global campaigns (Gomez, 2018). These campaigns span beyond pop trends and move into global movements that target political and systemic changes as seen with #MeToo and #BlackLivesMatter.

Defined as hashtag activism, and often dismissed as slacktivism, some hashtags have led a snowball effect of changes across the world, and seen governments bend to the cultural power of the hashtag and the corresponding global movement. One example of this started with the Facebook LGBT campaign in 2015, which ran in support of the US Supreme Court's ruling to legalise same-sex marriage. The campaign didn't demand any major time investment or commitment; it simply encouraged users to adopt a transparent 'rainbow flag' across their Facebook profile picture, and was adopted by more than 26 million people worldwide (Tombleson and Wolf, 2017). Whilst not initially a hashtag campaign, it led to the Human Rights Campaign using #LGBT and #SCOUTUS (Supreme Court of the United States) on Twitter and other social media platforms. This example of brand activism (with Facebook's support), in connection with a wider social media hashtag campaign, arguably represents one of the most successful activism campaigns run on social media, leading to actual global changes. The campaign highlighted the desire for change and in turn led to increased participation at physical protests. Tracking marriage equality and linking it directly to the hashtag campaign and subsequent protests is difficult to quantify any cause and effect, however since the #SCOUTUS campaign in 2015 the following countries have legalised gay marriage (entirely or in certain states in the country) (Wikipedia, 2022):

- 2015: US, Ireland, Vietnam, Finland, Puerto Rico, Greece
- 2016: Greenland, Colombia
- 2017: Finland, Germany, Australia
- 2019: Austria, Taiwan
- 2020: Northern Ireland, Costa Rica
- 2021: Switzerland, Chile

Although difficult to make a direct link, hashtag and social media campaigns are impacting social change on a level never seen before in history. As #BlackLivesMatter takes on new iterations each year, this campaign is shaping up to be the largest hashtag activism campaign in history; one that continually adapts to current trends to ensure it remains relevant. The collective narrative allows this story to live beyond its initial narrative.

CASE STUDY

XR Rebellion, the collective narrative

To understand the collective narrative and look at it in action, Extinction Rebellion, or XR, offers great insights into a collective approach to storytelling. XR seemingly appeared out of nowhere in 2019 and yet the movement has attracted worldwide participation from a diverse range of individuals and established activist groups. The call for a rebellion demanded action on climate change and used everything from drama, art, music, public protest and disruption to make XR's demands heard. At face value, these acts of public disobedience may be referred to as 'public relations' stunts, but on closer inspection, the group was using effective communication tactics and strategies far more sophisticated than a stand-alone publicity stunt. How does a little-known organisation mobilise worldwide protests in a short space of time? The answer lies in their collective narrative approach and ability to tap into the collective anxiety on climate change.

Storytelling and the collective narrative was at the heart of XR's campaign. Storylines have shifted from the traditionally dominant hero's narrative of brand storytelling to a collective narrative model. Gomez (2017) coined the term 'collective journey' to capture this shift, referring to it as a 'new modality of story itself' – one that is not linear and that can have many protagonists and multiple narratives (perspectives).

The global XR movement actively encourages the inclusion of a multitude of voices from around the world and a range of different backgrounds in its effort to demand action on climate change. In doing so XR departs from traditional approaches to brand and communication management. XR is a case study in brand building as much as it is in the power of the collective narrative. Current shifts in the origin of storytelling (i.e. the narrative being increasingly driven by audiences, as opposed to traditionally by brands and organisations) point to a greater need for practitioners to understand how collective narratives are built.

Background Extinction Rebellion

Extinction Rebellion was established in the UK in 2018 and is considered a civil disobedience movement, demanding immediate action on climate change. It defines itself as 'an international movement that uses non-violent civil disobedience in an attempt to halt mass extinction and minimise the risk of social collapse' (Extinction Rebellion, 2018). The original strategy for the global 2019 protests was to cause disruption, both metaphorically and literally. Even though XR emphasises the use of non-violent civil disobedience, multiple arrests have occurred as a result of protesters disrupting roads, trains and even airports. In April 2019, 5,000 activists shut down five key sites across London, including Parliament Square (Alibhai, 2019). Despite its status as a social movement, XR has become a highly recognisable, global brand in its own right.

Applying the collective narrative to XR Rebellion

The key elements of the collective narrative that XR Rebellion used during the 2019 protest and beyond were resonance, regenerative listening, super positioning, social self-organisation and change making. We'll discuss each one in detail.

Resonance

If we understand resonance in this case to mean a cultural element that taps into the public consciousness enough for individuals to take action, then XR exceeded in resonating with many different demographics across the globe. Like many behaviour change and activist groups that are successful, XR was very clear with their goals (Extinction Rebellion, 2018):

* Tell the truth: They sought for governments across the globe to declare a climate and ecological emergency.
* Act now: They asked governments to halt biodiversity loss and reduce greenhouse gas emissions to net zero by 2025.
* Beyond politics: They asked governments to create and consequently be led by the decisions of a Citizens' Assembly on climate and ecological justice.

Regenerative listening

The collective narrative requires communication and brand practitioners to take on a more fluid understanding of narrative. This is what Gomez (2017) refers to as 'regenerative listening'. The concept of resonance, while not new, plays a key role in regenerative listening and allows digital storytellers to tap into the 'deep inner yearnings held by massive numbers of people' (Gomez, 2017). Gomez describes it as a 'leaderless mating dance between story and people' (2017). Regenerative listening allows brands to be responsive to current events and build an authentic, relevant brand, in the image of the world around it.

XR's relevance to digital storytelling has moved beyond a focus on activism. The social movement has cultivated and activated a multitude of voices, ranging from Gen Z school kids, to Millennials, Gen X through to Baby Boomers. One of the key groups to emerge out of XR are XR Grandparents, with the tagline 'older, bolder and unstoppable' (Fletcher, 2019). As corporations and traditional brands have struggled with the perceived loss of control over their messaging as a result of the emergence of digital and in particular social media, XR has embraced the collective narrative and indeed sought to empower diverse voices, as opposed to 'managing' or indeed silencing them. XR's power lies in how it embraces the collective narrative across multiple channels, which allows it to develop a deep understanding of environmental responses.

Super positioning

XR took on a number of different ways to superposition themselves on the international stage in the form of protests and stunning visuals.

Protests held on certain days across the globe ensured worldwide coverage. A branding toolkit openly accessible via the XR website provided grassroots organisers and participants with the tools to stay 'on brand' (see: https://rebeltoolkit.extinctionrebellion.uk/).

XR understands the power of **semiotics and imagery** in the age of social media and ensured images caught attention and were used and shared on social media. In the UK, a street-performance group called the Invisible Circus took to protest in a different manner. They dressed up as 'ghostly-white figures cloaked in scarlet-red, drifting gracefully through lines of police and crowds of demonstrators' (Benjamin, 2019). The use of the colour red symbolises human blood or 'the blood of the species', but, in dual effect, also produced highly striking, symbolic images, guaranteeing their use on social media and television. Doug Francisco, founder of the Invisible Circus, said he wanted to create emotion with the costumes, and draw elements of art into the protest. He said, 'When you see the photographs, you have the police, the protesters, and these weird signature characters in-between. It's a powerful image' (Benjamin, 2019). Red-robed protests have now become associated with XR around the world, creating very distinct and shareable imagery.

Social self-organisation

One of the key tenets of Gomez's model of the collective narrative is self-organisation (2018), which is reflected in XR's self-organising system, which does not require permission to set up new local groups. This ability to quickly and spontaneously mobilise is largely helped by the 'pervasive communication technologies' that individuals and groups use (Gomez, 2018). Some organisations and public commentators have likened XR's tactics to publicity stunts, but seeing the movement's impact only in terms of a one-off event to gain publicity diminishes and indeed underestimates the group's ability to encourage large-scale, coordinated non-violent disobedience action around the world.

Change making

The ultimate goal for any social organisation or group is to bring about change. Change in terms of policy change, or even behaviour change, can be a long process. If we go back to the core goals of XR Rebellion, we can start to form an opinion on whether they achieved their endgame. XR Rebellion had three core demands:

1. Tell the truth: Perhaps the most achievable goal, governments across the world have had to become more transparent on their emissions and policies working towards minimising the effects of climate change. In many countries (e.g. the UK, Australia and many island nations) the climate is on the agenda for all key political parties.

2. Zero emissions by 2025: Critics have argued this was always going to be an impossible task, which was made even more challenging as a result of the global COVID-19 pandemic, which saw all non-pandemic issues take a back seat for at least two years. It can't be denied that Extinction Rebellion put climate on the (global) agenda and made it a more pertinent political issue. However, there's still a long way for most countries to reach zero emissions, with some setting a reduction rate of 80% by 2050 (UK).

3. Citizens' assembly: This target was primarily focused on an assembly set up in the UK. the UK Government and Parliament agreed in 2019 that the UK should do more to tackle climate change and the UK Climate Assembly met over six weekends in 2020. As a global brand aiming to get climate change on the agenda of the average person, and also policy makers, it could be argued XR Rebellion succeeded. The question is how will they continue to build momentum, particularly in a world that has been overshadowed by other issues?

A truly integrated branding approach

XR uses elements of transmedia storytelling in their digital storytelling approach. The brand itself has a strong anti-consumerist focus and all elements of branding follow this principle. The brand does not produce, and does not permit, merchandise, even to raise funds for its cause. The brand does however allow free use of its logo and artwork in a non-commercial manner (see: www.extinctionsymbol.info/).

Understanding younger generations, as well as what motivates the 'grey' generations, was key in XR's strategy. The self-organisation and ability to 'make the movement their own' had a lot to do with the initial success of Extinction Rebellion. So while branding was strong, and the guidance was provided, XR understood the nature of social media, protests and that climate change was highly topical (relevance and resonance). In terms of the collective narrative, the narrative is very much 'no one is coming to save you', emphasising that the citizens of the world must unite for climate change if there are to be lasting changes at government levels.

CHAPTER SUMMARY

This chapter provides an overall understanding of some of the key terminology and elements surrounding the traditional narrative, contrasted with the collective narrative. It discusses how a traditional story is constructed, especially within the context of some common marketing and public relations plots used in branding, alongside the use of archetypes that tap into the unconscious understanding of long-standing narratives. A modern understanding of digital storytelling – in terms of the collective narrative – is discussed alongside the key terms of resonance, regenerative listening, super positioning, social self-organisation, narrative reversal and change making.

The narrative arc and key plots

The narrative arc in its simplest form has a beginning, middle and an end that allows a story to progress and reach a resolution. Each part of the narrative builds on the previous act. This common arc has been used in film, television, novels and more. The most common narrative arc is the dramatic arc which includes five elements:

- **Exposition**: Background and introduction to the story.
- **Rising action**: Many scholars argue that the story is driven by conflict, and in this part of the narrative the first sign of conflict is shown.
- **Climax**: The pinnacle of the story and what everything is leading to.
- **Falling action**: Action that comes after a main decision by the key character at the climax.
- **Resolution**: How the story ends.

The hero's journey

The hero's journey has been a popular mode of storytelling for thousands of years, in which the hero is the main protagonist. This model follows the journey of the hero and encounters the challenges the hero comes across along the way. Joseph Campbell wrote about the hero's journey in this book *The Hero with a Thousand Faces* (Campbell, 2012) and defined story structure through the protagonist's journey.

The collective narrative

The collective narrative is a new way to define and understand how digital story-telling works. It is not the only narrative with the hero's journey still forming a part of common branding narrative, however many brands and campaigns, like Nike, Gillette, Dove, #BlackLivesMatter and #MeToo, are using the collective narrative as a powerful way to let the audience be a part of the story, and ensure a sustainable and enduring brand.

The collective narrative has six key elements:

1. **Resonance**
   Resonance can be defined as the ability of a brand or campaign to tap into a cultural trend, or zeitgeist, and link the brand in a meaningful way.

2. **Regenerative listening**

   Regenerative listening is a way to reinforce our beliefs and the fundamental core of our moral system. Gomez (2018) defines regenerative listening as 'a process where the storyteller listens so intently to the audience that the audience's language, attitudes and concerns start to show up in the story itself'.

3. **Super positioning**

   Super positioning can be defined as the way a brand (or organisation, person etc.) uses both the viral nature of social media and current trends to position themselves. Super positioning means even the smallest voices can be amplified well beyond their size, and the collective nature of this takes it even further.

4. **Social self-organisation**

   In what Gomez refers to as a level of self-determination, audiences can very quickly mobilise online campaigns and make them a real demonstration in a short space of time. Both the #BlackLivesMatter and #MeToo campaigns led to real-life demonstrations in a show of solidarity and support for the online campaigns.

5. **Narrative reversal**

   Narrative reversal is the ability of a brand or campaign to accept negative communication or an issue/crisis and address it openly and transparently. The key difference with narrative reversal in the collective model is understanding that the brand won't be able to control the message. Stories are shaped by the audience and hence are no longer one-sided.

6. **Change making**

   In an ideal collective narrative, the final step is lasting change to be made. This may be in terms of policy changes, government changes or as simple as a brand re-focus (smaller scale). Change making is the powerful culmination of all the elements of the collective narrative colliding and making long-lasting impacts on the world.

DISCUSSION QUESTIONS

1. Read the article The 7 Story Archetypes (www.socialmediatoday.com/content/7-story-archetypes-and-how-they-can-dramatically-improve-your-marketing) and in groups use the plot you are allocated by your facilitator to apply to an organisation of your choice. Come up with an 'angle' on how you could use this plot for an organisation/brand.

2. For each of the five plots (Kent, 2015), discuss one organisation, brand or company that is using that plot to tell their story. Think about why? Discuss your examples as a class:
   ○ Quest
   ○ Adventure
   ○ Rivalry
   ○ Underdog
   ○ Wretched excess

3. Reverse engineer a podcast: use digital storytelling elements from Chapter 1 ('Eleven elements of digital storytelling'), but also consider the narrative arc. Present a visual image of the podcast's structure. You can use any podcast but some highly structured narratives can be found at *This American Life* (www.thisamericanlife.org). Some elements you may consider:
   ○ Linear/chronological, fractured, framed, circular (story style)
   ○ Exposition, introduction, build-up, complication, rising action, tension, setting, characters, problem, solution, timeline, narrative style, audience, emotion, falling action, climax, resolution (narrative structure)

4. Find an example of the collective narrative from a brand perspective and analyse how they use participation, multi-narratives, regenerative listening, super positioning and social self-organisation. Create an infographic to share with the class.

READINGS

Kent, M.L. (2015). The power of storytelling in public relations: Introducing the 20 master plots. *Public Relations Review*, 41(4), 480–489. https://doi.org/10.1016/j.pubrev.2015.05.011

This reading is useful to understand narrative theory and how it is used in communications. Students will gain a broad understanding of 20 common plots used by storytellers and that can be used by brands.

Tombleson, B. and Wolf, K. (2017). Rethinking the circuit of culture: How participatory culture has transformed cross-cultural communication. *Public Relations Review*, 43(1), 14–25. http://dx.doi.org/10.1016/j.pubrev.2016.10.017

This reading looks at the influence of digital communication on cross-cultural communication. It seeks to understand how participatory culture has impacted on hashtag campaigns and how audiences create their own meaning from content.

REFERENCES

Alibhai, Z. (2019). What is Extinction Rebellion and where are the London protests being held? [online] *Metro*. Available at: https://metro.co.uk/2019/04/16/extinction-rebellion-london-protests-held-9220141/ [Accessed 31 October 2022].

Bartlett, E. (2022). 8 classic storytelling techniques for engaging presentations. [online] *blog.sparkol.com*. Available at: https://blog.sparkol.com/8-classic-storytelling-techniques-for-engaging-presentations [Accessed 31 October 2022].

Benjamin, P. (2019). The meaning behind Extinction Rebellion's red-robed protesters. [online] *Dazed*. Available at: www.dazeddigital.com/politics/article/44238/1/meaning-behind-extinction-rebellions-red-robed-protesters-london-climate-change [Accessed 31 October 2022].

Boyd, R.L., Blackburn, K.G. and Pennebaker, J.W. (2020). The narrative arc: Revealing core narrative structures through text analysis. *Science Advances*, 6(32). doi:10.1126/sciadv.aba2196.

Campbell, J. (2012). *The Hero with a Thousand Faces*. Washington, DC: New World Library.

Extinction Rebellion (2018). Find XR branches and events. [online] *Extinction Rebellion Global*. Available at: https://rebellion.global/ [Accessed 31 October 2022].

Fletcher, M. (2019). Extinction Rebellion: Green rebels with a cause. [online] *New Statesman*. Available at: www.newstatesman.com/politics/2019/10/extinction-rebellion-green-rebels-with-a-cause [Accessed 31 October 2022].

Freytag, G. (1894). *Freytag's Technique of the Drama (1900 Edition)*. 3rd ed. [online] Chicago, IL: Scott Foresman. Available at: https://openlibrary.org/books/OL7168981M/Freytags_Technique_of_the_drama [Accessed 31 October 2022].

Gomez, J. (2017). The hero's journey is no longer serving us. [online] *Medium – Collective Journey*. Available at: https://blog.collectivejourney.com/the-heros-journey-is-no-longer-serving-us-85c6f8152a50 [Accessed 31 October 2022].

Gomez, J. (2018). Embracing the narrative reversal. [online] *Medium – Collective Journey*. Available at: https://blog.collectivejourney.com/embracing-the-narrative-reversal-f56a0129e319 [Accessed 31 October 2022].

Gomez, J. (2022). The collective journey: A dynamic new storytelling model. [online] DW. Available at: www.dw.com/en/the-collective-journey-a-dynamic-new-storytelling-model/a-38872767 [Accessed 31 October 2022].

Holiday, S., Lewis, M.J., Nielsen, R., Anderson, H.D. and Elinzano, M. (2016). The Selfie Study: Archetypes and Motivations in Modern Self-Photography. Visual Communication Quarterly, 23(3), pp.175–187. doi:https://doi.org/10.1080/15551393.2016.1223548.

Jenkins, H. (2008). Sharing notes about collective intelligence. [online] *Henry Jenkins*. Available at: http://henryjenkins.org/blog/2008/02/last_week_my_travels_took.html [Accessed 31 October 2022].

Jung, C.G. (1969). *The Archetypes and the Collective Unconscious*. Princeton, NJ: Princeton University Press.

Kent, M.L. (2015). The power of storytelling in public relations: Introducing the 20 master plots. *Public Relations Review*, 41(4), 480–489. doi:10.1016/j.pubrev.2015.05.011.

Lulu, Rodriguez and Daniela V. Dimitrova. (2011). The levels of visual framing. *Journal of Visual Literacy*, 30(1), 48–65. doi: 10.1080/23796529.2011.11674684.

McKee, R. (2003). Storytelling that moves people: A conversation with screenwriting coach Robert McKee. *Harvard Business Review*, 81(6), 51–55, 136. https://pubmed.ncbi.nlm.nih.gov/12800716/

Muntasir, M. (2022). Genius or not? – Nike's 'Play New' advertisement campaign. [online] *Better Marketing*. Available at: https://bettermarketing.pub/genius-or-not-nikes-play-new-advertisement-campaign-eebb638abda1 [Accessed 26 October 2022].

Solomon, L. (2014). Creating Moments of Impact: Using Sparklines for Strategic Conversations. [online] Duarte. Available at: https://www.duarte.com/creating-moments-of-impact-using-sparklines-for-strategic-conversations/ [Accessed 16 Feb. 2023].

Tombleson, B. and Wolf, K. (2017). Rethinking the circuit of culture: How participatory culture has transformed cross-cultural communication. *Public Relations Review*, 43(1), 14–25. doi:10.1016/j.pubrev.2016.10.017.

Webster, L. (2020). Marvel, Star Wars and the risk of being a hero: Social responsibilities for transmedia storytellers in the age of collective journey. *Cultural Science Journal*, 12(1), 59–67. doi:10.5334/csci.138.

Wikipedia (2022). Timeline of same-sex marriage. [online] *Wikipedia*. Available at: https://en.wikipedia.org/wiki/Timeline_of_same-sex_marriage#2015 [Accessed 31 October 2022].

Woodside, A.G. (2010). Brand-consumer storytelling theory and research: Introduction to a Psychology & Marketing special issue. *Psychology & Marketing*, 27(6), 531–540. doi:10.1002/mar.20342.

5

TELLING STORIES ACROSS MULTIPLE PLATFORMS

OBJECTIVES

1. Develop different angles from a storyline
2. Learn how to create compelling and spreadable content
3. Understand the difference between short-form and long-form narrative
4. Understand the basic storytelling elements of social media platforms

This chapter identifies how to tell narratives from multiple angles, for suitable platforms and for an appropriate audience. It develops a communication/journalistic understanding of story 'angle', cultivates it for a brand context and highlights ways to curate different stories from one narrative. We discuss a range of social media tools that can help you tell stories, explore spreadable media and learn how to manage content across platforms.

CREATING ANGLES

> The public is exceptionally diverse. Though people may share certain characteristics or beliefs, they have an untold variety of concerns and interests. So anything can be news. But not everything is newsworthy. Journalism is a process in which a reporter uses verification and storytelling to make a subject newsworthy. (American Press Institute, 2019)

One of the key ideas around transmedia storytelling is that narratives shouldn't replicate themselves across platforms; they tell a different story on each platform, thereby collectively constructing a bigger, more engaging narrative. A core skill of both a journalist and a communication practitioner is to be able to create an 'angle' for a story. You may have heard the phrase that to create great stories you need to develop a 'nose' for them and may even know people that just seem to 'get' what makes a good story. Aside from having a 'good nose' for a story, an understanding of what makes a good story can be cultivated and it comes back to recognising what makes news. An angle or 'news angle' can be defined as something that is relevant to a particular audience or media outlet. In the world of transmedia storytelling, this idea is furthered in being able to create different angles from a single story. In terms of traditional angles and what makes a news story, Harcup and O'Neill (2017, p. 1471) identified the following top ten story angles in the traditional press:

1. **The power elite**: Stories concerning powerful individuals, organisations or institutions.
2. **Celebrity**: Stories concerning people who are already famous.
3. **Entertainment**: Stories concerning sex, show business, human interest, animals, an unfolding drama, or offering opportunities for humorous treatment, entertaining photographs or witty headlines.
4. **Surprise**: Stories that have an element of surprise and/or contrast.
5. **Bad news**: Stories with particularly negative overtones, such as conflict or tragedy.
6. **Good news**: Stories with particularly positive overtones, such as rescues and cures.
7. **Magnitude**: Stories that are perceived as sufficiently significant either in the numbers of people involved or in potential impact.
8. **Relevance**: Stories about issues, groups and nations perceived to be relevant to the audience.
9. **Follow-up**: Stories about subjects already in the news.
10. **Newspaper agenda**: Stories that set or fit the news organisation's own agenda.

Harcup and O'Neill's ranking of newsworthy angles was originally shared in their 2010 research paper, a revision of Galtung and Ruge's influential 1965 taxonomy of news values (Harcup and O'Neill, 2010). Since the advent of social media, Harcup and O'Neill (2017) have taken the original methodology and applied it to the top stories shared on social media. They discovered that while the order of importance changed, the actual newsworthiness of a story did not. Unsurprisingly, social media gave more precedence to stories around entertainment, surprise and bad news. Harcup and O'Neill (2017) point out that not all stories will fit under these banners, and there are at times unusual events that may lead to something being 'run' that otherwise may not catch the attention of news creators. In the age of social media, this in itself can lend more weight to news that falls into the 'zeitgeist' area, or that is 'of the moment'. In an unfortunate manner, bad news may still often lead and the saying 'if it bleeds it leads' can still mean a devastating event (i.e. natural disaster or mass shooting) will feature and indeed overshadow more traditionally successful (and arguably worthy) news angles. For most digital storytellers, however, the creation of positive stories for a brand is the focus.

Fog, Budtz and Yakaboylu (2005) consider the elements of places, process and products as important components in digital storytelling and these can be used in addition to the above elements.

Place can be important in digital storytelling and may add visceral elements to the story (for example the sounds and smell of a hospital in a public health story), which help to 'anchor' the narrative.

The **process** may consider how a product or service is made. Time-lapse photography has become an important element in building and construction to tell the story of the build. Confectionary organisations use visual content of the making of lollies to show the process involved prior to a customer buying the finished product, thereby building up excitement and a level of connection with the end product.

The **product** may consider how a product or service is sourced (if ethical) or made in a sustainable manner. The origin of products is becoming an important consideration in our climate-focused world. Consider how the Australian-based social enterprise Who Gives a Crap (whogivesacrap.org) uses its products to raise money to build sanitary toilets in countries where people don't have access to them.

These elements can all be used to create compelling narratives and can help storytellers come up with ideas for stories. Next, we are going to break down the creation of a story, from a journalistic and public relations perspective.

The lead

For written articles, the lead is an important element in digital storytelling. The lead is a short introductory sentence (usually 30 words or less) that defines who, what, when, where, how and why. Examples of leads are:

New York Times (7 June 2022)
Headline: As the Great Salt Lake Dries Up, Utah Faces an 'Environmental Nuclear Bomb'

Lead: Climate change and rapid population growth are shrinking the lake, creating a bowl of toxic dust that could poison the air around Salt Lake City.

The Guardian (7 June 2022)
Headline: Comedian John Oliver offers to buy Melbourne's 'demonic' banana statue
Lead: Comedian John Oliver has offered to buy a controversial banana statue that was pulled off the streets of Melbourne after being attacked by vandals.

The reason to make a headline and lead compelling is so the reader will continue to read the article. In social media, the lead translates to the caption or text under the key image and frequently may be the only part of the article someone will read before they move on to the next piece of content. Conveying the right information is important to get your message across. Because of the nature of social media, and the need to convey this information in a short amount of space, this has led to the creation of 'clickbait' headlines, or headlines that don't really represent what the article is about, in an effort to compel audiences to literally 'click' through. Good storytelling will avoid this and focus on the integrity of the story and the long-term reputation of your brand or the brand(s) you are representing.

How to find stories

Understanding what makes a great angle is the first step of any story, but how do you locate a great story to begin with? Once you develop your 'nose' for stories you'll be able to create them from many different sources (i.e. blog posts, conversations, newsletters), although sometimes you may need a little help to find them. The key here is listening and applying what you've learned about what makes a good story. For many brands, stories often already exist within the organisation and can be elicited from the CEO, staff, customers and volunteers. If you venture beyond your 'bubble', listen and ask the right questions, you'll find something intriguing that you can create an angle from.

Internal stories for brands can be used to persuade, motivate and inspire employees – if done well. An internal story, and the reason why someone resonates with it, is no different to how an external story works, although an internal audience may be more willing to listen in the first place, because there's a vested interest. With the rise of social media, internal storytelling has gained an important role as employees may act as ambassadors or detractors through social media channels. These actions may be approved or not, but either way, once the content is on social media, it is public and for everyone to see and engage with. Ensuring that your employees embrace the same narrative as the brand is important; so bringing them along as part of the storytelling process, and at times as the actual storytellers, will help ensure this. There are ways in which you can find stories to develop and build on a brand. They include:

- Continuous listening and environmental scanning via social media to gain an understanding of what your audience is saying about you, your competitors, the sector you are operating in, and indeed other current events that resonate with them.
- Using surveys or polls to create story ideas.
- Following the daily news, reading a trade journal or industry newsletters to gain an understanding about what is being said about your industry, including latest developments.
- Asking your audience what they want to know – thanks to social media this has never been easier.

The more you look for stories, the more you'll find. Sometimes the most unlikely people can give you the best stories. The only way you'll find them is by talking to people and developing your skills in linking stories to your brand objectives. This is a skill that takes time and much practice.

Establishing a culture of storytelling

In addition to finding stories, creating a culture of storytelling can ensure story-telling is top of mind for all employees and potentially even volunteers and others associated with your organisation. Employees can be encouraged to see their own lives as a story and apply that to their work environment. How an employee gets to work, how work has changed their lives, how their work is flexible and allows them to build their career while managing a family; these are all examples of stories that may add to brand value and encourage staff to become natural storytellers. Most importantly, it can shape an organisation's ability to retain and attract talent. As a part of this process, storytelling can help simplify the core of the brand; what an organisation does and what it stands for. This may help employees to make sense of their role, and the brand's role in their own lives, but also the lives of others. Establishing a culture of storytelling may include formal measures (for example, encouraging staff to submit a story idea on an intranet) or more informal measures (for example asking staff to share their stories during staff meetings). If both formal and informal measures are undertaken, a culture begins to form around the practice of sharing stories and the organisation will find them easier to source.

Developing different angles from a storyline

Knowing more about creating angles, a lead and finding stories is one thing, but actually getting pen to paper (or fingers on the keyboard) and crafting your angle is another. The best way to show how you create different angles for different audiences from a single story is to go through the process. In this example we have used some real statistics on melanoma (skin cancer) released by the Australian Government (see: www.canceraustralia.gov.au/cancer-types/melanoma/statistics). Some assumptions have been made based on the statistics. For example there is a breakdown of data based on the professions that have the highest rate of skin cancer.

A statistic drawn from the website indicates there were 16,878 new cases of melanoma diagnosed in 2021 (*estimate), representing 9,869 males and 7,009 females. In addition to this, of 1,315 melanoma deaths 64% were male and 36% female.

One simple angle that can be drawn from the statistics is that men account for more cases of skin cancer. Using the statistics from the Cancer Council website, the following angle might be created:

Men more at risk of death from melanoma than women in Australia.
New data suggests that Australian men are dying from melanoma at almost twice the rate of women in Australia.

This is a very broad angle however, and if the Cancer Council wants to highlight the particular issues in certain industries, they would use the data in a more targeted manner. For example, looking at the rate of melanoma amongst 'tradies' (skilled manual workers) or professions that work in building and construction, often working outside in the sun. The Cancer Council created the following angle for its media release:

Tradies aren't protecting against skin cancer despite up to ten times higher UV exposure.
New data reveals that Australia's tradies aren't acting to protect themselves from the sun despite exposure to skin cancer causing ultraviolet radiation (UV) up to ten times the rate of indoor workers.

Source: Media release from www.cancer.org.au/media-releases/2022/tradies-aren-t-protecting-against-skin-cancer-despite-up-to-ten-times-higher-uv-exposure

As a result of this media release the following news articles ran:

- **News.com.au** (national online news): The hidden danger killing Australian tradies (www.news.com.au/lifestyle/health/health-problems/the-hidden-danger-killing-australian-tradies/news-story/3031490d5d06ee8a4cf4247b28497ad6).

- **Inside Construction** (trade publication): Australian tradies aren't protecting against skin cancer (www.insideconstruction.com.au/section/research-analysis/australian-tradies-arent-protecting-against-skin-cancer/).
- **Yarrawonga Chronical** (local/regional publication): Victorian tradies aren't protecting against skin cancer. (https://www.yarrawongachronicle.com.au/news/victorian-tradies-arent-protecting-against-skin-cancer/)

This is one example of a story angle drawn from the statistics. Of course there are multiple other options, which could produce many different stories, targeted towards different media outlets, platforms and audiences. The angle of a story very much depends on both your target audience and the platform chosen. An angle targeted towards parents on Instagram would be significantly edited and may end up in a much shorter message, supported by an impactful graphic, than a media release would offer, as illustrated here.

Figure 5.1 Sunscreen for kids on Instagram, Photo by Leo Rivas on Unsplash

Figure 5.2 Sunscreen for kids on Instagram, Photo by Luke Michael on Unsplash

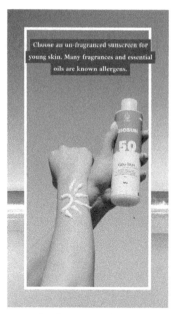

Figure 5.3 Sunscreen for kids on Instagram, Photo by Onela Ymeri on Unsplash

Figure 5.4 Sunscreen for kids on Instagram, Photo by Pawel Nolbert on Unsplash

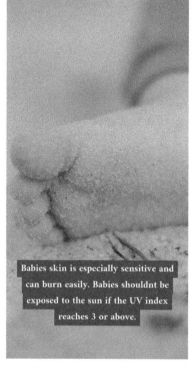

Figure 5.5 Sunscreen for kids on Instagram Photo by bady abbas on Unsplash

Drawing out different stories from a single narrative is an important part of digital storytelling. Understanding the platform it will appear on and who you are targeting will help to shape your story in a way that will be compelling and interesting to the intended audience.

Pitching

Once your angles are created you can prepare who to pitch your story to. It should be noted that for overarching statistics, like the ones released by the Cancer Council above, there may be more than ten different angles produced, depending on the objective of the campaign. You need to know the angle before you pitch your story, as for some media outlets a targeted angle will be more effective than a general one. For example, if you are pitching your sun aware story to a magazine for teenage girls, then the angle should focus on sun smart behaviour during the summer months, missing out on beach and/or pool fun if not dressed appropriately and/or burned, and the long-term health risk associated with sunburn. In contrast, a story targeted at a publication for tradespeople could focus on sun smart work gear and the impact of long-term health implications on their career, earning capabilities and business success – as well as family.

There's a slight nuance in the difference between how you might:

- pitch an angle to a journalist
- create different angles for a story for different platforms.

This all comes back to knowing your platforms and knowing your audience.

Pitching to a journalist involves understanding why the journalist may be interested in your story. For that, you need to understand the readers/viewers of their particular media outlet. A simple but often forgotten message in media relations is that if you want total control of your message, pay for an advertisement. When you engage a journalist for a story you will not have control over what they write, nor the angle chosen. Ideally you will pitch an angle that is desirable to the news outlet, however any well-trained journalist will seek to write an objective article that looks at the pros and cons of your story. This will result in more authentic content, which explains why media coverage is generally perceived as more valuable than an advertisement, however you need to be prepared that the ultimate story may not match what you had in mind in the first place.

There are two key times when you will typically engage the media: in the event of a crisis, or in the event of organisational success. As an advocacy organisation you may also reach out to the media to initiate a conversation about a wider issue, as for example in the RAC's Elephant in the Wheatbelt example. Here we are only discussing proactive media, i.e. when something good has happened for the organisation and you want to get coverage of it.

Before you pitch to a journalist, ask yourself if your news is actually news. Pitching fluffy, not newsworthy content will only undermine your personal reputation and future chances to gain coverage for your brand or organisation. You should have three key messages that you want to get across to a journalist and you need to provide something interesting, and that means 'What does it mean to the readers/viewers?' Keep in mind that as readers/viewers we always ask ourselves: WIIFM? (What's in it for me?), i.e. why should I read or engage with this particular piece of content? Why should I invest my time and energy, when there are so many other things that I could do instead?

For example, a government piece reporting on a newly passed piece of legislation in itself is not interesting to the average reader. However, if you can explain why that legislation is interesting and relevant to the audience (e.g. avoid a fine), then you'll have the journalist's attention. When speaking to a journalist, it's important to answer their questions. Journalists will know if you are avoiding discussing an issue, so the best thing is to have three key messages and address the issue. If the journalist has their own agenda/angle (and they often do), your story may not be the one they want to write, so try to insert your key messages when answering their questions.

The key element in pitching a story is understanding the 'So what'? does this mean (to me/my audience)? If you can't answer that, you should not be pitching a story. Journalists also want news so surprise them with some information they haven't heard before (positive information!) and remember it is possible to sell a story with a photo. News outlets, both online and physical, are all seeking that image, video or sound bite that connects with the audience. It's why stories of babies and children hearing for the first time following an operation are still run. There's an element of human emotion that is captured in the image or video that can't be replicated – it's authentic and heart-warming.

An example of pitching to engage a journalist is illustrated by the collaboration platform, Slack. They could write an article on how their software is a great collaboration tool for teams. In this case it is unlikely to get a run as the angle is business focused and isn't of interest to the reader. Instead, Slack could tell a journalist how their messaging application helped the NASA team put some robots on Mars. This is much more engaging and, for the right technology journalist, can be turned into an article that has interest to the readers (see: https://slack.com/intl/en-au/customer-stories/space-age-software-development).

CREATING COMPELLING AND SPREADABLE CONTENT

Knowing what is newsworthy and creating compelling narratives that people want to share are not necessarily mutually exclusive objectives. There's a dance between creating newsworthy content and balancing this with what your audience wants, and more to the point, what will resonate with them. For the digital storyteller, great stories have some key characteristics, including:

- Scope, scale and depth
- Consistency – across platforms
- Timeless themes – simple, but well presented
- Storylines and story arc development
- Cultivation, validation and celebration of your/their fan base
- Interwoven storylines and continuity across platforms

Content that is going to be shared needs to have some key elements to appeal to your audience. Heath and Heath (2016) came up with the following elements that create 'sticky' content:

1. **Simple**: A core element of all effective communication is to keep a message simple. The simpler the message the easier it is to understand and recall. The Perth Transperth Authority in Western Australia ran a behaviour change campaign to stop juveniles playing on the rail tracks and the key message was Stay Off The Tracks. It's simple, effective and illustrates exactly what the Transperth Authority hopes to achieve.
2. **Unexpected**: People love to be surprised (in a good way), so finding an element in a story that is unexpected means they will be more likely to share said content. A surprise element means people will pay attention for longer and mystery and curiosity are key drivers of human behaviour in terms of keeping their interest. Slack, a productivity tool to communicate, was used by the NASA Mars Mission team. This is a surprising use of the software and one likely to engage a reader.
3. **Concrete**: This means finding something that the audience can understand and relate to. For example to stop the spread of COVID-19 a key message was around the importance of hand washing. Often, that key message was presented as a graphic, and hence was something memorable, and an idea the audience is able to implement easily. Concrete language or images are easy to grasp.
4. **Credible**: People want to believe stories, so while the unexpected may delight an audience, they still need to believe in a narrative. This comes back to trustworthiness, and as a brand this is a key driver towards achieving authenticity. Nike's use of Colin Kaepernick in their 'Believe in something. Even if it means sacrificing everything' campaign was seen as credible as the brand has supported #BlackLivesMatter continuously.
5. **Emotional**: Emotion lies at the core of any successful story – if you can create emotion, people are more likely to remember your story and your brand.

Often, we may not remember facts, but we will remember how someone or an experience has made us feel. British retailer John Lewis is well known for its sentimental Christmas advertisements. For example, the 2022 Christmas advertisement 'The Beginner' pulls at the heartstrings, showing a foster parent learning to skateboard so he can connect with the child coming into his care who is a keen skateboarder. It's a powerful and emotional story that brings a heartfelt connection back to the brand.

6. **Story**: Heath and Heath (2016) list story as an element to increase stickiness. Story can be used as a strategy or a technique, and as mentioned throughout this book, creating something memorable is a way to connect with an audience, facilitating a sense of community. Going back to John Lewis' 'The Beginner', the advertisement is a compelling story that has the viewer asking why he is learning to skate at the beginning, shows growth (through his skill in learning) and the question is resolved at the end by the foster child arriving with a skateboard. It's a classic mountain narrative in a short 1.37 minute advertisement.

SPREADABLE MEDIA

Spreadable media is a key element of transmedia storytelling. You can design content to have a high element of spreadability. When the internet, and conse-quently social media, first started gaining traction, there was a lot of replication of content across platforms, which was somewhat supported – even encouraged – by cross-platform publishing tools. In other words, not a lot of strategic thought was given to the platform, or the audience, as the focus was on sharing a single piece of content as broadly as possible. We still see this on some level with some organisations and the level of sophistication in digital storytelling depends on the resources – human, technical and financial – that are being allocated. Not all content is created equal and there are patterns and motivations of content cir-culation. As humans we seek meaning, so understanding a particular audience's motivation and creating content based on that will improve the likelihood of content being shared. Jenkins, Ford and Green (2013) state that spreadability is determined by the process of social appraisal, but given what we now know about what people like to share on social media, we know content is more likely to be shared if it is:

- available when and where audiences want it
- portable – on the go – quotable
- easily reusable in a variety of ways

- relevant to multiple audiences
- part of a steady stream of material (building your reputation as a source of good, quality content).

(Jenkins, Ford and Green, 2013, pp. 195–228)

Content spreads when it acts as fodder for conversations audiences are already having (Jenkins, Ford and Green, 2013). Spreadable media must be fit for purpose for your brand. Hence, your understanding of the brand, the audience and platforms feeds back into your broader storytelling strategy around how you tell stories and who you are telling them to.

CREATING CONTENT FOR MULTIPLE PLATFORMS

Gigi Pritzker, CEO of Madison Wells Media, states that to be effective in creating content for multiple platforms there are a number of key elements to consider (Caprino, 2017):

- Be nimble about how content moves.
- Be platform agnostic.
- Work more efficiently.
- Grow your brand in more engaging ways.

Today, there is less pressure to provide content across all available platforms, and more focus on placing content on the right platforms, for the right audience. Many organisations have undergone a strategic streamlining of their platforms over the past years. Deciding where you want to make your content available is an important step in a digital storytelling strategy and brands need to ask themselves what the best formats to communicate their key messages are. Consideration needs to be given as to how portable you want your content to be. There may be a valid reason for not wanting people to share your content (i.e. if there's an issue with mis- or disinformation, or a copyright issue).

Halvorson and Rach (2012) highlight that people use several channels over the course of their relationship with a brand. They may not always be on the same platform. So while you may have different content across your platforms, it's also important that it is consistent and complementary, to avoid any confusion. You don't want to send out any mixed messages. This is also in line with transmedia storytelling principles where a core assumption is that anyone can enter your brand journey via any platform at any point in time. The stories need to show that they make sense without prior context, considering your audience may not have a previous interaction with your brand.

Understand how to develop short-form and long-form narrative

Short-form narrative

Short-form narrative is a condensed way of telling a story. A short-form narrative could be as short as a tweet on Twitter (which is now substantially longer than it was only a few years ago). Multiple short-form narratives can make up a bigger story, transmedia style, and contribute to the overall brand narrative. On social media, most brand-related posts are short-form narratives; however, they may link to a longer narrative on another platform (i.e. website). In general, social media is mostly for short-form narrative. This has as much to do with the way people are using social media (scrolling through) as it has with declining attention spans.

Long-form narrative

Long-form narrative generally refers to longer, journalistic style writing that differs from standard news items. Examples of long-form journalism can be seen in *The Washington Post* or *The New York Times*. These articles may be anywhere from 1,000 to 2,000 words long, with links to additional articles. In terms of brand storytelling, a long-form story is a narrative of 800 words or more that expands on a shorter narrative.

You can design a narrative to use both short- and long-form narratives, each building on the other, adding depth to the overall brand narrative. Deciding on the right narrative style will depend on your audience and your platform. As a quick guide, the best content will be tailored for your audience, however there are certain posts that do well on each platform.

Social media posts

Instagram

Figure 5.6   Instagram logo

Instagram is a platform that changes regularly and its algorithm along with it. While it is hard to predict what will get the best engagement at any given moment in time, there are universal posts that typically do well on Instagram. Instagram posts are short-form narrative, but can link to bigger platforms (i.e. websites or blogs) for a deeper narrative. Instagram now offers a Creators Lab that uses the success stories of other creators to help brands and individuals earn money on Instagram.

Reels (video): Video has become a key feature of Instagram and with Reels taking the place of video, content creators now have the option to remix their videos. Video is given preference over images and with the use of Stories to highlight a reel for 24 hours, there's an added focus. The general recommendation is to post five stories per day to ensure a good retention rate.

Image stories vs Reels: There's a slight nuance in that image stories (static images rather than video) may perform slightly better than video stories in reaching people. This may be due to the nature of how people use Instagram. Images provide the option to hold and read the content. Content that works best tends to use real faces, offers a clean visual palette (either through colours or background), and uses images that elicit our senses (i.e. strong semiotics elements that evoke sounds, taste, touch) (Hernandez, 2021). Stories can now be easily converted to Reels, so there's still the option to post static images and convert them into a video, adding effects and music.

Posts: While video/Reels may be getting all the attention, there are still important 'traditional' posts on Instagram that work well. A static image may gain traction if it is shared/user-generated content with the appropriate hashtags. A study of hashtags on Instagram has found that more is better and posts with 20 hashtags see the highest reach rate. Posts with 30 hashtags (the maximum currently allowed on Instagram) did well in generating engagement. However, just because you can include up to 30 hashtags doesn't necessarily mean you should. Instagram itself recommends limiting hashtags to be specific. More is not always better. Indeed, Instagram has become known for shadow bans, in an effort to weed out accounts that use too many hashtags or appear to be driven by bots. Your hashtag choice should be informed by the content and most importantly your target audience (Hutchinson, 2021). Authenticity and a well thought out strategy always come out ahead!

Carousels: Recently Instagram carousel posts have been shown to generate 1.4 times more reach and 3.1 times more engagement (Sehl, 2022). A carousel is a post that has more than one photo or video – the platform allows you to add up to 10 images or videos. Users can swipe through to view the images/videos. They act in a similar way to a single post but because of the ability to add multiple images, they can build a story, show before and afters, include moving images, provide how to and step-by-step guides, show micro detail of images (i.e. zoom in), etc. Sehl (2022) points out that due to the nature of scrolling, carousels may increase engagement as they make the user stop and swipe and hence tend to be more interactive and engaging than a static post.

Facebook

Figure 5.7 Facebook logo

Facebook is similar to Instagram in that it offers many different options for posts. Here we will discuss the ones that are most useful for brands in digital storytelling. While brands may have control over what they post to their platform, keep in mind that most users have set their profile to private, so you aren't privy to the conversations taking place between audience members. This has a major impact on your (social) monitoring abilities. If appropriate to the brand (e.g. BlackMilk) creating communities and brand pages where your community can speak may be of benefit. This doesn't mean that you should guide or continuously interfere in conversations, but it provides your fan or support community with a safe space to come together with like-minded people, whilst providing you with an opportunity to listen – and to clarify any issues if needed.

Post: Posts, with or without images, are the basic bread and butter of Facebook. Generally speaking, posts that are just text are unlikely to create much engagement, purely due to the algorithm and inability to attract attention when someone is scrolling. A great image can still gain attention on Facebook, particularly when mixed with the right caption and hashtag. During the early days of the COVID-19 pandemic, some governments across the world used graphical posts (much like a short infographic) to summarise the number of infections, the number of hospitalisations and similar data to quickly show viewers daily updates.

Video posts: When people scroll through Facebook, a video is more likely to be seen, however there's only about 2–3 seconds to engage your viewer if you want them to stay. Facebook gives precedence to native videos uploaded to the platform (over a YouTube link for example) so brands will experience better engagement if they upload directly. Most advice suggests keeping videos short on Facebook (about 60–90 seconds), however sometimes longer videos (2–3 minutes) may still go viral if they are compelling.

Live: Facebook live is similar to Instagram and offers the opportunity to engage with audiences and answer questions. Usually these are updates, show and tells and question and answer sessions. Lives should be unscripted in order to bring a level of authenticity to the brand, including the presentation of a real face to the organisation. Despite being unscripted, they should have a focus and goal, and be advertised prior to the event to ensure the audience is aware it's happening.

Stories: Facebook offers the option for stories (much like Instagram), and indeed many brands post the same stories to both platforms. Stories can give a behind-the-scenes look at product development or 'a day in the life' of the brand and add authenticity to the posts. They also offer interactivity, similar to Instagram, inviting questions or responses to polls.

Events: One of the popular features of Facebook is the ability to create an event page, post updates and images, and also have people who are 'interested' or 'going' post questions. This is one of the most useful functions of Facebook and if your brand or organisation is involved in events; it's an easy way to reach and engage with your audience.

Infographics: Because of Facebook's layout, for brands, there's the ability to add graphics that provide much more detail than what you would see on Instagram. Facebook allows images to be uploaded in larger format than Instagram and hence brands can use infographics to include detail for their audiences. This can be useful for governments, corporations and any brand that wants to visually show data. Infographics are powerful tools to distil complex information visually.

Brand community pages: Branded community pages work best when they are facilitated by the brand, but led by the fans. Super fans can be appointed admins and 'moderate' the pages, to add a level of authenticity and an emphasis on community, as opposed to brand control. As illustrated in the BlackMilk case study, these sites work best when fans are allowed to express themselves and share their interests and information related to the brand. For particular brands, real-life events may also occur and the page can be used to facilitate engagement with like-minded people.

Blog posts: Some brands still have blogs, and Facebook is a great way to encourage engagement and share the blog page. As this is a medium best used to share another platform, rather than copying and pasting the entire blog a shortened version may be included encouraging the user to visit the blog site. The key is to include a compelling photo or video, then a 'sound bite' that will entice the reader to read more on the linked platform.

TikTok

Figure 5.8   TikTok logo

TikTok, the rising star of social media, was the fastest growing platform in 2022 (West, 2022) and is a platform that rewards authentic content. TikTok's success lies as much in the creative nature of the platform as it does in the generational focus. TikTok posts are all in a video format, however the platform itself highlights the most effective storytelling approaches for brands, which include:

- Telling the story of your brand (product/service) through using user-generated content and outlining the value of the product or service.
- Stories that show the results first and then work backwards (think reverse narrative). An adventure story works well as it generates excitement, then works back.
- Stories that get to the point or show the 'elevator pitch'. This is a succinct introduction into the brand and why they deserve attention.
- Step-by-step stories – showing the audience how to do something in an engaging way, this can also include user-generated content.
- Stories that are a day in the life or process focused; again user-generated content is used heavily here.
- Stories that show how something is easy, fast or reliable; this may include a call to action at the end.

Source: (TikTok, 2021)

Most important on TikTok is the understanding of key digital storytelling principles like being aware of the zeitgeist (what is trending and what are people sharing), the use of songs that are heavily played on TikTok, and also ASMR (autonomous sensory meridian response) principles, as discussed in Chapter 2.

LinkedIn

Figure 5.9 LinkedIn logo

LinkedIn, like most platforms, offers a different number of options for posting. Its demographic tends to be professionals, but as it is a scroll-based social media network, content should be relevant and shareable, as well as visual to ensure it gets noticed. LinkedIn is a platform designed to put across your opinion, comment on others' opinions (respectfully) and even share interesting or amusing anecdotes from the workplace (keeping names confidential). LinkedIn's algorithms result in content being available over a longer period of time compared to Twitter, for example. This means traffic and engagement may build slower and over time. On the other hand, this also means that even those users who only log into their account once a week or less will still be able to see relevant content days and weeks after it has been posted. Here, quality content is certainly valued over quantity.

Blog posts: Blog posts do well on the platform as long as they are authentic and relevant to your audience. LinkedIn audiences are there to network, so don't be afraid to ask questions of the audience. This is an ideal way to present a long-form narrative with links to other platforms, encouraging cross-platform promotion. Blog posts can be shortened to around 200 words, or longer at around 1,000 words.

Re-shares: People who share quality and interesting content will get engagement. The trick is to share something people haven't seen and make a comment linking the original post back to your industry and network.

Native video: Native video, as in video you post directly to your LinkedIn feed, will be highlighted in your network. People love seeing a familiar face on the platform, so if you have something to say, consider filming it. The platform has seen an uptick in authentic content so don't worry about producing something too polished or scripted.

Plain text: If your topic is timely, share it with a question to your network, alongside appropriate hashtags. You don't always have to have a visual, and sometimes the best conversations will happen independently of images.

Images: These gain attention, but LinkedIn is a very specific platform that focuses on business, networking and organisations. There has been some backlash when people post more 'social content' (i.e. holiday snaps) that is seen as off-topic. However, if carefully selected, appropriate images can assist your content in standing out. There is a carousel option on LinkedIn and you can showcase more than one image or PDF.

The defining commonality in all LinkedIn posts is the ability to use hashtags (relevant to your industry) and also tag relevant connections to superposition your content.

YouTube

Figure 5.10   YouTube logo

YouTube was one of the first internet platforms to encourage participatory culture and online sharing. Today many brands use YouTube as a depository for brand-related content. The nature of YouTube means videos should be longer than would be posted on Facebook, Instagram or TikTok for example. It's very much a brand extension platform and offers the transmedia element of providing deeper information should audiences want it. The key here is the brand's audience – what sort of content do they want, what will they watch, and for how long?

Company culture videos: These offer a great way to showcase the authenticity of your brand and why someone may want to work for you. While you may have the ability to produce a glossy, corporate video, authenticity works best, even on this platform, and audiences will want to see real people.

Product/service videos: Many people prefer watching videos over reading so providing engaging content that is relatively short may gain attention.

Event videos: Event videos can be used to document an event, but also include engaging content for future events. The YouTube version would be the longer extended version of what is shown on Instagram/TikTok.

Timelapse videos: These are useful for mining companies, building and construction, land development, product development or any process that spans over a long time. They can be satisfying to watch, but are usually a brand extension.

Interviews: This is a transmedia approach that provides a deeper level of content that can be both with staff, and with customers. Interviews should be unique and provide a new insight into the brand and the people associated with it.

Twitter

Figure 5.11 Twitter logo

Preferred by some communities and sectors as a primary form of engagement, Twitter is usually more text driven, but note the increased emergence of images to highlight content. Twitter conversations are fast moving, anchored in contemporary debate, and because of this, it is easy to be left behind if you do not log into your account for a few days or even hours. For brands, Twitter offers the ability to engage in a meaningful way. Although the platform is fast paced and offers more of a broadcast model, with the right resources in place, brands can respond personally, building trust and a reputation for authenticity with individuals who want to engage with their brand. Consumers or other stakeholders frequently use Twitter to raise concerns or demand timely responses to an issue, so even if your brand may not be active on Twitter in terms of content generation and storytelling, it is crucial that you monitor conversations and have the ability to respond to any posts warranting further clarification from your end. Issues are best handled offline or via direct messages. However, you want to avoid an issue escalating due to a failure by the brand to respond. Although different to other platforms, Twitter still offers ways to highlight content.

Hashtags: A key feature of Twitter and one that brings in elements of relevance and resonance if brands can be agile and respond (appropriately) to trending hashtags.

Twitter chats: Twitter chats are still used to discuss topics and engage with audiences.

Links and posts: Twitter can link to just about all content on other platforms so it's an opportunity to cross-promote in a shorter, micro-detail manner.

CASE STUDY

Spotify Wrapped

The case study of Spotify Wrapped will be discussed to understand how the value of brand, community and fans (see Chapter 3) fits with telling a story across platforms. Spotify launched in 2008 and is a music streaming service which people can access for free, or by paying for a subscription (premium) service. Spotify identifies 422 million users including 182 million subscribers (Spotify, 2022). Spotify Wrapped is a personalised digital storytelling strategy that uses big data, obtained via its users, to create

Figure 5.12   Spotify logo, Photo by Alexander Shatov on Unsplash

individual, shareable stories to feature across multiple channels. For the audience it uses nostalgia and personalisation to increase shareability and also stickiness. Spotify says that initially the purpose of Wrapped was to 'give back to users' and it had no promotional intentions. They also said that their message strategy was designed to be a 'cultural brand campaign', or in other words seeking to tap into the zeitgeist of the music year to show the bigger narrative.

Their platforms

The Wrapped campaign allows for easy sharing from the Spotify app or website via Messages, Facebook, Twitter, Instagram, TikTok and more. It is ephemeral content in that it is only available in December and January, although the songs from most-listened-to content are available in a personal playlist after this time.

Their audience

Spotify uses big data and yet personalises it for their audience. The broader advertising campaigns tell the bigger narrative of what people are listening to, and the shareable content provides a personalised version. The platform's audience is diverse as it is large, and hence the personalisation lets each user tell their individual story. This is the duality of big data - large amounts of data allow platforms to tell big stories about its users, and yet, the data can be used on such a small level that it also allows for individual stories.

Their storytelling strategy

The #spotifywrapped campaign is simple in its execution. Spotify already has data of its users, and hence with the number of users on its platform there is sufficient content to create creative overarching and micro stories. As the stories are personalised, they provide a snapshot of a user's taste in music to their followers. Spotify maximises on trends and the 'zeitgeist' of each year to tell bigger stories as well. In 2016 they used interesting statistics to feature on a UK billboard, to increase brand awareness (Shakespeare, 2017).

'Dear 3,749 people who streamed "It's the End of the World as We Know It" the day of the Brexit vote, Hang in there.'

Figure 5.13　Example of copy on Spotify billboard

Spotify understands its audience well and knows a lot of people listen to music travelling to or from work, hence they run a lot of advertisements at train stations, airports and bus stops. In following the trends of its audience, in 2020 Spotify celebrated a decade of the #spotifywrapped campaign, focusing on the song of the decade (Spotify, 2020). Knowing the year had been a difficult one for many of its users (when the global COVID-19 pandemic resulted in many lockdowns with related economic impacts around the world), the promise of nostalgia facilitated via the music from the previous decade provided great comfort to users.

Data visualisation

The visualisation of big data is important, so it can be both easily shared and understood. Data is only meaningful to people if it's personalised, and Spotify understands this. They create easy ways to customise the look and feel of their #spotifywrapped images and in terms of increasing accessibility they also make Wrapped available to audiences that use the platform for free, as well as subscribers. In addition to the social media campaign, Spotify use targeted billboard advertising to discuss the bigger narrative. This is done in a humorous manner and further connects with the audience. Spotify also helps users share their Wrapped experience by offering tips on how to get more out of the experience – they have included voice commands, interactive Instagram story lenses, TikTok effects and customisation of the share cards. This adds to further personalisation of the experience.

Shareability

The key element in the campaign, as well as telling the 'music narrative' of the year, is shareability. Spotify makes it easy to generate personalised data, but then facilitates the sharing of key insights across multiple, external platforms.

Fans

In terms of fandom, Spotify is appealing to social connection, identification, pride and advocacy for music fans to share the personal music tastes. Also important is the way in which Spotify shares bite-size information that is able to be viewed 'at a snapshot' moment. This enhances its engagement as it appeals to the nature of social media platforms. The Spotify user is at the core of the campaign and hence the campaign holds an element of authenticity, and the use of a hashtag #spotifywrapped allows the content to be compared and tracked.

Conclusion

Spotify's Wrapped campaign is as much a story of data personalisation and digital story-telling as it is branding. The clever campaign furthers brand loyalty with existing users, but also becomes a brand awareness campaign in itself, reaching out to new and casual users. Big data has the ability to tell both large and small stories for brands, and as we know small stories create big stories, this is a sure way for Spotify to engage the hearts and minds of its users.

CHAPTER SUMMARY

This chapter discusses the theory behind telling stories across multiple platforms. It looks at the key reasons why people share content and how to create differ-ent angles for different platforms. It is important to understand what news stories media outlets are interested in and may print. Harcup and O'Neill (2017, p. 1471) defined the top ten stories in the traditional press:

1. **The power elite**: Stories concerning powerful individuals, organisations or institutions.
2. **Celebrity**: Stories concerning people who are already famous.
3. **Entertainment**: Stories concerning sex, show business, human interest, animals, an unfolding drama, or offering opportunities for humorous treatment, entertaining photographs or witty headlines.
4. **Surprise**: Stories that have an element of surprise and/or contrast.
5. **Bad news**: Stories with particularly negative overtones, such as conflict or tragedy.
6. **Good news**: Stories with particularly positive overtones, such as rescues and cures.
7. **Magnitude**: Stories that are perceived as sufficiently significant either in the numbers of people involved or in potential impact.
8. **Relevance**: Stories about issues, groups and nations perceived to be relevant to the audience.
9. **Follow-up**: Stories about subjects already in the news.
10. **Newspaper agenda**: Stories that set or fit the news organisation's own agenda.

This chapter discusses how to identify and expand on stories as a brand. This includes:

- Listening on social media (as well as offline) to what your audience is saying about you, your competitors, your industry and contemporary events
- Using surveys or polls to create story ideas

- Reading the newspaper or trade journal about what is being said about your industry
- Asking your audience what they want to know – social media has never made it easier

Shareability is an important concept in digital storytelling and how to create spreadable media that is more likely to be shared is a required skill. Spreadability is a social process that requires the content to appeal to certain elements that make it easier to share; content should be:

- available when and where audiences want it
- portable – on the go – quotable
- easily reusable in a variety of ways
- relevant to multiple audiences
- part of a steady stream of material.

(Jenkins, Ford and Green, 2013, pp. 195–228)

Building your fan base also provides a way to ensure your content is distributed. The Spotify Wrapped case study illustrates how fans can be used to share content for brand awareness, but also to tell micro narratives of brand data.

DISCUSSION QUESTIONS

1. Based on the following organisations, explore how a story is told on different platforms. Try to find one example of a story that has used different angles for different audiences and/or platforms.
   a. World Health Organisation
   b. Burberry
   c. Uber
   d. Transport authority (your local one)
2. Using transmedia storytelling and participatory culture elements, devise a strategy for a real-life client. Focus on doing certain elements well – not all elements – and show how you'll build a digital community.
3. Take a media release from a government organisation/brand/NGO and show how you would adapt that story across different platforms. Think about tone and audience, as well as the objective and call to action of the campaign.

READINGS

Lund, N.F, Cohen, S.A and Scarles, C. (2018) The power of social media storytelling in destination branding. *Journal of Destination Marketing & Management*, 8 (June), 271–280.

This reading focuses on the shared experience of tourism and using others to tell stories in destination branding. It gives the example of the VisitDenmark campaign as a case study in the use of user-generated content as part of the campaign.

REFERENCES

American Press Institute (2019). What makes a good story? [online] *American Press Institute*. Available at: www.americanpressinstitute.org/journalism-essentials/makes-good-story/ [Accessed 2 November 2022].

Caprino, K. (2017). Cofounder of one of the most innovative Hollywood firms shares her vision. [online] *Forbes*. Available at: www.forbes.com/sites/kathycaprino/2017/10/03/co-founder-of-one-of-the-most-innovative-hollywood-firms-shares-her-vision/?sh=375082f82127 [Accessed 2 November 2022].

Fog, K., Budtz, C. and Yakaboylu, B. (2005). *Storytelling*. Berlin/Heidelberg: Springer-Verlag. doi:10.1007/b138635.

Halvorson, K. and Rach, M. (2012). *Content Strategy for the Web*. Berkeley, CA: New Riders.

Harcup, T. and O'Neill, D. (2010). What is news? Galtung and Ruge revisited. *Journalism Studies*, 2(2), 261–280. doi:10.1080/14616700118449.

Harcup, T. and O'Neill, D. (2017). What is news? *Journalism Studies*, 18(12), 1470–1488. www.tandfonline.com/doi/full/10.1080/1461670X.2016.1150193

Heath, C. and Heath, D. (2016). *Made to Stick*. Colchester: Random House.

Hernandez, S. (2021). How to get the most visual attention on your content. [online] *Social Media Today*. Available at: www.socialmediatoday.com/spons/how-to-get-the-most-visual-attention-on-your-content/608678/ [Accessed 2 November 2022].

Hutchinson, A. (2021). New study looks at optimal hashtag usage in Instagram feed posts, based on 18m examples. [online] *Social Media Today*. Available at: www.socialmediatoday.com/news/new-study-looks-at-optimal-hashtag-usage-in-instagram-feed-posts-based-on/610377/ [Accessed 2 November 2022].

Jenkins, H., Ford, S. and Green, J. (2013). *Spreadable Media: Creating Value and Meaning in a Networked Culture*. New York: New York University Press.

Sehl, K. (2022). How to use Instagram carousels to 10x engagement. [online] *Social Media Marketing & Management Dashboard*. Available at: https://blog.hootsuite.com/instagram-carousel/#:~:text=Instagram%20carousel%20posts%20are%20one [Accessed 2 November 2022].

Shakespeare, S. (2017). Spotify's 'Thanks 2016' campaign cues it up for a prosperous New Year. [online] *YouGov*. Available at: https://yougov.co.uk/topics/politics/articles-reports/2017/01/11/spotifys-thanks-2016-campaign-cues-it-prosperous-n [Accessed 2 November 2022].

Spotify (2020). How it's made: Wrapped. [online] *YouTube*. Available at: www.youtube.com/watch?v=hpwv5tiQGKk&t=6s [Accessed 2 November 2022].

Spotify (2022). About Spotify. [online] *Spotify*. Available at: https://newsroom.spotify.com/company-info/ [Accessed 2 November 2022].

TikTok (2021). Get creative: 6 frameworks to tell your story on TikTok. [online] *TikTok For Business*. Available at: www.tiktok.com/business/en-US/blog/get-creative-6-storytelling-frameworks [Accessed 2 November 2022].

West, C. (2022). TikTok marketing: The complete guide for brands in 2022. [online] *Sprout Social*. Available at: https://sproutsocial.com/insights/tiktok-marketing/ [Accessed 2 November 2022].

6

BECOMING A
STORY CURATOR

OBJECTIVES

1. Understand the theory of co-creation and related key terms such as authenticity, zeitgeist, crowdsourcing, slacktivism and hashtag hijacking
2. Understand how user-generated campaigns fit into the realm of digital storytelling through the #MeToo case study
3. Learn about the evolution of the influencer and how they have shaped the media, including challenges and successes across the years

We learn to develop stories, but also how to encourage others to tell stories on our behalf. This chapter explores how brands can use digital audiences to collaborate and co-create. We discuss key concepts around how to become a story curator – a specific skill needed for digital storytelling. There are some key terms in story curating we need to understand in depth; hence we'll discuss what authenticity, zeitgeist, crowdsourcing, slacktivism and hashtags activism mean. The theory of co-creation is examined, as well as the advantages and disadvantages of others (e.g. influencers and advocates) telling stories on our behalf in terms of brand reputation. We explore the ethical dilemmas associated with using influencers and why getting the right collaboration for storytelling is important.

THEORY OF CO-CREATION

The theory of co-creation has been evolving steadily since the introduction of the internet (although it did of course exist prior to the internet). We have already discussed co-creation as being a key element of participatory culture. A main shift in organisational branding that we have seen over the last 20 years is the move away from an organisation-centric branding strategy towards one of co-creation, where the brand is built through multiple channels. The natural progression of co-creation with the rise of digital storytelling and influencers is a natural shift – as these elements become more powerful in their ability to persuade consumers, so too does their power relationship with brands increase. Co-creation in brand storytelling in the era of the collective narrative is almost essential to survival. For too long brands that have tried to hold on too tightly to their interpretations of 'reality'. Now, they are being held accountable for not being inclusive, failing to facilitate input by key audiences.

In its simplest form, there are two main types of co-creation that brands take part in. The first is a dedicated campaign that invites the audience to be a part of the campaign. It often requires little more than a hashtag and has a low barrier to entry. Examples of this are #shotoniphone #shareacoke #icebucketchallenge and even social movement campaigns like #MeToo. The other type of co-creation is more holistic and involves the deliberate inclusion of stakeholders and the audience to build a brand and become involved in brand direction and innovative ideas. An example of this is Ikea's 2018 digital platform 'Co-Create Ikea' that encouraged customers to share product ideas, collaborated with universities and ran entrepreneurial and innovation labs around the world (see: https://about.ikea.com/en/life-at-home/co-creation). This approach is strategic, deliberate and long-term, requiring significant resources. Most importantly, it needs to align with the brand positioning, to ensure engagement is meaningful, as opposed to being perceived as a token gesture.

Why do we use others to tell stories?

There are many reasons why we use others to tell our stories. We have discussed some in relation to participatory culture and the collective narrative. Other reasons include:

- Co-creation is rooted in open participation and innovation.
- Co-creation gives brands a chance to engage with consumers on a deeper level.
- Collaboration and co-creation humanise the product development process.
- It is important to recognise the value and attributes of different audience members.
- Co-creation can boost consumer engagement with new product offerings.

(Muscroft and Needham, 2013)

Specific to brands, using others to tell our stories has many advantages including:

- Brands can learn and improve from engaging the audience in conversations, rather than making assumptions about consumers' needs and wants.
- Earned media have a multiplier effect, intensifying and spreading the communication messages everywhere online.
- The audience becomes involved through individual conversations on blogs, product review sites, news sites and many other places.
- The company, customers and other members of the public can initiate a story.
- Stories from others might increase the authenticity of brand narratives – and by extension the authenticity of the brand.

Different members of the audience engage differently with digital stories. According to Strauss (2016), there are five levels of audience engagement:

1. The least engaged internet users only **consume** online content. They read blogs, view videos and photos, listen to podcasts, and read the reviews and opinions expressed by others occupying higher levels of engagement.
2. The next level consists of those who **connect** with others and brands through digital channels. For example, by liking a particular YouTube channel.
3. There are members of the audience who **collect** information and go through a process of filtering content, tagging what they find valuable in social media sites. This could include 'liking' someone's content or sharing posts in a Facebook channel.
4. Next, there are those who are **creators** in their own right and develop their own original materials, such as Instagram photos and YouTube videos. They may write product reviews or contribute to a brand's Wikipedia page, for instance.
5. Finally, the most engaged audience members **collaborate** with the company whilst working with others to identify ways in which products or processes could be improved. For example, CNN offers iReporter, which enables users to send in videos of breaking news as observed first-hand. This type of collaboration aims at helping companies and brands to improve and develop products and communication materials, whilst drawing on the collective knowledge – and passion – of their stakeholder community.

Authenticity

In the digital storytelling space, there is a shift away from the traditional corporate communication model relying on carefully crafted and controlled messages to a move characterised by more authentic and organic communication. Authors like Valentini and Kruckeberg (2012) state that social media and related networks need to be 'conceptualized as online social environments that enable people to engage in relationships of a different nature for example, professional, personal, and spiritual ones' (p. 8). As a brand or organisation, this represents a fundamental shift in thinking. Digital storytelling is a space where you may not create a story, but instead, you harness the participatory nature of the social space as you share and co-create stories with your wider audience. In doing so you build an emotional connection with the audience and allow their experiences to build that connection with your brand.

In digital storytelling 'authenticity' has become one of the most essential elements as audiences want to connect with something real. The concept is a core value of social media. For brands authenticity is a key element in building and maintaining trust and represents the foundation of a good reputation. Authenticity can be a broad term and viewers can perceive authenticity differently according to their background and culture. The term authenticity varies across the literature and has been applied in many different disciplines including psychology, marketing, communications and tourism, extending to 'staged authenticity', referring to the re-creation of ethnic or cultural traditions, such as for example the now globalised version of the Scottish Highland Games (Chhabra, Healy and Sills, 2003). In a marketing and communication context, authenticity is viewed as a part of the brand narrative that delivers an honest representation of the organisation and hence increases trust.

The issue with this is that authenticity will mean different things within different organisational contexts, hence an internal definition is needed to ensure it delivers on building trust between audiences and the organisation. The Cambridge Dictionary defines authenticity as the 'quality of being real or true', hence the link to brand trust here is evident (Cambridge University Press, 2023). Conlon, Smart and McIntosh (2020) discuss the importance of authenticity in digital storytelling, highlighting that audiences recognise it when 'the experience is intense and deeply trusted as being "true" to a reality that connects symbiotically with their own unique world' (p. 269). Built into the concept of authenticity is the emotion the audience feels from storytelling, and its relevance and resonance to the audiences' world. In the digital world, relevance and resonance are intertwined with current affairs, events and campaigns and underpin some of the reasons why digital stories are shared. 'Can Creativity Make You Bleed?' is an example of using emotion to build an authentic digital story that spans across different platforms but allows the audience to feel different emotions based on their interaction with the campaign. Andy Fergusson from Leo Burnett outlines the experiment.

CASE STUDY

Rigg Award, Leo Burnett, 'Can Creativity Make You Bleed?'

Written by: Andy Fergusson, November 2022

Now in its ninth edition, the triennial Rigg Design Prize is Australia's highest national accolade for contemporary design bestowed by an Australian public gallery (National

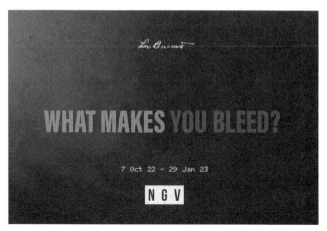

Figure 6.1   What Makes You Bleed? campaign
Printed with permission of Leo Burnett

Gallery of Victoria) and seeks to profile a different field of design practice every three years. In 2022, for the first time, the National Gallery of Victoria exhibited work from the communication and advertising industry.

Figure 6.2   Leo Burnett, National Gallery of Victoria space
Printed with permission of Leo Burnett

Eight agencies were challenged to create a campaign that articulated the potential of creativity to accelerate positive social, cultural, economic or environmental change. The eight exhibited campaigns represent a call to action for Australia to realise its 'creative potential'.

Each agency was tasked with using the same five channels to communicate their idea – social media, a billboard, street furniture, a street poster and a digital screen.

Leo Burnett once said that 'Creativity has the power to transform human behaviour', so we saw this brief as an opportunity to prove the potential of creativity, by actually motivating people to do something tangible. And learn more about people in the process.

Our concept posed the question 'Can creativity make you bleed?' It put creative potential to the test, by finding out which human emotion would motivate people to give blood.

We chose blood donation because it's a universal human need. But only 3% of Australians give blood, so it is clear that finding the right motivation is very important.

We created a series of distinct campaign elements, which all used a different core emotional driver: anger, joy, sadness, surprise, fear and disgust. And we encouraged people to vote on which one was the most motivating by scanning an accompanying QR code.

The emotions chosen were based on the 'core basic emotions' proposed by behavioural psychologist Paul Eckman, a pioneer in the study of emotions, and a collaborator on Pixar's movie *Inside Out*.

Each piece was created in a bespoke way to take advantage of the assigned media format and each piece used storytelling in a unique way to ensure it elicited the required emotion.

To motivate using **JOY**, we created a social media film that used the true story of a blood donor, James Harrison – whose blood has helped save more than two million babies' lives – as an example of the wonderful impact your blood can have.

Figure 6.3   What Makes You Bleed? Joy
Printed with permission of Leo Burnett

To motivate using **FEAR**, we created a digital screen that demonstrated the terrifying reality of what happens when our community runs out of blood. As the blood level dropped, the societal consequences became more extreme.

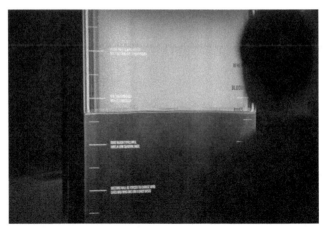

Figure 6.4　What Makes You Bleed? Fear
Printed with permission of Leo Burnett

To motivate using **SADNESS**, we created a billboard that juxtaposed heart-wrenching stories of loss written on empty blood bags. Demonstrating how giving blood equates to giving people more time with their loved ones.

Figure 6.5　What Makes You Bleed? Sadness
Printed with permission of Leo Burnett

To motivate using **ANGER**, we created street posters that showed how some of the most fringe groups of people in Australia have greater numbers than there are blood donors. And that should make your blood boil.

Figure 6.6 What Makes You Bleed? Anger
Printed with permission of Leo Burnett

To motivate using **DISGUST**, we created a funny yet disturbing film that documented the story of a niche pair of 'blood drinkers'. Demonstrating a disgusting alternative way to share a pint of blood with someone.

Figure 6.7 What Makes You Bleed? Disgust
Printed with permission of Leo Burnett

And to motivate using **SURPRISE**, we showed the results in real time of which emotions were the most motivating based on which QR codes people had scanned the most.

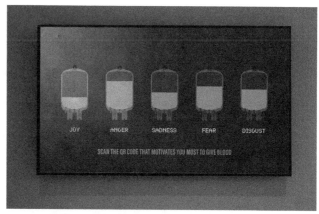

Figure 6.8 What Makes You Bleed? Surprise
Printed with permission of Leo Burnett

Figure 6.9 What Makes You Bleed? Surprise
Printed with permission of Leo Burnett

To date, the current front runners are 'sadness' and 'disgust'. The former is to be expected, as we know that sadness and empathy is a strong driver. But when it comes to 'disgust', it may be down to the humour of the piece, or perhaps it was just such an unexpected way to promote blood donation that people simply paid more attention.

It is very rare that you get to experiment with different emotions and storytelling techniques to achieve the same goal. So, this project has been a great exercise in stretching our creative muscles and experimenting with approaches that are outside the norm.

We hope that this project will inspire people to tell stories in different ways, but more importantly we hope people will be inspired to give blood.

Although authenticity can be built through others telling the brand story, creating real emotion can also build a strong authenticity for a brand or campaign through connecting in a personal manner. In other words, real stories that build emotion create authenticity. As social media and digital storytelling have evolved, the desire for authenticity has also grown as audiences seek out the 'real' online. Simply put, the more digital we become, the more we crave to feel human.

Zeitgeist

If you look in the Oxford Dictionary, zeitgeist is described as 'the defining spirit or mood of a particular period of history as shown by the ideas and beliefs of the time'. In the age of the internet, or indeed social media, the term defines 'an idea that is iconic to a particular moment in time'. There is limited academic and even media discussion on the role of the zeitgeist in digital storytelling. The reason for this is that it is a difficult concept to capture, clearly define or indeed recreate. It's hard to predict what will be the zeitgeist of the moment, and it can change from one day to the next. When it happens, however, like an unpredictable viral meme, it can be incredibly powerful and, if harnessed well, transform brands. In the collective narrative the zeitgeist fits a number of elements including resonance and super positioning, however the organic nature of these trends, and hence authenticity, is what drives the popularity. This is not to say brands can't capitalise on a trend once it is happening. The case study we will look at to define the zeitgeist in digital storytelling is of the brand Ocean Spray.

CASE STUDY
Ocean Spray cranberry juice

During the global COVID-19 pandemic an unassuming video using the Fleetwood Mac song 'Dreams' went viral and racked up almost 26 million views on TikTok. The video was uploaded by @420doggface208 or Nathan Apodaca on 25 September 2020 and has since been seen more than 85 million times and inspired many people to replicate it, including 73-year-old Fleetwood Mac's drummer, Mick Fleetwood. In the video, Nathan is filming himself serenely skateboarding while drinking a bottle of Ocean Spray cranberry juice and lip-synching to the song. Early on, Ocean Spray let the video play out and enjoyed the organic marketing, as they watched bottles of their product sell in large numbers. As time went on, the brand reached out to Nathan Apodaca and gifted him a new truck to replace the one that had broken down and prompted the production of the video, as he jumped on his skateboard to prevent him being late for work. Next, the CEO of Ocean Spray, Tom Hayes, filmed himself replicating the video, as did multiple celebrities and more traditional content creators. There is no doubt Ocean Spray benefited from the viral video and Hayes came out and said the brand 'had disproportionately benefited from the pandemic' (Weissman and Weissman, 2021). In a moment of zeitgeist, Fleetwood Mac also saw their 1977 song 'Dreams' trending on the iTunes and Spotify singles charts. TikTok, as the platform on which the video shot to fame, equally capitalised on the 'good vibes' video trend, featuring Nathan and multiple 'Dreams' co-creators in a commercial.

Ocean Spray is a 91-year-old company that had a traditional approach to social media and yet moved to an approach that was 'a little more edgy, and to be a little more attractive to the younger consumer' after the viral TikTok (Weissman and Weissman, 2021). The question remaining is why did this video go viral? Much discussion has been around the stage of the pandemic and that the video summed up the freedom and carefree nature of the human spirit, something people (particularly young people) were craving after the unknowns and restrictions that had been placed on them early in the pandemic. It also captures a sense of uniqueness and ability to simply roll with the punches and get on with life in the face of adversity (the pandemic, the broken down car). The point of the zeitgeist is that it can rarely be predicted. Instead, it is more something that can be harnessed and built on. This requires ongoing monitoring of trends and influencers to determine if something is building momentum that may be capitalised on for the purpose of your own brand or the brand you are representing.

Can brands use the zeitgeist to their advantage?

There is no doubt the chance video was of benefit to Ocean Spray. They did see an uptick in sales, and hence an increase in profits. However, the real question is: can this be sustained, once the popularity of the video has worn off? The answer really depends on the brand's evolution and ability to tap into the cultural zeitgeist, as audiences may feel everything that comes after seems inauthentic. There are a few ways brands can seek to build on the zeitgeist:

- **Keep the momentum going**: Brands can use moments on social media to extend their advertising, communication and connection with audiences.
- **Consider more native content**: If a particular video has been popular, consider how you might use this in future content creation for the brand, and hence as a part of your digital storytelling; for Ocean Spray, the series could lead perhaps to content of people drinking cranberry juice on a number of different, unconventional means of transport, e.g. a surfboard, a bike etc.
- **Think transmedia storytelling**: While a zeitgeist moment is desirable, it's only ever going to be a part of the story, not the entire story.
- **Give back**: Depending on the nature of the content shared, if a brand is benefitting from something that was created organically and it can positively affect the lives of those involved, it should do so. In the case of Ocean Spray, the company reached out to Nathan Apodaca, without fanfare or media, and replaced his broken down car with a new one (plus plenty of bottles of Cran-Raspberry).

Crowdsourcing

Crowdsourcing is an open-source approach to digital storytelling that has been used for many years to encourage innovation and creativity. The idea of crowdsourcing is based on the collection of ideas from a broader community, and often facilitated through social media and/or a dedicated crowdsourcing platform (Steils and Hanine, 2022). It is not only ideas in the form of product innovations that exist in crowdsourcing, but also digital storytelling in itself, with the ability to ask the community to create and share content. This works well in campaigns in which it is not only the content production that is desired, but also the sharing and amplification of the message. In the following case study, we look at how the UN used the #CovidOpenBrief in a crowdsourcing manner, and as part of the collective narrative, to curate images and content for use in spreading the message about hand washing and other public health measures to ensure good hygiene during the peak of the global pandemic. User-generated content is a micro term that can be seen as a part of crowdsourcing, and ultimately is a form of this approach.

CASE STUDY

UN COVID-19 open brief #CovidOpenBrief

In early 2020, as the COVID-19 pandemic began to grip the world, the UN called creatives to step up and create artwork to be submitted to their 'creative content hub' (https://unitednations.talenthouse.com/). The aim was to help communicate important and unifying messages that could 'combat the spread of COVID-19 and unite the world during the pandemic' (United Nations, 2022). There were six predetermined key elements to the call to action:

1 Personal hygiene
2 Physical distancing
3 Know the symptoms
4 Myth-busting
5 Spread kindness
6 Solidarity

A key element of the open brief was that artwork was free to be shared and available in multiple creative formats and languages, furthering its ability to be used across the globe in an open manner. The artwork covered images, videos, audio, gifs and copy.

This type of crowdsourcing campaign has a two-fold effect. First, the UN was asking for artwork which it might use itself, but was also available on a microsite for anyone to use, thereby reducing the total production costs. Second the act of the creators creating the artwork increased topic engagement and visibility, as they were encouraged to share their work with their own online communities via predetermined social tags and hastags including:

@WHO @UN @UnitedNations @Talenthouse #CovidOpenBrief #UNCovid19Brief #FlattenTheCurve #SafeHands #AloneTogether #ViralKindness #StopTheSpread #Coronavirus #Covid19

While the campaign did have 'winners' chosen from a field, the cleverness of the crowd-sourced campaign was that it became a part of the awareness campaign the UN was trying to implement, and thereby helps get the message out as a part of a broader awareness-raising and education campaign.

Slacktivism

A few years ago, slacktivism (sometimes referred to as clicktivism) was a popular term that was used in relation to some user-generated activist campaigns. The term slacktivism was derived from the original idea of hashtag activism. Hashtag activism is defined as the 'act of fighting for or supporting a cause with the use of hashtags as the primary channel to raise awareness of an issue and encourage debate via social media' (Tombleson and Wolf, 2017, p. 15). 'Slacktivism' as a term grew out of this, based on the public grabbing onto hashtags and using them, often with little effort or change. The term slacktivism has been defined as a 'willingness to perform a relatively costless, token display of support for a social cause, with an accompanying lack of willingness to devote significant effort to enact meaningful change' (Kristofferson, White and Peloza, 2013, p. 1149).

There's been great debate on whether hashtag activism can make a meaningful contribution or offers only token support that makes the poster feel good but doesn't bring about any change. There's no doubt that there have been many campaigns that have failed to go beyond the status of more than a 'like' on Facebook. However, the notion that hashtags and likes 'do nothing' is simplistic at best when more and more evidence is showing that online activism is more effective than it first appears, and more importantly may have lasting behaviour change impacts (see Bennett and Segerberg, 2012). In 2013 UNICEF ran a campaign entitled 'Give Money, Not Facebook Likes'. It was a harsh advertisement and blatantly called out slacktivists to do more. The caption to the advertisement read: 'Like us on Facebook, and we will vaccinate zero children against polio'.

In an article in *The Atlantic, Vice* columnist Brian Moylan said 'right now, gay activism needs all the help it can get. But do you know what's not helping? Changing your Facebook profile picture to a silly red-and-pink equal sign' (Khazan, 2013).

In a similar sentiment to UNICEF, the comment at the time was not misguided, but focused on the lack of immediate change and not looking to the bigger picture, and the more widespread worldwide movement and narrative that was occurring. Many corporations and not for profits rely on quarterly financial results for financial reporting. Even not for profits, like UNICEF, where funding is often urgent and needed quickly, require a quick turnaround on results for campaigns. Profile image filters and hashtag campaigns, despite the speed of the internet, can be powerful campaigns but work a lot more behind the scenes on behaviour change and long-term political change. Two years after the UNICEF campaign and the comment in *Vice*, academic research indicated that changing a profile image or sharing a hashtag was increasing peer-influence and challenging the status quo; as State and Adamic (2015) noted, 'individuals changed their profile picture to a variant of the equal sign only after observing several of their friends do it first' (p. 1749). Furthermore, not only was it changing peer behaviour, but the academics also argued it was increasing participation in offline activism as 'the likelihood to engage in activism increases with the observation of other individual's activism' (p. 1741). For some campaigns, like #MeToo and #BlackLivesMatter, behaviour change is the goal, and hence these hashtag campaigns become highly successful activist campaigns, creating long-term and far-reaching political, policy and behaviour change. The timescale of these campaigns however is years, and success is unlikely to be achieved in a matter of months. Since the beginning of hashtag campaigns and profile picture support the biggest misconceptions have been proven wrong – firstly that slacktivism or clicktivism does not do anything (it does) and secondly that it is separate to offline activism (it is not).

Hashtag hijacking

While hashtag campaigns are proving effective, and showing longevity, there is a downside as we see more hashtag hijacking when popular hashtags begin trending. As a part of the idea of the collective narrative, while collective stories can be positive, some people are seeing this as an opportunity to interrupt conversations. Trolls and non-progressive activists may use a trending hashtag to get their voice heard. So, while there are many benefits, an opportunity to engage online audiences may lead to brands 'losing control' of the intended messages. Sometimes, it is not trolls hijacking a hashtag, but rather the public with a different view of an organisation. Two examples of failed hashtags include:

- #myNYPD (New York Police Department)
- #mcdstories (MacDonalds)

Both campaigns had negative comments that were not in support of the organisation or brand. The #myNYPD campaign 'prompted a flood pictures of officers mistreating people and old newspaper headlines about unarmed people being shot dead by police. It also sparked similar hashtag trends – including #myLAPD – and attracted international attention' (Tran, 2014). #mcdstories was promoted for less than 2 hours after many negative comments were shared around obesity, animal rights, food poisoning, poor hygiene and much more (Lubin, 2012). For brands engaging in the use of hashtag campaigns, particularly in the space of user-generated campaigns, it is important to play devil's advocate before using the hashtag. The decision to run a hashtag-focused campaign should not be taken lightly, but carefully planned through and determined as a suitable strategic fit for your brand and positioning. For example, if you are an industry body representing the Australian coal lobby, a hashtag campaign is most likely targeting the wrong audience and inviting more criticism than the endorsement you may desire (just in case you are wondering, yes, 'Coal. It's an amazing thing', supported by the #coalsamazing hashtag were actual campaign ideas that did not result in the type of engagement that the Minerals Council of Australia would have had in mind). If you are asking others to share your hashtag, think of every viable way this may be taken out of context. Sometimes even the best thought out hashtags can be taken over by internet trolls or haters. It is important to monitor hashtags and intervene if someone is using your hashtag to trash your brand or 'spam' your hashtag feed.

CASE STUDY
#MeToo

We discussed user-generation campaigns in Chapter 3 as an introduction to how they are a participatory approach to digital storytelling. This case study seeks to understand hashtags campaigns (a form of user-generated campaign) and how they are a collective narrative style that is enduring and unpredictable.

To illustrate the power of a simple hashtag, the #MeToo movement is one that has shown not only can hashtag campaigns endure across time, but also across cultural contexts, leading to social and political changes. #MeToo is a worldwide campaign that aims to bring attention to sexual harassment and assault. The hashtag campaign as we know it began in 2017 when actor Alyssa Milano wanted to demonstrate evidence of sexual assault in Hollywood. This was quickly followed by other celebrities, but then average women, and some men, began sharing their stories. #MeToo is an example of the power of the collective narrative as thousands and thousands of personal stories were shared across the globe. While Milano may have sparked the online movement, the #MeToo campaign did not start with Alyssa Milano, it was a campaign against rape culture started originally by Tarana Burke in 2006 and reignited by Milano after a series of public claims from notable celebrities and senior executives. The timeline of #MeToo spans from 2006 to present (see: www.chicagotribune.com/lifes tyles/ct-me-too-timeline-20171208-htmlstory.html) and involves Hollywood actors and executives, high-profile executives, sports coaches, politicians and talk show hosts.

The 'safety in numbers' approach to the hashtag campaign saw thousands of stories shared that in turn turned a spotlight on the scale of the issue. As such a single story – or experience – becomes part of a truly collectivist storytelling effort. It is important to remember that by observing others, one forms rules of behaviour, and on future occasions, this coded information serves as guides for action. In this way, social norms and behaviours observed among celebrities displaying symbolic information of what is applauded and accepted in societies allows viewers to have access to and to emerge into different realities (Bandura, 1986).

The collective stories put pressure on politicians, high-profile media personalities and sport coaches and saw reporting and legal action against sexual assault increase. While the campaign may have started in earnest in 2006, it did not gain worldwide attention until 2017. Five years later, the campaign is still seeing policy and government changes across the globe. A recent report in Australia for Gymnastics Australia reported on the toxic culture and sexual abuse that have been a part of the sport for decades. While it is difficult to explicitly draw a link between these independent reviews and the #MeToo campaign, it is compelling that the collective action of hundreds of thousands of people worldwide has drawn attention to bigger issues in society and in turn empowered other individuals to speak up and have their voice heard – often after years and decades of feeling unheard and marginalised. Hence as a society we need to look deeper into online engagement and how it exposes audiences to different views and how they make sense of the world.

After #MeToo, using the zeitgeist for social issues

A number of brands undertook brand activism as a result of the #MeToo campaign. While it cannot be verified if all the campaigns were developed as a result of #MeToo, some directly addressed the issue, such as Gillette – with mixed results. There has been an uptick in brand campaigns with a highlight on better equality for women, and this can be seen in:

- Always, Fight like a Girl
- Gillette, The Best Men Can Be
- Durex, Consent #Timesup
- Twitter, #HereWeAre
- Uncommon Goods, support for RAINN (sexual assault)
- Schweppes, Dress for Respect

Each campaign had different rates of success, with some being very controversial in nature (e.g. Gillette and Schweppes). However, as noted previously, brands need to be conscious of increasingly skeptical and savvy audiences to avoid being accused of cause washing. The alignment with a cause needs to fit the overall brand narrative, i.e. it shouldn't be a departure from traditional marketing and positioning approaches, which will likely be interpreted as a ploy to exploit a social phenomenon for marketing gain. There's a very fine line between using the collective narrative successfully and using it for marketing gain.

INFLUENCERS

It is impossible to talk about digital storytelling without references to the use and role of influencers. In curating a brand's digital story, influencers may be an important part of building an authentic and sustainable brand. Love them or hate them, they are an integral part of the digital environment and in some instances have been incredibly successful at building a brand narrative (either their own or for someone else). On the flip side, influencers have also been known for some spectacular fails and poor business ethics (see e.g. Fyre Festival). Influencers have become powerful prosumers in their own right – consumers who are now producing content and sharing their ideas... and influence. Influencers are not limited to words (bloggers) but can be micro bloggers and visual influencers as seen on Instagram, YouTube, Twitter and TikTok.

This desire for authenticity has fed into the rise of the influencer to connect with audiences via the 'everyday voice', but also in turn has led to influencers not disclosing payment for content, thereby selling a modern version of staged, carefully created 'authenticity'. There are a number of reasons why people are attracted to influencers:

- Emphasis on content marketing: Content is king and it is impossible for brands to create it all, so influencers offer a third-party option.
- Relevance and resonance: Influencers have relevance to their audience and resonate more as they are perceived as 'word-of-mouth' and not 'advertising' (often despite the fact they are).
- Trust: We trust people 'just like us' so that means influencers (who are often everyday people) are more likely to be trusted. However, within this context it should be noted that the trust influencers enjoyed in the mid-2010s, then perceived as 'people like me', has since rapidly declined, as audiences become more critical and indeed savvy (see e.g. the Edelman Trust Barometer, Edelman, 2022).

There are many ways organisations define the different types of influencers. In terms of number of followers, the definition varies from agency to agency. Due to increased visibility associated with social media, everyone is already famous to a certain degree and within a social network (Gamson, 2011). Social media provides the means to make one's private life a public story and anyone can become an influential storyteller, irrespective of their location and background. Influencers use typical storytelling techniques to gain fans and ensure people keep coming back. As a result, there has been an explosion of 'micro-celebrities' and social influencers (Ouvrein et al., 2021). A micro-celebrity is famous in a particular (digital) subculture; thus, this person has a 'niche' audience (Marwick and Boyd, 2011). Despite a small(-ish) following, micro-influencers and even nano-influencers (those

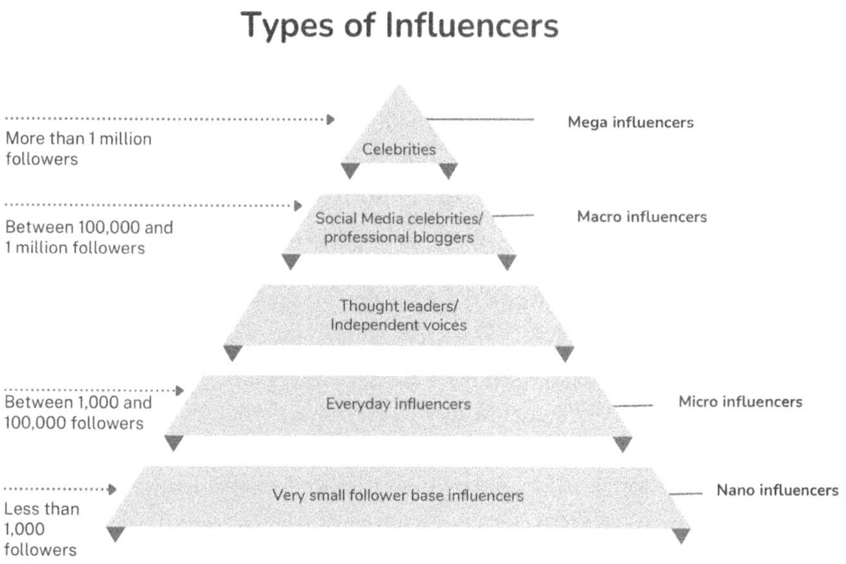

Types of Influencers

Figure 6.10 The influencer pyramid, Source: Based on Ouvrein et al. (2021)

with fewer than 10,000 followers) can be extremely powerful, as they may carry a lot of weight and influence within a particular (niche) community, e.g. the home-schooling community in your local city/region, extreme sports enthusiasts or a collective of craftivists. However, the nature of social media is constantly changing the way people use the platforms, which means micro-celebrities are not the only type of influencer that is gaining attention.

Mega-influencers: Celebrities (actors, athletes, artists) who have a following of more than 1 million followers. This generally equates to 2–5% engagement per post. Think professional athletes like Serena Williams or Justin Bieber, who have utilised their existing profile to build huge online followings.

Macro-influencers: Professional bloggers, YouTubers with 100,000 to 1 million followers. This may equate to 5–20% engagement. Macro-influencers offer the best of both worlds: a sizeable following, plus an engaged audience in a particular niche, e.g. fashion, gaming, music, etc. Think lifestyle bloggers.

Micro-influencers: Everyday influencers who have 1,000 to 100,000 followers. This may equate to 25–50% engagement per post. Micro-influencers have at times shown themselves to be more effective than celebrity influencers, particularly with hyper-local campaigns. They have a loyal audience and are highly influential. Depending on the product or campaign, the type of influencer used will vary according to the core objectives.

Nano-influencers: Everyday social media users with fewer than 1,000 followers. They are not professional influencers, although they can wield considerable influence within their network. However, their content focuses more on personal events, family, friends and memes.

Selecting the right influencer

Selecting the right influencer/s for a particular campaign, brand, product or service is key in reaching the right audience. Most of the research in this area uses the source credibility model as the main framework on why you might choose to use an influencer (Erdogan, 1999). This framework consists of three key elements: expertise, trustworthiness and attractiveness (Erdogan, 1999). The research around this model more than a decade ago suggests that trustworthiness is the most important dimension, followed by expertise (Amos et al., 2008), and other scholars have followed suggesting influencers should be chosen in relation to building brand reputation (Vodák et al., 2019) and brand connectedness (Bakker, 2018). However recent studies have shown that it is trustworthiness followed by attractiveness that is most important to the online brand campaign and brand perception, with expertise having little importance (Wiedmann and von Mettenheim, 2020). This is a significant shift, although in line with anecdotal observations from many communicators and marketers that influencers do not need to have any expertise in the product or service they are promoting in order to sell it.

The principle of role models (or key opinion leaders) has always been around in society, and influencers represent a form of role model on social media. Celebrities were used in advertising long before the rise of the internet, and people related to and engaged with them (albeit in a one-sided manner usually). Social comparison theory proposes that people determine their own worth by comparing themselves to others, and within the social media context this theory is both relevant and troubling. Developed by Leon Festinger in 1954, this theory still holds up today as we see social media users finding motivation from those online, as well as dissatisfaction, guilt and more serious conditions like body dysmorphia and eating disorders (Festinger, 1954; Zimmer-Gembeck, Hawes and Pariz, 2020). Choosing the right influencer hence comes down to knowing who they are, who their audience is and if they match your brand values and storytelling objectives.

Types of posts

The regulation of influencer posts can be a grey area. Depending on the regulatory context in which you are operating, there may be individual licensing requirements (e.g. United Arab Emirates), legal requirements (e.g. the need to align with consumer law) or a reliance on industry guidelines, often co-created by key industry bodies to pre-empt further regulation. There are four key types of posts that should be defined when creating an agreement with an influencer. These posts do not include an actual advertisement-style post, which is usually brand-led (even if an influencer is used).

Sponsored post #spon #sponsored

A sponsored post is where a brand pays an influencer to write a post/share content about a brand. The influencer shares content through their social media channels using their voice. There are guidelines that the sponsorship needs to be communicated to the audience.

Free samples/gifts #gifted

Many social media influencers are willing to share content in return for a free sample or gift. This is another grey area in terms of regulation, and one that various regulatory bodies around the world continue to watch closely. Brands do not have any control in regard to the content being shared as there are no contractual bonds. Brands may also provide gifts to be given away by influencers. It is important to note that the Public Relations Society of America considers excessive gifts unethical. Many Australian organisations also ban the use of gifts (i.e. gifting food or alcohol to journalists). Even with guidelines and protocols by professional bodies, gifting can be a grey area if no disclosure is required. Ethical considerations suggest that if in doubt: disclose!

Pay-per-click influencer post

Pay-per-click links still exist. In this model an influencer shares a link through social media channel and the brand only pays based on the number of clicks generated. It is considered a low-involvement relationship between influencer and brand and a low-budget option. The brand does not have control over the message being shared with the link, although the rise of influencer agencies has seen an increased level of control over the content of individual influencer posts.

Collaborations #collab #collaboration #paidpartnership

A collaboration is when brands engage with influencers to create content. This is an area of activity that captures the core of public relations, simply moving traditional engagement and collaboration models into the online domain (Wolf and Archer, 2018). Brands may develop short- or long-term collaborations with social influencers. It is recommended that contractual agreements are in place when using any kind of influencer. Key elements that need to be included in an influencer agreement include:

- Terms of agreement (i.e. parties involved, dates, what is contract for)
- Timeline of agreement
- Deliverables (what is the influencer to deliver)
- Cancellation reasons (i.e. poor performance etc.)

- Contract requirements (i.e. approval process)
- Confidentiality and exclusivity
- Compensation and payment terms
- Intellectual property rights

Measuring influencer effectiveness

Measuring influencer effectiveness is difficult in that there's no one-size-fits-all approach and much of the definition of 'effectiveness' will come down to the individual brand and purpose, and indeed the objectives set at the beginning of any campaign. According to Tribe (a major influencer platform in Australia, the US and the UK), there are three common objectives used in assessing partnerships:

1. Content quality
2. Engagement
3. Follower reach

However, many brands use a range of measures to track performance of influencers or return on investment, including:

- Custom URLs and hashtags, swipe up links and brand tags, dedicated landing pages
- Affiliate links
- Discount codes
- Reach and impressions (metrics)
- Audience engagement and audience growth
- Brand mentions
- Traffic from social channels
- Conversations and revenue from social media

The type of tracking will again depend on the goal or objective of the campaign. AMEC, the International Association for the Measurement and Evaluation of Communication, strongly advocates for the holistic measurement of communication, including all relevant online and offline channels. Influencer engagement – or even a single post by an influencer – will only ever tell a very small part of your brand story.

Ethics and influencers

The issue arising in recent years is the role of ethics in influencer communication. While media are organised bodies often a part of a professional alliance, and hence have a code of ethics to adhere to (see www.meaa.org/), influencers are individuals (and often not journalists). They are not guided by a set of ethics. In Australia, the Australian Association of National Advertisers (AANA) is the national body that regulates advertising to promote fair marketing practices: it encourages transparency and honesty. The AANA recommends influencers use #ad for sponsored posts.

Influencer platforms and relevant industry guidelines sometimes recommend using #spon and others use #ambassador.

However, there is a wide variation of usage, and some influencers do not use recommended hashtags, with little repercussions.

Influencer codes of ethics continue to be a work in progress, although approaches vary across countries and jurisdictions. In Australia the Association of National Advertisers is responsible for the relevant self-regulated industry codes applicable to social media influencers. The AANA Code of Ethics contains a set of standards and overarching principles with which advertising in any medium must comply. The underlying principle is that advertising should not be disguised as user-generated content or independent market research. Given the wide range of influencer content, it cannot be assumed that audiences recognise influencer posts as advertising, as opposed to a personal opinion or impartial review. However, the Code does not have the force of law. Intead, it relies on education, guidance and the assumption that public shaming or calling out of brands (and influencers) failing to act transparently and ethically will risk reputational damage. In July 2020, the newly established Australian Influencer Marketing Council (AiMCO) introduced a voluntary self-regulation initiative through its Influencer Marketing Code of Practice. The Code provides guidance on how and when advertisers and influencers should make relevant disclosures, informed by a focus on best practice, measurement and industry knowledge. Its focus is on informing contractual arrangements, including disclosure requirements, between brands and influencers.

Some areas are gaining more scrutiny however – particularly in the areas of health and finance. From July 2022 social media posts claiming health benefits now constitute 'marketing' under the Therapeutic Goods Association guidelines if influencers mention any product claiming to 'remove toxins', 'relieve pain' or 'reduce inflammation' (testimonials). In the financial sector a recent crackdown by corporate watchdog, the Australian Securities and Investments Commission (ASIC), on unlicensed financial advice has caught out many finfluencers, by (threatening jail time and/or fines if making recommendations about stocks, investment funds or financial products. However the ASIC rules don't cover cryptocurrency or property, which are ironically two areas that have received much influencer attention. Regulation around influencer engagement is rapidly developing and varies widely, from individual licensing requirements for local and visiting influencers (United Arab Emirates) to more of an industry informed and guided approach (e.g. the USA), or the application and adaptation of existing laws to the influencer context (e.g. Germany). Take the time to investigate the status quo of influencer-related regulation in your country.

CHAPTER SUMMARY

This chapter discusses the theory of co-creation and how brands can become story curators using co-creation as a meaningful way to build an authentic narrative. **Co-creation** is a critical part of participatory culture and a large part of digital storytelling and showing **authenticity**. Brands that are able to curate content created by others, and invite others to be a part of that content creation, may better resonate with their audiences on a larger scale. There are many styles of co-creation campaigns and these include hashtag campaigns, user-generated campaigns, crowdsourcing and an organic zeitgeist.

An example of a **crowdsourced campaign** that is discussed in this chapter is the #CovidOpenBrief that asked artists all over the world to submit media relating to six key themes during the COVID-19 pandemic. In terms of authenticity, user-generated campaigns may be more effective than carefully designed, organisation-driven approaches, as they are not brand-centric and are amplified by the creators sharing their content (as well as the brand).

The chapter discusses the role of the **zeitgeist** in digital storytelling and how, for brands that are actively listening to their channels, it provides another opportunity to curate content that may be powerful. The example of Ocean Spray is discussed as a successful zeitgeist moment that pushed the brand's social media strategy in a new direction.

The chapter discusses the notion of **slacktivism** and urges caution in applying the term too quickly to campaigns that may be gradually changing opinions, attitudes and even policy over time. Initially some of these campaigns may look like they are inviting token gestures that do little to further an issue, but long-term they are raising awareness (and sometimes funds – see the ALS #icebucketchallenge) and may motivate further action and involvement to bring behaviour change.

The importance of **user-generated campaigns** is discussed based on the #MeToo movement, including the power and far-reaching implications of a hashtag that became a worldwide political campaign.

A key element of co-creation is the use of influencers in digital storytelling. This chapter discusses the types of different influencers including:

- Celebrities – mega-influencer
- Social media celebrities/professional bloggers – macro-influencer
- Thought leaders – macro-influencer
- Every day influencers – micro-influencer
- Smaller influencers – nano-influencer

DISCUSSION QUESTIONS

1. Have you ever been engaged in slacktivism or hashtag activism? What motivated you to become engaged? What were the consequences of your involvement in this cause?
2. Research influencer guidelines in your country. Are there any surprises? Create a shareable infographic summarising your key findings.
3. In groups discuss: Do social media influencers need to be accurate and truthful about expressions of personal support for a product on the one hand and also disclose rewards and commercial connections with brands and products on the other? Discuss in groups and decide on your group's position. Prepare a statement to deliver to the class.
4. Explore and discuss authenticity within the influencer marketing context. Is 'staged authenticity' an acceptable norm within this context?
5. Discuss the best and worst examples of hashtag hijacking that you are aware of and share your insights with your group/class.

READINGS

Tombleson, B. and Wolf, K. (2017). Rethinking the circuit of culture: How participatory culture has transformed cross-cultural communication. *Public Relations Review*, 43(1), 14–25. https://dx.doi.org/10.1016/j.pubrev.2016.10.017

This paper discusses the role of the circuit of culture in cross-cultural communication and looks at the role hashtag campaigns have to play in activism. It discusses the role of the public relations practitioner in curating content and acting as a cultural intermediary.

Khamis, S. (2016). Self-branding, 'micro-celebrity' and the rise of social media influencers. *Celebrity Studies*, 8(2), 191–208. https://doi.org/10.1080/19392397.2016.1218292

This paper discusses the meaning of self-branding and where it fits in the role of marketing and social media influencers.

Borchers, N.S. and Enke, N. (2022). I've never seen a client say: 'Tell the influencer not to label this as sponsored': An exploration into influencer industry ethics. *Public Relations Review*, 48(5), 102235. https://doi.org/10.1016/j.pubrev.2022.102235

This article concerns ethical issues in relation to influencers and identifies ten key ethical issues. It discusses the need for 'a broad perspective on influencer industry ethics that positions influencer communication at the intersection between Public Relations, advertising, and journalism' (p. 1).

REFERENCES

Amos, C., Holmes, G. and Strutton, D. (2008). Exploring the relationship between celebrity endorser effects and advertising effectiveness. *International Journal of Advertising*, 27(2), pp.209–234.

Bakker, D. (2018). Conceptualising influencer marketing. *Journal of Emerging Trends in Marketing and Management*, 1(1), 79–87.

Bandura, A. (1986). *Social Foundations of Thought and Action: A Social Cognitive Theory*. Englewood Cliffs, NJ: Prentice-Hall.

Bennett, W.L. and Segerberg, A. (2012). The logic of connective action. *Information, Communication & Society*, 15(5), 739–768. doi:10.1080/1369118x.2012.670661.

Cambridge University Press (2023). Cambridge Dictionary | English Dictionary, Translations & Thesaurus. [online] Cambridge.org. Available at: https://dictionary.cambridge.org/.

Chhabra, D., Healy, R. and Sills, E. (2003). Staged authenticity and heritage tourism. *Annals of Tourism Research*, 30(3), 702–719. doi:10.1016/s0160-7383(03)00044-6.

Conlon, M.M.M., Smart, F. and McIntosh, G. (2020). Does technology flatten authenticity? Exploring the use of digital storytelling as a learning tool in mental health nurse education. *Technology, Pedagogy and Education*, 29(3), 269–278. doi:10.1080/1475939x.2020.1760127.

Edelman (2022). *Edelman Trust Barometer*. [online] Available at: www.edelman.com/trust/trust-barometer [Accessed 2 November 2022].

Erdogan, B.Z. (1999). Celebrity endorsement: A literature review. *Journal of Marketing Management*, 15(4), 291–314. doi:10.1362/026725799784870379.

Festinger, L. (1954). A theory of social comparison processes. *Human Relations*, 7(2), 117–140. doi:10.1177/001872675400700202.

Gamson, J. (2011). The unwatched life is not worth living: The elevation of the ordinary in celebrity culture. *PMLA*, 126(4), 1061–1069. doi:10.1632/pmla.2011.126.4.1061.

Khazan, O. (2013). UNICEF tells slacktivists: Give money, not facebook likes. [online] *The Atlantic*. Available at: www.theatlantic.com/international/archive/2013/04/unicef-tells-slacktivists-give-money-not-facebook-likes/275429/ [Accessed 2 November 2022].

Kristofferson, K., White, K. and Peloza, J. (2013). The nature of slacktivism: How the social observability of an initial act of token support affects subsequent prosocial action. *Journal of Consumer Research*, 40(6), 1149–1166. doi:10.1086/674137.

Lubin, G. (2012). McDonald's Twitter Campaign Goes Horribly Wrong #McDStories. [online] Business Insider. Available at: https://www.businessinsider.com/mcdonalds-twitter-campaign-goes-horribly-wrong-mcdstories-2012-1.

Marwick, A. and Boyd, D. (2011). To see and be seen: Celebrity practice on Twitter. *Convergence: The International Journal of Research into New Media Technologies*, 17(2), 139–158. doi:10.1177/1354856510394539.

Muscroft, J. and Needham, A. (2013). Managing co-creation. [online] *Slideshare*. Available at: www.slideshare.net/Facegroup/managing-cocreation [Accessed 3 November 2022].

Ouvrein, G., Pabian, S., Giles, D., Hudders, L. and De Backer, C. (2021). The web of influencers: A marketing-audience classification of (potential) social media influencers. *Journal of Marketing Management*, 37(13–14), 1–30. doi:10.1080/02672 57x.2021.1912142.

State B. and Adamic L. (2015). The Diffusion of Support in an Online Social Movement: Evidence from the Adoption of Equal-Sign Profile Pictures. Paper presented at the Proceedings of the 18th ACM Conference on Computer Supported Cooperative Work & Social Computing, Vancouver, BC, Canada.

Steils, N. and Hanine, S. (2022). Effective creative crowdsourcing: A multi-dimensional evaluation framework. *Creativity and Innovation Management*. doi:10.1111/caim.12497.

Strauss, J. (2016). *E-Marketing*. Abingdon: Routledge.

Tombleson, B. and Wolf, K. (2017). Rethinking the circuit of culture: How participatory culture has transformed cross-cultural communication. *Public Relations Review*, 43(1), 14–25. doi:10.1016/j.pubrev.2016.10.017.

Tran, Mark. (2014). #myNYPD Twitter callout backfires for New York police department. [online] The Guardian. Available at: https://www.theguardian.com/world/2014/apr/23/mynypd-twitter-call-out-new-york-police-backfires.

United Nations (2022). *United Nations COVID-19 Response Creative Content Hub*. [online] Available at: https://unitednations.talenthouse.com/ [Accessed 3 November 2022].

Valentini, C. and Kruckeberg, D. (2012). New Media Versus Social Media: A Conceptualization of their Meanings, Uses, and Implications for Public Relations. in S Duhé (ed.), New Media and Public Relations. 2. edn, Peter Lang, New York, pp. 3-12.

Vodák, J., Novysedlák, M., Čakanová, L. and Pekár, M. (2019). Who is influencer and how to choose the right one to improve brand reputation? *Managing Global Transitions*, 17(2). doi:10.26493/1854-6935.17.149-162.

Weissman, C.G. and Weissman, C.G. (2021). 'Disproportionately benefited': Ocean Spray CEO Tom Hayes on going viral and expanding into new categories. [online] *Modern Retail*. Available at: www.modernretail.co/retailers/disproportionately-benefited-ocean-spray-ceo-tom-hayes-on-going-viral-and-expanding-into-new-categories/ [Accessed 3 November 2022].

Wiedmann, K.-P. and von Mettenheim, W. (2020). An adaptation of the source credibility model on social influencers: An abstract. *Enlightened Marketing in Challenging Times*. doi:10.1007/978-3-030-42545-6_65.

Wolf, K. and Archer, C. (2018). Public relations at the crossroads. *Journal of Communication Management*, 22(4), 494–509. doi:10.1108/jcom-08-2018-0080.

Zimmer-Gembeck, M.J., Hawes, T. and Pariz, J. (2020). A closer look at appearance and social media: Measuring activity, self-presentation, and social comparison and their associations with emotional adjustment. *Psychology of Popular Media*, 10(1). doi:10.1037/ppm0000277.

7

STORYTELLING DESIGN AND COMPOSITION

OBJECTIVES

1. Apply your knowledge to create a storyboard for a digital story
2. Learn how to develop a digital storytelling strategy for an organisation or brand

The ability to tell digital stories is a crucial part of digital storytelling, but using them strategically for an organisation or brand, and knowing how to develop a digital storytelling strategy, is another skill separate to the act of telling a digital story.

This chapter uses the original seven elements of digital storytelling, as identified by the Centre for Digital Storytelling in Berkeley, California (Lambert, 2002; Storycenter, 2022) and expanded by the University of Houston (2015).

Students learn how to create an overall story strategy and break it down into a manageable, shareable and actionable plan. In this chapter we analyse the Croatian osiguranje campaign, (Skoko and Gluvacevic, 2020), to highlight key points in strategy development.

CREATE A STORYBOARD FOR A DIGITAL STORY

Storyboards have been used by many different creative professionals for the purpose of mapping key ideas. The idea of the storyboard first emerged within the context of filmmaking, but it provides many benefits for other practice areas and professions. Disney, the film company, developed the idea of storyboarding in the 1930s by drawing sequential cartoon scenes that represented the film and its storyline (Disney, 2018). It is essentially a visual planning document and a roadmap for what you will create. In the marketing, communication and advertising industries, storyboards are a way to gain key stakeholder approval and endorsement for an idea prior to incurring any cost to produce the actual content.

A storyboard represents the visual sequence of your ideas. It will show the images (or representation of images), graphics and copy, voiceover and music that will appear for each frame. A storyboard could be hand drawn or developed via templates available on platforms like Wix and Canva that provide you with a structure into which you can enter your content. In branding and the business world storyboards are useful to pitch ideas, present ideas to a CEO or (line) manager, or generally to show steps in a story for approval purposes.

Using templates to create a storyboard

There are many different templates you can use to create a storyboard and even websites that will walk you through the process (see e.g. www.storyboardthat.com/). At the simplest level, the free-to-use graphic design platform Canva offers generic storyboard templates to download and enter your own material: www.canva.com. An example of a template is shown in Figure 7.1.

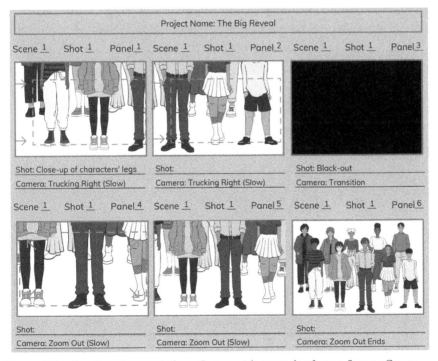

Figure 7.1   Storyboard example from Canva, with example of story, Source: Canva

How to create a digital storytelling strategy for an organisation or brand

While any storyboard can be used to plan and showcase a video, digital story or social media post, in the case of building a digital story, it helps to understand at least the basic structure prior to creating a storyboard.

Eleven elements of digital storytelling

These building blocks are important to gain a holistic understanding of the digital storytelling environment. Drawing on the 11 elements of digital storytelling (Lambert, 2002; Storycenter, 2022; University of Houston, 2015) we discussed back in Chapter 1, you can consider each element when constructing a storyboard. For reference, Figure 7.2 is a handy graphic of the 11 elements to help refresh your memory.

WHAT IS STRATEGY IN DIGITAL STORYTELLING?

The definition of strategy, according to the Oxford Dictionary, is 'a plan or action designed to achieve a long-term or overall aim' (Oxford English Dictionary, 2023). Myerson (2018) specifically defines brand strategy as: 'An articulation of the ideas upon which a brand is built and/or the plan for systematically expressing those ideas through identity and brand experience(s)'. Essentially, strategy is all about the position you are in right now, and where you want to be. Indeed, strategy is all about how you get to that desired end point. However, also note the emphasis on 'experience' in the brand context. Strategy is:

- Where are we now?
- Where do we want to be? (the final stage but we need to know this in order to understand the 'how')
- How will we get there? (this is what a strategy is – detailing the 'how')

The best way to answer these questions is to compile a gap analysis. This can be done by answering the questions in the table below.

Step 1	Step 2	Step 3
Where are we now?	Where do we want to be?	How do we get there?
Describe and list the current situation	Describe ideal outcome (goals and objectives)	Finally list what you need to do to get from where you are to where you want to be
Example: New business entrant, struggling to attract quality staff	*Example: Be recognised as the employer of choice in your particular business sector*	*Example: Amplify the staff voice via profiling and co-created content, curating quality, engaging insights into our company culture based on humorous, but educational digital short stories, targeted at potential talent and amplified via word of mouth*
Add your own example:		

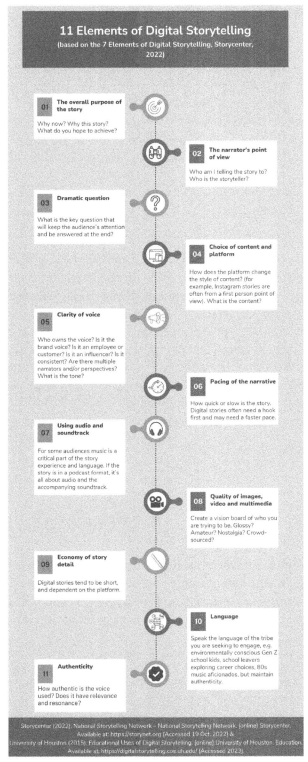

Figure 7.2 Eleven elements of digital storytelling, Source: Based on Lambert (2002), Storycenter (2022) & University of Houston (2015)

Auditing a current brand/digital story

The audit is an important part of any digital storytelling strategy as it will high-light areas for improvement, but also emphasise existing areas of strengths. If your brand is new, then only the competitor analysis part of the audit will be relevant. The audit forms a part of the 'where we are now' and allows you to build a picture for the PESTLE and SWOT part of your strategy. Beware: we are often tempted to make assumptions about where we are at. Do not skip this step! If approached with an open mind, you'll be amazed about the new insights you'll gain.

Audit

An audit can be as simple as taking the time to critically look at your current digital storytelling strategy and determine if it is effective. It offers brands a baseline to improve on and can be used in a strategy to create measurable objectives. It also allows brands to become aware of their best-performing posts and content. In a digital storytelling context this will often mean auditing your social media, website and digital content to determine what type and style of material attracts the most engagement. After completing an audit you should be able to identify your most effective platforms, see what posts are getting the most engagement, determine gaps and where you can improve your strategy.

There are many paid-for social media analytics tools including:

• Sprout Social
• HubSpot
• Brandwatch
• Talkwalker
• Social Studio
• Hootsuite (both paid-for and free versions)

And many, many more. Which one is best for your brand is entirely dependent on your strategy, financial resources and size – and indeed your preference may change over time. Beware though, many of these packaged tools can be very expensive and hence are often only available to established, major brands with sizable marketing and monitoring budgets.

Essentially, the type of data and insights that you need to capture are:

• **Share of voice**: What percentage of the conversation is about you and your brand, as opposed to your competitors?
• **Sentiment**: What is the mood of the conversation about you and your brand vs conversations that are happening in the broader sector and/or in relation to competitors?

- **Relevant hashtags and keywords**: Based on each platform you are operating on, which keywords are picked up most frequently – based on your own posts, but also sector wide?
- **Trend**: What are your audiences talking about? Within the context of your business, industry and/or service, but also within a broader context. What are they passionate about? Are there any particular memes emerging? Is there any potential for collaborations?
- **Return on investment (ROI)**: Is your social engagement paying off? How much engagement are you attracting for each dollar invested? Are there any platforms that may warrant a greater focus, or indeed should you reconsider your presence on some platforms due to a lack of ROI?

If you do not have a sufficient budget for paid tools, there are many basic tools that can give you a good idea of what is happening on your social media channels free of charge. The key is to curate a toolkit that works for you, and that you can easily draw on when needed. Indeed, many professional communicators believe in the superior value of a carefully curated (social) dashboard, which allows them to track exactly the types of things they like to focus on, based on their favourite tools. These may include:

- Nexalogy
- Mentionlytics
- Service and product review sites
- Platform-based analytics tools, e.g. Facebook, Google
- Google Alerts
- Answer the Public
- Followerwonk (free and paid-for versions)
- Buffer (free and paid-for versions)
- Sprout Social, Hootsuite and many others also offer free templates to manually audit your channels
- RivalIQ by NetBase Quid offers social media industry benchmarking and key takeaways from each year on social media use

Please note that these tools, their availability and pricing structures change frequently. As a professional communicator you continuously need to keep an eye out for the most appropriate tools to use and integrate in your personal and/or brand dashboard. Most audit templates will identify the key platforms for each brand and then break down performance and audience goals and incorporate a SWOT.

You can download free templates at Hootsuite and similar platforms, but most audits include the following information:

Account

- **Platform**: e.g. Instagram
- **Handle**: i.e. your @username

- **Hashtags**: ones the organisation uses regularly
- **Link in profile**: this might be the organisational website or a blog etc.
- **Verified**: is the account verified, or is there an application underway?
- **Channel owner**: is it the business, what staff member is responsible?
- **Mission statement**: what's the purpose of the platform? Link to a key performance indicator, e.g. grow brand awareness by 20% in 2023.
- **Top content/pinned post**: what is the content people engage with the most?
- **Most recent post**: include the date to see if account is up to date (as opposed to largely lying dormant).

Performance

- **# of posts**: Total number of posts over a specific period.
- **KPIs for platform**: Note what you are tracking, e.g. engagement rate, click-through rate, likes etc.
- **Year on year change**: Note if platform is improving.

Audience

- **Demographics**: Use your analytics platform to determine who is engaging with you.
- **# followers**: How many do you have?
- **Year on year change**: Note if numbers are improving.

Hootsuite identifies six main elements to audit your social media channels, including:

1. Create a list of all your social media accounts.
2. Check in on your branding and make sure it's consistent across all your platforms – logos, images, colours etc.
3. Identify your top-performing social media content (including hashtags, type of content, and time of posting; some content may perform better with certain audiences and/or subgroups that you are trying to engage).
4. Evaluate each channel's performance based on your KPIs (e.g. followers, likes, engagement, conversion).
5. Understand your audience(s) on each platform.
6. Take action: update your social media marketing strategy.

Source: (Newberry, 2018)

Competitor analysis

A competitor analysis is undertaken to determine what your competitors are doing so you understand their brand position in relation to yours. It does not mean you need to be doing what they are doing. Indeed, even though you may sometimes decide to follow their lead, often you will seek to do something entirely different, to build and strengthen your own unique identity. To undertake a competitor analysis you can use the same audit templates as for your own branding. The key difference is that you'll only have access to publicly accessible data, i.e. you may have to make some assumptions. A competitor analysis may be used to differentiate your brand and highlight why your brand's features are superior or different.

DESIGNING A DIGITAL STORYTELLING STRATEGY

Throughout this section we'll use the Croatian osiguranje campaign to highlight specific elements of a digital storytelling strategy and how it was used (Skoko and Gluvacevic, 2020). Croatian osignuranje is the largest insurance company in Croatia and has been operating since 1884 (Skoko and Gluvacevic, 2020). 2014 saw the organisation celebrate 130 years of existence by highlighting the history of the company as a way to differentiate its brand and offerings (Skoko and Gluvacevic, 2020). A creative communications campaign was devised that focussed on the organisation's history and designed 'a project that would show the social role of the corporation, its size, historical significance, and role in the development of the Croatian economy' (Skoko and Gluvacevic, 2020, p.8). The campaign involved a multimedia exhibition around the history of both Croatia and the organisation, as well as a participatory campaign that invited Croatians to share their own thoughts on the country's history.

Throughout this section, we will analyse the Croatian osignuranje campaign in relation to the key elements of strategy creation. A full reading of the case study can be found in Readings at the end of this chapter. In the appendix is a full digital storytelling strategy as presented by a postgraduate student to show its application in higher education. The components that make up a digital storytelling strategy include:

1. Executive summary
2. Contents page
3. Introduction
4. About us
5. Research
6. Situational analysis
7. Goals and objectives
8. Target audiences
9. Strategy
10. Timeline
11. Budget

Executive summary

An executive summary should not be a synopsis of what is in your report but instead a snapshot of your report, which summarises its main points. The idea behind an executive summary is that the reader will gain a broad understanding of the key points/ideas/stories of the campaign and motivates them to read on to learn more about your proposal. Think of it as your 'highlights reel'. Executive summaries can be written, but are much better presented and engaged with visually.

Introduction

An introduction provides context to the report and talks about the digital storytelling environment and even key issues facing the organisation. You don't have to go into depth on the background, but instead provide a short synopsis of why the report is being written and what it hopes to achieve. Some context on the particular issues facing the organisation may be included here. This section is also useful to highlight the structure of the report and what the reader may expect – tell them what you are going to tell them.

About us

This section is for competitive processes where you know you'll be competing against other businesses. It's the section to highlight the skills and expertise of your team and really show how their strengths will build the strongest storytelling campaign.

Research

The research section should include (at minimum) a competitor analysis, social media audit, PESTLE, SWOT and situational analysis. All of these elements are discussed.

Competitor analysis

Depending on the campaign, undertaking research into your competitors and their situation may be relevant to the digital storytelling campaign. Potentially, a competitor analysis may not be necessary as it's included in an overall business plan, but nevertheless understanding what your competitors are doing may encourage you to adjust your strategy.

Social media audit

Again depending on the campaign and who you are writing the digital storytelling strategy for, you may need to include your audit material in the strategy. This will provide you with a good baseline, detailing where the organisation/campaign is at, and where you want to go. It may help you to develop your SMART objectives.

PESTLE and SWOT

The research section should include your PESTLE and SWOT. The PESTLE analysis informs your SWOT and hence should be done first.

PESTLE is an analysis tool and stands for:

Political – things that affect the economy or industry the client exists within. This could be policy changes, upcoming elections, taxation and much more.

Economic – the current economic environment and how it is impacting the industry. For example during the COVID-19 pandemic the economic outlook was unstable, but provided opportunities for some (e.g. streaming services and the activewear industry).

Social – all social factors including demographics and culture that may impact the industry. This may include religion, health, media, education etc.

Technological – technological elements that may impact the client or industry including communication, automation licensing, technology use etc. Access to technology may also become a valuable consideration, depending on your target audience.

Legal – anything legal that has the ability to affect the client or industry, including employment laws, regulations, industry requirements.

Environmental – environmental factors that may affect the client or industry such as climate, geography etc.

For particular clients not all elements may be relevant, but going through them will prompt you to consider factors that you may have ignored previously and provide you with a solid understanding of the industry and the challenges they are facing.

PESTLE is a scan of your external environment. Hence insights should inform the Opportunities and Threat sections of your SWOT analysis.

SWOT is another analysis tool and stands for:

Strengths – strengths are things that your organisation or brand do particularly well, and which distinguish it from its competitors. Insights should be drawn from your earlier audit and other research, with an eye on how it can help you to shape and strengthen your digital storytelling campaign. For example this may be that you have a large following on Instagram.

Weaknesses – weaknesses are those elements that prevent your organisation or brand from performing at its optimum level. These are areas that you will want to improve on to remain competitive. For example a lack of brand awareness or limited to no employee engagement in your storytelling efforts would be a weakness.

Opportunities – opportunities are areas that while they may be a weakness at present, with the right campaign, may grow and help the campaign/business grow. Your PESTLE may help you to identify areas for further improvement.

Threats – threats are external factors that may negatively impact on your organisation, brand or indeed campaign. This may include changing government policy, intense competition or takeovers of popular social media platforms that you have traditionally relied on for your storytelling efforts.

Situational analysis

After undertaking the research it's important to analyse and synthesise key insights and highlight the key areas your campaign will be focusing on. It's rare a strategy will address every aspect of your background research, so it's important to articulate why you've chosen a particular area or two that will be the focus of your strategy. You can use your research to strengthen your argument and justify why investment in particular areas is expected to provide you with the best return on investment.

In the case study, Croatian osiguranje (Skoko and Gluvacevic, 2020) research was used to differentiate the organisation against the other 20 insurance companies on the market. The proposed campaign aimed to do this through using Croatian identity and a focus on social responsibility.

Goals and objectives

Goals and objectives are two different concepts, but they are related. Your goals should look at big picture ideas, be achievable and generally longer term. In terms of digital storytelling a goal might be:

• Increase brand awareness amongst Millennials.

So this is a perfectly good and achievable goal – but it doesn't tell you the steps involved.

Outcome objectives are the next step after you have a goal and you break it down into something that is Specific, Measurable, Achievable, Relevant and Timely (SMART).

> **Specific**: Objectives need to be specific. Be clear on elements the digital storytelling strategy can measure.
>
> **Measurable**: Make the objectives measurable so you can evaluate the outcome and know when and if you've achieved it.
>
> **Achievable**: An objective needs to be something you will be able to achieve.
>
> **Relevant**: The objective needs to align to your goal and also the brand's values.
>
> **Timely (or time-bound, time-limited)**: Set a deadline by when you'll assess your progress, otherwise your campaign would run indefinitely.

Note: do NOT create an objective for each of these characteristics. Each of your objectives should be SMART in its own right.

Using the above goal a SMART digital storytelling objective might be:

- To achieve 30% awareness of <insert brand name> on Instagram amongst the Millennial target group, by the end of the financial year <insert year>.
- To achieve 20% comprehension of the main elements of the product line among key target media by a specific date (based on a 'test' to be included in an evaluative questionnaire).

Outcome objectives could also relate to the impact of the intervening publics (media) on primary publics (e.g. teenagers). You can easily measure this with surveys, opinion polls or focus groups. A word of caution: if your objective seeks out to *increase* for example brand awareness or audience engagement, you need to establish a baseline first! You can only ever measure an increase based on what you already know! Using the case study of the Croatian osiguranje (Skoko and Gluvacevic, 2020), the campaign had a number of objectives that were directly related to the campaign and could be measured easily as shown by the following examples:

1. During the 45 days of the exhibition, attract a minimum of 30,000 visitors and 'educate' them about Croatian history and the role of the Croatia osiguranje.
2. Position the exhibition as a cultural (as opposed to a corporate) project and ensure that in at least 70% of media publications the exhibition is characterised as a multimedia-interactive project of an educational nature.
3. Inform citizens about the possibility of participating in the exhibition and ensure that they participate over a period of 45 days with a minimum of 2000 of their own photographs.

(Skoko and Gluvacevic, 2020)

Target audiences

A digital storytelling strategy relates to how messages are delivered to pre-identified and predetermined target audiences and platforms. The steps involved to determine an audience include:

- Identify target audience that you seek to reach; you need to gain a comprehensive understanding of their characteristics, including:

    o Demographic – Statistical characteristics of your target audience and or market segment, including age, gender, ethnicity, income, level of education, occupation, etc.

    o Psychographic – The qualitative equivalent of your demographics, capturing your target audience's values, desires, goals, interests and lifestyle choices.

    o Behavioural – Within a marketing context behavioural segmentation divides customers and target audiences based on how they interact with your company or brand and beyond. This could include likes and dislikes, response to a particular service or your brand per se, purchasing behaviour, buyer journey stages, purchasing patterns, such as timing coinciding with holidays, seasonal events, etc.

    o Geographic – Capturing where your audience(s) are based, lie and/or work. Depending on your brand, this may reflect countries, but also smaller geographic divisions, such as regions, cities or even postcodes.

- Define medium/media characteristics used to deliver messages. Your decision is based on intent to influence target audience behaviour.

Using the case study Croatian osiguranje (Skoko and Gluvacevic, 2020) the 'primary target group consisted of young and middle-aged people (35–49), employed, highly educated, those living in families with average and above-average household incomes. The secondary target group consisted of local Croatians aged 25–55 who have at least one insurance, employees, and retirees with an average household income' (Skoko and Gluvacevic, 2020).

Strategy

The digital storytelling strategy should be detailed. You should highlight your platforms and detail how each will develop the story. The platforms must be synergistic with each other and build on the 'story'. The platforms should effectively convey the key messages to primary and secondary target audiences. In a true transmedia storytelling approach, the narrative should unfold across a number of different platforms, i.e. traditional media, Twitter, Facebook, Snapchat, Pinterest, podcast, blog, TikTok, YouTube, Instagram etc. However, you may also like to include offline platforms and communication channels into your transmedia mix. The platforms must connect or link in some way, but the story should be adapted and extended for each platform.

The strategy for Croatian osiguranje focused on two elements: an exhibition showcasing the 133 years of the organisation, using a tunnel below Zagreb which was turned into a multimedia project, and the digital space using #wewriteourownhistory for citizens to showcase their own historical account (Skoko and Gluvacevic, 2020). The two elements were linked as attendees at the exhibition were invited to share their own historic photos using #PovijestPisemoSami. As outlined in the case study, the physical event was the main experience with all other channels leading to it (Facebook, Instagram, Google, Twitter, traditional media). There were three phases during the campaign:

1. Communications campaign to gain interest and showcase the history of Croatian osiguranje (26 August – 10 September, 2017). This is a brand/campaign awareness phase.
2. Individual stories about the exhibition, including a press conference inside the tunnel (where some of the exhibition was housed). This phase included the grand opening and communication on social media (10 September – 1 October, 2017). This is a brand story phase.
3. The last phase highlighted citizen stories and their own historical photos and digital platforms, and some were included in the exhibition (1 October – 1 November, 2017). This is a participatory community story phase.

(Skoko and Gluvacevic, 2020)

A simple way to ensure your strategy links well is to include a roadmap of your goals, narratives, tactics and metrics (measurement), as shown in Figure 7.4.

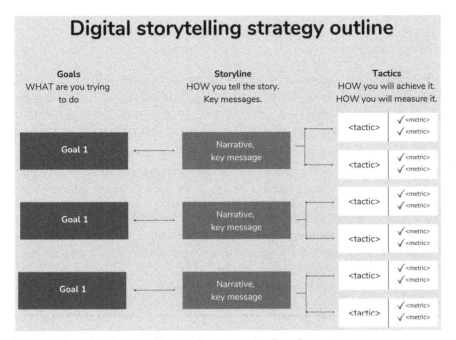

Figure 7.3 Digital storytelling outline, mapping key elements

Figure 7.4   Example of a story wheel

Story wheel

A story wheel is a useful element to include in a digital storytelling strategy as it highlights the key narrative and shows smaller narratives that are linked to the bigger narrative. How your story wheel looks may depend on the narrative structure you choose. The most used story wheel has an overarching narrative and smaller narratives that feed into the bigger narrative.

Key messages

A key message is the succinct narrative of the overarching message, and sometimes separates individual messages that you want to pitch at convenient target audiences/ groups. Any focused strategy should have no more than three key messages. With more than three your audience is unlikely to remember them, and may be confused by the number of messages. The simpler the better and this will allow people to remember and recall your message. Sometimes a campaign may only have one single message pitched to all target audience groups. A few hints for key messages include:

- Don't try to communicate too many messages in one campaign.
- Consider your story and how the key messages relate.
- Key messages need to be complementary, easy to remember and reinforce the organisation's vision, mission and values.
- Visuals used also need to support the key messages.
- You may consider combining this section with your story lines and key stakeholders.

A key message can be an actual message, or sometimes a hashtag, and this is shown in the case study of the Croatian osiguranje campaign. Croatian osiguranje was celebrating its 130th anniversary and wanted to mark the occasion with an inclusive communication project that showed 'presence and sustainability through social change – world and local wars, and changes in state and social arrangements' (Skoko and Gluvacevic, 2020, p.8). In this case the key message was a hashtag #wewriteourownhistory – a clear message that invites stories from the community and simultaneously provides a way to share them.

Timeline

The timeline for a storytelling strategy should outline the key elements of how long each element will take. In the case of Croatian osiguranje, there were three clear phases (mentioned above) that built on each other and were able to be measured. A timeline does not need to be complex, but should highlight key milestones.

Budget

The budget outlines the costs of all elements of your strategy. This ensures activities align to business expectations of cost. The Croatian osiguranje campaign had a media budget of 80,000 euros.

An additional example of a postgraduate strategy for the Perth Observatory, which outlines all these states – some visually – can be found in the Appendix.

CHAPTER SUMMARY

The chapter discusses the role of the storyboard and how it can be used to visually represent ideas. It discusses how to use templates and highlights the adapted 11 digital storytelling elements.

The role of strategy is discussed, as is how its purpose is to build on ideas and to provide a long-term plan of action, by looking at where the brand is now and where it wants to be. The strategy is essentially the roadmap to get there.

How to audit an existing strategy or digital story is discussed by looking at the elements of a PESTLE and SWOT. An audit can be as simple as taking the time to critically look at your current digital storytelling strategy and determine if it is effective. It offers brands a baseline to improve on, and can be used in a strategy to create measurable objectives. An audit can also include competitors to see how the brand or organisation is performing against key brand competitors.

This chapter discusses the key elements of a digital storytelling strategy and includes examples on how to present it. It looks at the key parts of a (written) strategy including:

1. Executive summary
2. Contents page
3. Introduction
4. About us
5. Research
6. Situational analysis
7. Goals and objectives
8. Target audiences
9. Strategy
10. Timeline
11. Budget

The case study of Croatian osiguranje is used throughout this chapter to highlight creative storytelling strategy development in action.

DISCUSSION QUESTIONS

1. Using a client/brand, audit their existing storytelling strategy and use this as a guide to create a new strategy.
2. Create an 'I Am From' story - create a digital story around 'I Am From' without stating your geographical location. Show the use of a storyboard in the planning phase. Use any platform to create the video, but consider the 11 elements of digital storytelling. See 'The power of digital storytelling' (https://youtu.be/jA2cTZK9hzw) for inspiration (Bailin, 2014).
3. Using the case study in the readings, workshop the following elements:
   a. Explain the creative process used in the campaign and key issues that may arise. Create an infographic on the process.
   b. Using Canva or a similar tool, create a snapshot of the Croatia osiguranje's insurance campaign. Note the digital storytelling measures used.

READINGS

Skoko, B. and Gluvacevic, D. (2020). Creativity in public relations: The case from Croatia – How to make the history of the insurance company 'cool'. [online] IntechOpen. Available at: www.intechopen.com/chapters/73320 [Accessed 2 November 2022].

This case study is discussed throughout this chapter and provides an industry example of a strategy and its key outcomes. It also highlights the creative process that is a part of the development of strategy.

REFERENCES

Bailin, E. (2014). The Power of Digital Storytelling. [online] *YouTube*. Available at: https://youtu.be/jA2cTZK9hzw [Accessed 9 November 2022].

Disney (2018). *Disney Institute*. [online] Available at: www.disneyinstitute.com/blog/storyboarding-a-communication-tool-to-foster-employee-engagement/ [Accessed 2 November 2022].

Lambert, J. (2002). Digital Storytelling Cookbook. Berkeley, CA: Digital Diner Press.

Myerson, R. (2018). Home. [online] *How Brands Are Built*. Available at: https://howbrandsarebuilt.com/ [Accessed 1 November 2022].

Newberry, C. (2018). How to conduct a social media audit (includes free template). [online] *Hootsuite Social Media Management*. Available at: https://blog.hootsuite.com/social-media-audit-template/ [Accessed 2 November 2022].

Oxford English Dictionary, (2023). Oxford English Dictionary. [online] OED.com. Available at: https://www.oed.com/

Skoko, B. and Gluvacevic, D. (2020). Creativity in public relations: The case from Croatia – How to make the history of the insurance company 'cool'. [online] IntechOpen. Available at: www.intechopen.com/chapters/73320 [Accessed 2 November 2022].

Storycenter (2022). National Storytelling Network. [online] *Storycenter*. Available at: https://storynet.org [Accessed 19 October 2022].

University of Houston (2015). Educational Uses of Digital Storytelling. [online] University of Houston, Education. Available at: https://digitalstorytelling.coe.uh.edu/ [Accessed 2023].

8

STORYTELLING THROUGH VIDEO AND SCROLLYTELLING

OBJECTIVES

1. Apply storytelling principles to video and explore its application across different digital platforms and brands
2. Understand scrollytelling and how it is used in digital storytelling

This chapter identifies different types of digital stories and explores diverse styles of video and scrollytelling for digital storytelling for brands across platforms like You-Tube, Facebook, Instagram, Snapchat and TikTok. Creativity is a focus of this chapter, as well as looking at how different campaigns have used different platforms for their branding and storytelling efforts. The use of scrollytelling – a long-form multimodal story – in digital storytelling is also considered. This chapter includes insights into the development of a scrollytelling script, mapping the evolution of the Black Lives Matter (BLM) movement and a case study on a video story produced by the UN to challenge gender inequality.

TYPES OF VIDEO STORYTELLING

As platforms now offer diverse ways to tell stories, a number of different styles of video storytelling have emerged. A critical analysis of the different platforms can provide an insight into how brands use video to develop their digital stories. The more our worlds become digital, the more people want to connect and feel human. Authenticity is key and there are elements of video that can immerse someone into human emotion and senses.

The algorithm and the rise of video

How social media platforms promote content has a profound impact on the content audiences see and engage with, and on the content brands create. Platforms' algorithms change frequently but the latest trend has seen a preference given to video, and given the nature of most social media platforms, even more so to short-form video content. An algorithm in this context is basically a way of ranking content on a platform. It does this through analysing content already on the platform and looking at its metadata – including captions, alt text, hashtags and engagement metrics (McLachlan and Mikolajczyk, 2022). The algorithm then takes this information and delivers content to its intended audience, generally based on how someone behaves on a platform and the content they typically engage with. For brands, understanding how the algorithm works means you can target your content better to the audiences you want to see and engage with your content. However, each platform has a different algorithm and different focus that changes so frequently that it becomes impossible to identify any one strategy that will work into the future. Whilst you should consider and understand current algorithms, strong campaigns are characterised by a clear message and target audience, as well as a focus on building an audience, rather than trying to manipulate the algorithm of a given platform.

VIDEO STORYTELLING EXAMPLES

Rather than discuss individual platforms (which are always subject to change) we are going to look at a number of campaigns that have used video storytelling to great effect. Some of these campaigns benefited from a sizeable budget; others required minimal expense but nevertheless had a profound effect on their audience. These micro case studies provide examples of differing budgets and approaches, followed by the final case study – a call to action for a humanitarian cause – which provides a deep dive into the many elements that make up a digital story.

Case study: It's a Nurse campaign

https://youtu.be/64EilXiMQxk

The It's a Nurse campaign is an exemplar in digital storytelling for its ability to create a powerful emotional bond with its audience, showcasing how a powerful narrative can outshine a sophisticated video produced with a large budget. The video was created by Health First in conjunction with 321Agency and is based on a letter from a mother (Kathy Taylor) to the Health First hospital, following the death of her son, Cory (Gerrell and Hatter, 2017). The original letter, with Kathy's permission, was narrated word for word in the video.

Campaign goals

Based on details provided in the Shorty Award application the campaign goals were to:
- create a powerful informational video for nurses and obtain 5,000 video views
- generate social media buzz for the video by garnering 500 shares of the video on Facebook
- obtain one local media story from this effort
- create camaraderie and boost morale among nurses internally.

(Gerrell and Hatter, 2017)

Storytelling techniques

This video is powerful mostly due to its simplicity. The seriousness of the film is understood using the black screen. The voice over (an actor) reads the letter in Kathy's own words, as the video shows photographic stills of different hospital vignettes, including patients and nurses. The power of the video lies in the letter, which is narrated using a natural cadence to appeal to the listener and repetition of the phrase 'the boy in the bed' to evoke strong images of the situation. The letter is almost poetic in its delivery and its heartfelt words, pauses and use of voice technique (cracking voice) is powerful in its ability to connect with the audience, build empathy and care for the writer of the letter. Coming back to a term that digital storytelling pivots on, the video is authentic and shows a level of authenticity that is often hard to replicate in marketing and communications. 321Agency explains:

> It showcases the importance of brand authenticity and the power of storytelling – two attributes that, when executed properly, have proven time and time again to resonate with audiences. While this story was particularly compelling (not to mention timely, given the nationwide focus on the opioid epidemic), the biggest takeaway for brands looking to create a 'viral video' or 'viral marketing campaign' is that, regardless of your industry, if you look hard enough and pay

close enough attention to the impact your product or service has on the end user, you'll find that there are stories just waiting to be told. (321Agency, 2018)

Most striking about this video is the basic image transitions which would have cost very little to produce, and yet the power of the story and ability to place the viewer in the moment is profound.

Case study: Airbnb Wall and Chain campaign

https://youtu.be/BpAdyFdE3-c
    Some brands are lucky enough to have storytelling at their core. Travel brands, like Airbnb, have access to stories not only from their Airbnb hosts, but also from the people visiting these places. Storytelling can transcend a brand and connect with the hearts and minds of people when a smaller story tells a larger story, and one that connects with a moment in time (the zeitgeist). The Airbnb Wall and Chain story was a true story that followed a typical hero's journey trajectory, with the main character Jörg going back to visit Berlin to see the vibrant city it had become since the fall of the Berlin Wall in 1989. It is a moving story that uses animation rather than real-life recreation. The animation provides a creative licence for more semiotic elements to be used, such as the colour blue (a calming colour) juxtaposed with the colour red (the Airbnb logo colour). Growing evidence suggests that consumers are now more focused on their relationship with a brand than the actual product (Pera and Viglia, 2016) and for brands like Airbnb, this is important as they provide a service rather than product brand. This video ran as an advertisement during the 25th anniversary of the fall of the Berlin Wall. Berlin is a popular and prominent travel location, featuring a wide range of Airbnb homestays and experiences. Its execution highlighted great relevance and resonance with its audience. Tapping into the zeitgeist (and having foresight of events relevant to their brand), Airbnb was able to use storytelling to tell a deeper story on travel, history and personal growth, by drawing on nostalgia. Nostalgia and the personal story appeal to audiences and build an emotional connection – both with the story, its main character, and by extension the brand.

Using others to tell your stories

The Airbnb campaign is a wonderful example of not only finding stories in your organisation, but also using others to tell your stories. The actual story was emailed to Airbnb by a customer, and the organisation recognised its ability to appeal to a broader audience.

Metaphors are powerful

Metaphors connect with people, and in this story the use of the wall is used in many ways – breaking down barriers, breaking through issues from the past etc. Dennis Goedegebuure who led the Airbnb team for this campaign said, 'the narrative of the story is focused on how travel can break down walls through staying in people's homes, getting in touch with the local culture' (Handley, 2014).

Case study: The Reluctant Sea Shanty campaign

https://youtu.be/UPBOkiPUcpc

The Reluctant Sea Shanty was a campaign devised by BMF Agency and FINCH for the UN Refugee Agency and released on World Refugee Day 2022 on TikTok. The UN Refugee Agency (Australian division) collaborated with TikTok star Nathan Evans to launch 'The Reluctant Sea Shanty' with the aim to resonate with a younger audience.

Zeitgeist and the sea shanty

The sea shanty is a style of folk song sung by sailors acapella aboard ships to keep morale up on boats. It is usually a story in itself and at times improvised. The sea shanty has a chant-like element to its song and has a typical three-act story structure with a beginning, middle and end. The sea shanty immediately announces itself as a story and often starts with 'there once was a...', a take on the classic 'once upon a time' fairy-tale beginning. Nathan Evans posted his own sea shanty version via his TikTok account (@natanevanss) and explained how he teamed up with the UN Refugee Agency to create the song. In 2021 and throughout 2022 sea shanties were trending on TikTok as a collaborative moment where people could come together and join in the singing. There's an element of human connection taking place; the precise emotion the UN wanted to evoke in audiences – a connection with refugees. The exact reason behind the popularity of the sea shanty on TikTok is unknown, but it most likely became popular as a result of the global COVID-19 pandemic and out of people's desire to connect (much like the Ocean Spray TikTok). In using this song format and style, the UN Refugee Agency was tapping into the zeitgeist and connected with a younger audience that might be familiar with shanties on TikTok but had not thought about the refugee journey – away from their homeland, towards an unknown future.

Nathan Evans' TikTok video again appeals to emotion by re-telling the journey of a sailor (or multiple sailors), but uses a more downbeat version of the sea shanty, which is usually upbeat and thunderous. The execution of the video is dark and evokes the unknown. The UN asked the audience to simply 'share this film to support people feeling conflict and persecution', in an attempt to raise awareness change behaviour – and indeed attitudes. Cross-platform stories are told as the TikTok leads to a website with individual refugee stories, which includes a donation tab for those seeking to support the UN Refugee Agency's efforts.

SCROLLYTELLING

Scrollytelling is a contemporary hybrid format of storytelling that uses multimedia as a part of its narrative and unfolds as the user scrolls (Schneiders, 2020). This may include video, infographics, images, maps and much more. Scrollytelling is predominantly used in long-form journalism (see e.g. *The Washington Post*, *The Guardian* and *The New York Times* – including its 'Snow Fall: The Avalanche at Tunnel Creek': www.nytimes.com/proj ects/2012/snow-fall/index.html#/?part=tunnel-creek – and also TASS, the Russian News Agency, detailing Napoleon's journey in 1812: https://1812.tass.ru/en). However, some organisations are using scrollytelling to tell a deeper story, by drawing on interactive content that takes the reader on a journey, providing unique and engaging storytelling experiences that traditional platforms, such as television, radio or print, cannot provide alone (Wolf and Godulla, 2016). In this context see for example the United Nation's 'A Wilderness of Water' (https://feature.undp.org/ wilderness-of-water/), which tells the unique and important story of our oceans, inviting audiences on an immersive and educational story, which ends in a call to action (donations, but also actionable examples of personal behavioural change).

Scrollytelling is captivating and multi-sensory and is used by researchers, medical professionals, weather bureaus and government agencies to tell complex elements of a story, as well as showcase multiple stories in one location. Think of scrollytelling as a visual story that draws you into its narrative. It starts with a typical one-page landing page that then prompts you to scroll further as the story evolves. The structure of scrollytelling is usually 'linear or elastic', meaning it follows a timeline but it may branch off in sections (Seyser and Zeiller, 2018).

Despite the focus on (digital) storytelling in public relations and communication scholarship and practice, Honours research student and Immersive Visualisation e-scholarship recipient Grace Jones noted that scrollytelling remains under explored in the public relations and communication literature. Interestingly, this is within the context of an increased focus on data visualisation in the discipline over the past decade (Cope and Wells, 2018).

Illustrating the value of scrollytelling in seeking to communicate complex developments over time in an immersive, engaging and informative way, Grace created a scrollytelling data visualisation of the Black Lives Matter (BLM) movement and its global reach over time.

Figure 8.1 Mapbox visualisation of BLM movement, Source: Grace Jones, Curtin University

Grace completed her first-class Honours thesis exploring the contextualisation of the BLM movement in Western Australia, noting an increased focus on Indigenous Australians' rights, alongside the adoption and adaptation of BLM symbols and messaging. However, for her scholarship she wanted to track and visually represent the evolution of the movement from its origins in 2013, following the acquittal of George Zimmerman in the shooting dead of African-American teen Trayvon Martin 17 months earlier in Sanford, Florida, to a truly global movement, with localised protests from Brussels and Paris, to Rio de Janeiro and Osaka, all the way to Perth, Western Australia. She found that although several powerful interactive online maps documenting BLM existed, they were all very much focused on the US-based movement. A small number of existing maps visualised protests across the world and even over time, but failed to tell the actual story of BLM and its evolution over time and space. What Grace's work did was bring multiple maps, resources and stories of localised protests together to create an overlay of multiple datasets (protests, social media activity, legislative changes), thereby providing a global record of the BLM movement, including opportunities to explore location-based storylines further.

The resulting scrollytelling record enabled audiences to explore the evolution of the movement over time, whilst gaining an insight into localised adaptations and interpretations in key locations. The layering and contextualising of existing, previously dispersed information demonstrated that movements like BLM should not be dismissed as 'slacktivism' or tokenistic, as when you join up all the datapoints, you not only gain the big, complete picture of protests across the globe, you also gain an understanding of the impact the movement has had in terms of visibility, media coverage, social media engagement, physical participation and eventually legislative changes.

Case study: How the UN made a film to challenge gender inequality

https://finchcompany.com/news/the-story-of-our-final-frontier/
This case study has been reproduced with the permission of FINCH Company.

The message of 'Equality: Our Final Frontier', a new film for UN Women Australia directed by FINCH's Jonny Kofoed, is simple: humans have, through their sheer ingenuity and determination, made the world a comfier, happier, and more expansive place. For some of us, at least.

The film centres on a woman - really, any woman at all, for her experiences are sadly universal - as she moves through a futuristic society, experiencing age-old sexism in a world that is stridently modern. The film's simple, urgent statement is thus: even as we continue to make huge strides in technological advancements, we still have a long way to go when it comes to true gender parity.

The statistics on the issue of women's rights are grim. The official report from the UN puts equal access for women 135 years into our future. Though discussions relating to

Figure 8.2 UN 'Equality, Our Final Frontier' video still, women standing in futuristic environment
Printed with permission of FINCH

gender, sexuality and bodies are more in the front of our collective consciousness than ever before, that has not yet translated into direct action.

We are stalling, and we are stalling in a way that draws glaring and painful attention to just how easy it could be for this problem to be fixed. As 'Equality: Our Final Frontier' shows, we can put a man on the moon. What we can't do – not for lack of capacity, or financial resources – is make this planet, our one true home, a just and fair one.

Described by Kofoed as essentially being a 'one-shot' film, the short plunges through a world replete with great developments in hardware and innovation, from a deliberately very phallic rocket ship to a base established on the moon. It's all rendered in a mix between live action footage and cutting-edge animation, a style that walks an elegant line between the real and the fantastical.

Figure 8.3 UN 'Equality, Our Final Frontier' video still, TransAtlantic train image
Printed with permission of FINCH

And yet even as a world made entirely by human hands flowers before our hero character, still she encounters problems that have beset women for time immemorial – the experience of being shut out of boardrooms, and made to feel uncomfortable and vulnerable on public transport. The point of the film is clear: these new gadgets and gizmos do a lot, but they are wallpaper slapped on a decaying wall until we sort the widespread and systemic exclusion of individuals based on their gender.

'You're talking about colonizing Mars; and colonizing the moon', Kofoed says. 'And yet there are still these ridiculous comments about beauty. You realise that the truth is stranger than fiction. You stop yourself, and you say, "That's crazy. There's so much going on, and yet this one thing can't seem to be fixed"'.

Figure 8.4   UN 'Equality, Our Final Frontier' video still, look 70 years younger advertisement

Printed with permission of FINCH

When the brief for the film from The Monkeys landed on Kofoed's desk, it was this simplicity that drew him to the project. 'I loved the idea', Kofoed explains. 'The heart of the problem is the notion that we're capable of great things, and if you glance into the future, there's some pretty amazing things that are about to happen. But somehow, gender equality is still 135 years away. So that's a pretty good starting point for an animation screenplay'.

Kofoed is talking over Zoom from his offices at Assembly, the animation and live action filmmaking collective that he co-founded. In the background, there are walls and walls of books, and a drum set, tucked away in the corner. It is, in fact, a nice reminder of one of the central themes of the film – a mix between the old, represented by the leather-bound volumes behind Kofoed's head, and the newness of the grainy, digital window through which he is speaking.

This, indeed, has been part of Kofoed's process for about as long as he has been working in the world of commercials. His understanding of technology is vast, but he has always balanced that technical skill with what he calls an emphasis on 'soul'. Whether it be his work for Amnesty International or Women's Refuge, he has never utilised mere technical trickery to tell his stories. He has always searched for a way that those gizmos can reveal something essential about us; about who we are, and what we want.

'For someone who works on computers all day, I don't really like computers, and I don't think they like me either', Kofoed says, beanie on his head, silver ring on his finger, glimpsed when he becomes particularly animated, and begins to gesticulate. 'We're constantly trying to reject the digital world'.

From the beginning, 'Equality: Our Final Frontier' was conceived as an animation project, though initial conversations circled around the idea of bringing it to life in 2D. 'I kind of felt like there was a real opportunity with animation with this project, because of the open-endedness in terms of creating a PSA', Kofoed explains. 'It was about not being held back from very specific casting, and the animation was going to make it very open-ended'.

The key, after all, was to ensure that this was not one person's story, limiting its scope. There needed to be no barriers to entry for audiences. Women's rights are a global issue, and though they take many different forms across cultures, the heart of the matter is always the same.

Even with this universal quality established as a central part of the film, the briefing was defined by that pressing question, which Kofoed brings up over the Zoom conversation himself – 'Why animation?' For Kofoed, the answer he kept returning to was simple. 'Animation allows you to go places', he says.

'A kitchen table shot is the same as a helicopter shot in animation land. They cost the same. We needed to walk down the street; we needed to go down a big escalator; and we also needed to fly to the moon. And those things with animation don't have the same constraints. It's all the same thing'.

Early discussions, during this briefing stage, used Matt Groening's *Futurama* as a visual reference. Kofoed took that as an opportunity to explore a heightened world, but one with a deep grounding in the human condition. 'That for me was a way of saying, 'we're talking about the future and about reality, but there's something whimsical about it as well'. It was interesting, in how we walked that tightrope of looking at the future in a surreal way, but keeping it relevant'.

In the early days of the project, Kofoed explored the idea of making the film a solitary walk through a timeline – a visual metaphor for the journey through the next hundred or so years, and how they can shape the battle for the rights of women. But over the course of that development, even as the central narrative thrust remained the same, the approach changed and altered. 'Initially, there were dates all around her; she was literally walking through a timeline', Kofoed says.

'And as we were working through it, we realised that there were certain things that we could weed out, and not be so heavy-handed. It was a really interesting process; pulling stuff out, and seeing if people are getting the right theme. Sometimes you have to pull yourself out of the individual shots, and realise that you're constructing this very simple narrative'.

When production rolled around, Kofoed worked fast – the shoot for the live action footage lasted precisely one day. 'It was a really small cast', Kofoed explains. 'We've got our hero, and we've got a couple of extras. So everything about the animation technique was driven by the fact that we didn't have a lot of time to shoot it'.

That made the film more of what Kofoed calls a 'design' or an 'editing' job. He didn't have the usual devices that storytellers can fall back on. The story itself was breathtakingly simple, the character more of a signifier than a flesh and blood human being. 'It was quite pictorial', he says. 'A lot of the environment does a lot of the communication'.

Figure 8.5 UN 'Equality, Our Final Frontier' video still, woman walking through futuristic environment
Printed with permission of FINCH

Kofoed and his creative collaborators saw this story as a sadly lonely one. This is one woman, passing by herself through an overpopulated and oversaturated world that she cannot connect with; that has made no real space for her.

The film is, of course, a rallying cry for support, and it ends with a message of hope. This is not a journey that has to be taken alone. Indeed, any real structural change that will bring about a future in which everybody on the gender spectrum can take their own place at the table will only happen thanks to a collective. But still, for Kofoed, it kept coming back to that one image – a body, moving through space.

'The film ends with her coming all this way, but there's one thing missing', he says. 'So it's simple, there aren't many close-ups. And it's important that it lands'.

One of the key moments in the film features the hero character sitting by herself on a train, her body shrouded in the whorling colours of animation. A faceless man – faceless in the way that the anonymised, controlling players of the patriarchy always are – sits next to her. She shuffles away. He shuffles towards her. It is a tiny, almost imperceptible exertion of the privilege and influence that men hold over women, summed up in two characters moving back and forth, as though in a sad dance. He feels safe. She does not.

'There was a good month where with that shot of the hero character on the train, it wasn't coming across that this woman is really vulnerable', Kofoed says of the moment. 'And it was just about being able to use the green screen footage, and getting the man on the carriage to sit slightly closer. It's like comedy editing, almost – you get one or two frames either side, work out where the "laugh" is'.

It was the philosopher Miranda Fricker, a powerhouse of modern feminist thought, who gave a phrase to what is lacking from this kind of depressingly normal interaction; this dance. She called it 'epistemic friction'. We are all of us in the bubbles of our own experience, tied to who we are as social players – I'm a man, and you're a woman, so we move through the world differently. That's just the way it goes. We are perceived differently, and we hold ourselves differently, and the world understands us differently.

But the problem becomes when there is no overlap between those bubbles. We are defined by the way that our gender is built and seen by society, and it is hard to imagine that changing. What we can do is try to make ourselves usefully uncomfortable by encountering different ways of being in the world. We want to unsettle ourselves; to experience that friction Fricker describes. That's a way of expanding our horizons, and better understanding how the people around us live.

The faceless man on the train has no friction. He sees the world as being made up of people who are, if not like him, then able to be pushed around and shaped by him. He doesn't understand that there are any other ways that he could be, and he's locked in a way of expressing himself that means that he can make someone feel uncomfortable without necessarily even understanding that he has made them uncomfortable.

In order to achieve gender parity, it's that kind of useful friction that will help us. Men need to be unsettled – not in a damaging or destructive way, but in a way that helps them understand all the things that they cannot even see. Discrimination is a big, complex issue, and one that we need to work on constantly, in a multitude of different ways. If we remember to always search for the things that shake us up a bit, then we'll see that brighter future much faster.

That, after all, is part of the power of 'Equality: Our Final Frontier', one that Kofoed acknowledges up top. A key element of the target audience for the film is those men who have perhaps forgotten, or need to be reminded, that there are other ways of being than their own. It's Kofoed's way of referencing what might have been the elephant in the room – this film is, in some ways, a woman's story, and it's being directed by a man.

'I'm part of the intended audience for this piece', he says. 'So that was quite interesting. And furthermore, as an employer, I have the potential to be part of the problem. So I'm working on a job and being educated at the same time'.

He takes a brief moment; reflects. 'And also, as being the father of a daughter, I'm heavily invested in affecting the change as well. I think those are the best jobs, where you're asking yourself, "What are you trying to say and who are you trying to say it to? And is it going to work? Is it going to affect behaviour?" So it's a personal project, in that respect'.

Appropriately, given the film is about the intersection between technology and the humanist project of making the world a better place – not to mention the problems that come when these two things pull apart – 'Equality: Our Final Frontier' uses cutting-edge technology to tell a very natural story.

To create the film's polished final look, Kofoed and his team at Assembly deployed an AI process that applied a pre-established visual style to the footage that he shot in front of a green screen. The computer program was given its design inputs, and then it produced an output, one that overlaid a cohesive visual language on top of the very human movement of the actors that Kofoed shot.

According to Kofoed, this style is only going to become more popular as the years go on. 'We're seeing it more and more every month', he said. This is art being made on the very frontiers of technology, and about those very frontiers, and what they lack.

It's also meaningfully different from that prior technological advancement that mixes animation and live-action footage, rotoscoping. Whereas rotoscoping sees animation laid over shot footage 'by hand', which Kofoed calls 'painstaking', this new process was much simpler. 'We just used the green screen – we had a 2D character we could drop into 3D scenes. We could re-light really quickly'.

In turn, this process allowed the post-production to move fast, and for the team to test out different ideas. One of the most dreaded words in the animator's dictionary is 'render' – the artform is hard going on computers, and requires a lot of processing time before anything approaching a finalised shot can be watched back. But Kofoed's technology knocked render times out of the picture.

'With every shot we make, there's probably ten in the bin that didn't make it', he says. 'We like working that way'.

'Equality: Our Final Frontier' is a PSA. It is designed to change hearts and minds; to raise awareness of an issue that, thanks to powerful (and male) forces, has been allowed to languish in the shadows. But Kofoed and those who he worked with on the project across Assembly, FINCH and agency The Monkeys never wanted to merely lecture. This was a film that had to be entertaining first; to engage in a way that saved it from being a dusty classroom lecture.

'We're trying to be taken seriously, but also, we are competing for the same eyeballs as traditional advertising', Kofoed explains. 'And I guess with PSAs, you can't just expect people to listen. You need to entertain. So just like with any short film, or a short story, it needs a good hook'.

That desire to joyously unsettle in the way that great entertainment always does began with an idea from The Monkeys to open with what Kofoed calls a 'cock rocket' – that spaceship shaped like a male appendage that opens the short.

It was, the director says, about not giving the audience any opportunity to look away, and remained a principle throughout the making of the entire film. 'We're buying audience attention in ten second chunks', Kofoed says, simply. 'Luckily the future is very odd. So that's where the entertainment was driven from'.

Precisely how the film gets taken up by audiences remains to be seen. But Kofoed is proud of the project, and understandably so. In particular, he likes the fact that it can fit any screen; be absorbed in any context. 'It works on cinema screens, and it works on your phone', he says. 'It's the same deliverable. It's not an edited version. It's the simplicity of the graphics, with enough texture there – it holds up'.

And anyway, the director has already shown the project to some of his most important critics – those who helped him make it. Throughout the process, he kept key people from both Assembly and FINCH from seeing the project, so that he could garner their input at just the right moment. 'We're quite strategic, knowing who gets to see it at work, knowing that there are only a few people who can see it fresh'.

Throughout, when he needed help, he brought the cut home and threw it on the telly so that his family could watch. As Kofoed says, the film can and should be watched anywhere. Its call for change and equality, supported by the UN, is universal, and should transcend culture and upbringing. But what an important viewing context that is – the home. It's a message of hope, and a call to action, that meets people precisely, and intimately, where they live.

CHAPTER SUMMARY

The chapter discusses how digital stories are told through video and scrollytelling – i.e. multimodal narratives. The different types of video storytelling are discussed through three examples – a low-budget video (It's a Nurse), a user-generated story (Wall and Chain) and a zeitgeist theme with high production involved (The Reluctant Sea Shanty). The overarching theme in all these stories is that small stories create big ones; the more personalised a narrative, the more the audience can apply it to their own lives.

This chapter also discusses the concept of scrollytelling, a digital long-form story that uses multimedia to tell an immersive and multi-sensory story.

Finally the case study of 'Equality: Our Final Frontier', a film for UN Women Australia directed by FINCH, discusses the different elements of digital storytelling found within this one video, as well as metaphors, visual semiotics, narrative structure, animation and the character's journey. It is a showcase of many different elements discussed in the book so far.

DISCUSSION QUESTIONS

1. What videos have you watched that enabled you find out more about a company/organisation/brand? Think about the reasons why you wanted to know more and apply digital storytelling techniques to discuss them.
2. How has <brand chosen by your facilitator> used video to develop their brand and overall digital story?
3. Discuss in groups what the purpose of digital storytelling is - why do brands invest in it? Give some examples.
4. Source examples of scrollytelling where multimode storytelling has been used (video, images, sound, maps etc.). Can you find an example of a brand using scrollytelling? Can you think of any topics or stories worth exploring in a scrollytelling format?

READINGS

Planer, R., Wolf, C. and Godulla, A. (2020). Digital storytelling beyond flagship projects: Exploring multimedia work routines in higher education practical training. *Journalism Practice*, 16(6), 1–18. doi:10.1080/17512786.2020.1832140.

This journal article goes into depth about long-form story and multimedia storytelling for smaller productions. The article discusses the multimedia skills required in related professions and offers reflection opportunities for students on what skills they need to build. It has particular relevance to journalism students.

Seyser, D. and Zeiller, M. (2018). Scrollytelling – An analysis of visual storytelling in online journalism. 2018 22nd International Conference Information Visualisation (IV). doi:https://doi.org/10.1109/iv.2018.00075.

This article discusses scrollytelling and investigates which types of infographics are used for visualizing complex data in long-form journalism published online. The analysis focuses on the utilization of infographics in scrollytelling and how infographics are integrated in long-form articles'.

REFERENCES

321Agency (2018). 321 wins PR award for 'it's a nurse' video. [online] *321 Blog*. Available at: https://321theagency.com/insights/community/321-wins-pr-award-for-its-a-nurse-video/ [Accessed 15 November 2022].

Cope, J. and Wells, M. (2018). Picturing statistical narratives: A century of data visualisation in public relations practice. In: S. Collister and S. Roberts-Bowman (eds.), *Visual Public Relations*. Abingdon: Routledge, pp. 53–82.

Gerrell, M. and Hatter, J. (2017). 'It's a nurse' video – The Shorty Awards. [online] *shortyawards.com*. Available at: https://shortyawards.com/9th/its-a-nurse-video [Accessed 15 November 2022].

Handley, A. (2014). The Airbnb Berlin Wall anniversary film: A Q&A with its creator #BelongAnywhere. [online] *Ann Handley*. Available at: https://annhandley.com/back-story-marketing-takeaways-airbnb-berlin-wall-anniversary-film/ [Accessed 15 November 2022].

McLachlan, S. and Mikolajczyk, K. (2022). 2022 Instagram algorithm solved: How to get your content seen. [online] *Hootsuite Social Media Management*. Available at: https://blog.hootsuite.com/instagram-algorithm/ [Accessed 15 November 2022].

Pera, R. and Viglia, G. (2016). Exploring how video digital storytelling builds relationship experiences. *Psychology & Marketing*, 33(12), 1142–1150. doi:10.1002/mar.20951.

Schneiders, P. (2020). What remains in mind? Effectiveness and efficiency of explainers at conveying information. *Media and Communication*, 8(1), 218–231.

Seyser, D. and Zeiller, M. (2018). Scrollytelling – An analysis of visual storytelling in online journalism. *2018 22nd International Conference Information Visualisation (IV)*. doi:https://doi.org/10.1109/iv.2018.00075.

Wolf, C. and Godulla, A. (2016). Potentials of digital longforms in journalism: A survey among mobile internet users about the relevance of online devices, internet-specific qualities, and modes of payment. *Journal of Media Business Studies*, 13(4), 199–221. doi:10.1080/16522354.2016.1184922.

9

PODCASTS FOR BRAND STORYTELLING

OBJECTIVES

1. Explore the role of podcasts in brand storytelling
2. Understand how brands are using podcasts within a digital storytelling context
3. Learn key podcast terminology, based on standard podcasting platforms
4. Understand key podcasting concepts, including structure, narrative, and interview technique

The fact that we have dedicated an entire chapter exclusively to podcasts should provide you with an indication of how important podcasts have become in the world of digital storytelling. As one of the fastest growing channels, podcasts are used by brands in innovative – and indeed highly immersive – ways to develop and extend brand narrative. Building a podcast series relevant to a brand takes skill, creativity and a fair amount of planning. This chapter outlines the leaders in brand podcasts and discusses podcast narrative, key turning points, tension build up and how to keep the audience engaged and interested. It outlines the pre-production, production and post-production elements of podcasting for brands.

THE ROLE OF PODCASTS IN BRAND STORYTELLING

> If you look at a sky full of stars you can't make sense of it. If you take a few
> stars, link them together and make a constellation – now you've got a cool
> picture of a bear and that's memorable. It's the same with storytelling – you
> need to reduce it down to something essential that people can engage with.
> (Stevenson, 2022)

Podcasts have been used by organisations as innovative ways to develop brand narrative for at least ten years. Brands such as General Electric, Ford, BMW and Microsoft have used podcasts in various formats that are explored in this chapter, with the aim to build a deep, sustainable relationship with their audiences. In his online class on podcasting, Alex Blumberg (2022) states that audio is the most visual medium – it is a strange statement but when we hear something, we automatically create visuals in our mind. Hence, audio becomes a powerful medium for storytelling and can create deep memories. The other essential element to audio is that it provides an intimate experience that conveys honesty, and this is because when everything else is stripped away, the language becomes more powerful and, hence, emotional. Blumberg (2022) asserts that podcasts are the most honest medium; you can hear the truth, you can hear a lie. As previously mentioned in this book, the more the world around us becomes digital, the more we crave for human connections, which is exactly what storytelling podcasts provide us with. We believe it is for this reason podcasts have increased in popularity in recent years.

Podcasts as they are known today emerged in the 21st century and truly increased in popularity with the 2014 investigative journalism podcast *Serial*, produced by WBEZ Chicago public radio and the American monthly hour-long radio programme *This American Life*, which is available as a free monthly podcast. Although the format was not new, it was a revolutionary new way of presenting investigative journalism, and the 12 weekly instalments were written and read by journalist Sarah Koenig in a dramatic and engaging way (McCracken, 2017). The impact of *Serial* cannot be underestimated; it sparked a genuine interest in investigative journalism, and simultaneously an interest in podcasting and digital storytelling.

Reflecting on the rise and success of *Serial*, Hardey and James (2022) summarise:

> The podcast – a mix of first-person narration and documentary storytelling – is composed of 12 episodes, narrated by Koenig, which aired at weekly
> intervals starting October 3, 2014. The original Serial reached 10 million
> downloads in seven weeks; by mid-February 2015, the podcast had been
> downloaded more than 68 million times, making it the most popular podcast in the short history of the medium. (p. 75)

The Australian, a national Australian newspaper, produced a similar podcast in 2018 called *The Teacher's Pet*, which investigated the cold case disappearance of Lynette Dawson, a nurse and mother, who vanished in 1982 without a trace. The podcast investigated details of her marriage and highlighted flaws in the police investigation. Two further episodes were added to the original 14, as the case evolved, followed by a podcast called *The Teacher's Trial*, which was released every Friday, summarising key events when the case finally returned to court. Lynette's husband, former rugby league player and teacher and Chris Dawson, was found guilty on 30 August 2022 for her murder.

In both examples, narrative techniques were used to build a relationship with the audience and garner their interest, information was given out in breadcrumbs, not all at once, so the listener had a reason to come back in the next episode to literally follow the trail. While this was an innovative approach to investigative journalism, the serial format of podcasting is not new and is reminiscent of the radio show *The War of the Worlds* that was performed and broadcast on 30 October in 1938, made famous for the compelling narration by Orson Welles that convinced listeners that the world was indeed experiencing a real time Martian invasion (Wikipedia, 2019). In this case the narrative was fiction, however *Serial* applied a very similar approach to a real-life unsolved murder case and used 'co-consumptive practice' to involve the audience in reviewing evidence and sharing their opinions (Hardey and James, 2022). Applying Jenkins' elements of participatory culture (2006) and also the role of the fan, *Serial* created an emotional relationship with the audience through intrigue and shared connection. For the radio station WBEZ Chicago and also *This American Life* – the production team behind *Serial* – the podcast was key in making a local radio station and national radio show known and recognisable worldwide. It was very much a case of everything old is new again: a podcast is a serial format – taking the idea of Charles Dickens' Victorian novel that was serialised in a newspaper (discussed in Chapter 1), to a serialised fictional radio show in 1938, to a real-life serialised digital radio show in 2014 that was made available on demand, all over the world.

Similar to the notion that if you want to write a novel, you need to read a lot, anyone considering podcasting for brand storytelling should listen to the *Serial* podcast (and others) in order to understand structure, narrative technique and the use of sound. If this kind of popularity can be gained for a true crime series, what might be the possibilities for brands keen to harness this interest in podcasting?

Building a podcast series relevant to a brand takes skill and creativity, and just because you can have a podcast, it doesn't mean you should. Like most aspects of branding, podcasts need to have a purpose and fit with the brand in order to have meaning. Across the last ten years a growing number of different brands have used podcasts in different styles, and some of these include:

- Storytelling podcasts: Narratives that may be fictional or non-fiction (i.e. General Electric, *The Message* and WBEZ Chicago, *Serial* respectively).

- Interview podcasts: A host interviews guests around a specific topic (i.e. Microsoft Stories or Ford, *Bring Back Bronco*).
- Mono or co-hosted podcasts: One, two or more hosts discuss their opinions on specific topics, sometimes with audiences that call in (i.e. Dave Ramsey's *The Ramsey Show*).
- Panel podcasts: A particular subject is discussed by a group of people and moderated by a host (i.e. *The Global Pillage*).

Podcasts have become a popular tool in the communication mix, as they are accessible, can be listened to anywhere and allow the user to multi-task (e.g. listen on the commute, on a walk, whilst doing chores around the house). The rise of digital radios and Bluetooth technology in cars has allowed podcast platforms to increase in numbers; podcasts are convenient to consume. Podcasts are different to listening to a radio show, however, and they offer a much more intimate listening experience. In part this is because they are available on demand and often listened to via ear- or headphones, enabling the listener to truly immerse themselves in the narrative. However more importantly this is due to the quality of the recording and the use of natural language that makes consuming a podcast more akin to listening to a friend on the phone. Podcasts are also expanding into areas that previously did not get much airtime, with academics and journalists joining forces to bring research to an interested audience, as Rogers and Herbert (2019) explain:

> In an environment where research papers are buried behind publishers' paywalls, podcasting allows academics to communicate their research beyond the university.

As audio and recording equipment are now so easily accessible, podcasts are increasingly becoming a part of historical documentation. For example, Rogers et al.'s (2020) podcast project became an important part of documenting cities during the peak of the global COVID-19 pandemic.

The podcast hook, the XY formula

In the book *Out on the Wire: The Storytelling Secrets of the New Masters of Radio*, Abel (2016) analyses successful podcasts like *This American Life* and *Planet Money* to discern the formula to create a compelling podcast. While podcasts rely on creativity and connection, there is a story formula, referred to as the XY formula, that ensures a compelling hook both for the overall narrative, as well as for each individual episode. The formula was devised by Alex Blumberg, formerly of *This American Life* and *Planet Money* and now of Gimlet Media:

'I'm doing a story about X. And what's interesting about it is Y'.

A simple statement, and yet it emphasises the importance of a hook, clearly stating what's interesting about a particular podcast and why your audience should be interested in it. If this statement is applied to *Serial*, you might get something like:

'I'm doing a story about the murder of Hae Min Lee. And what's interesting about it is that Adnan Syed says it's impossible that he killed her, despite being found guilty'.

The 'what's interesting' statement should raise questions and already have the listener wondering 'why is that and how can I know more?' Abel (2016) says:

It's a way of looking at that character and conflict, or that character-free 'topic', and deciding how interesting it is – how much do we need this story to exist in the world? As a counterpart to the focus sentence, it helps clarify a very important piece: maybe you've got your narrative arc, you've [got] conflict.

For brands, this same formula can be used, and should be used to clarify the overall story, but then also completed for each individual podcast. The key is to clearly identify and state why the story should be of interest to listeners. Dave Ramsey runs an American podcast called *The Ramsey Show*. In the show he talks about money issues and financial solutions and yet he does so in a way that engages millions of listeners across the nation, who would not traditionally have tuned into a financial programme. A key element of successful podcasting is that small stories create big stories, and Dave understands this. Most episodes involve listeners calling in with their issues, based on which Dave quickly unravels the problem and identifies the real issues. These often include big issues like domestic abuse, financial abuse and much more. Based on these small personal stories he highlights greater (societal) issues and brings them to light in a moving and powerful way.

Who is listening?

In 2022, Australia overtook the US as the world's biggest podcast listening audience per capita. 'The infinite dial 2022 Australia' noted:

Monthly podcast listening hits 40% among Australians 18+, up from 37% in 2021. Weekly podcast listening is steady at 26%, the same as in 2021, and the same as weekly podcast listening in the US. (Edison Research, 2022)

Insights from the report noted that among Australians aged 12 years and above who listen to podcasts, 20% listen every day, and more than half (57%) listen to the entire episode. These are not small numbers, and they reflect a similar trend across the world; people love listening to podcasts and they listen for similar reasons, such as to get a deeper understanding of an issue or concept, for the convenience of accessible information, to gain a wider perspective and to be entertained (Edison Research, 2022). Interestingly, there is growth across most age groups, so for brands, it is important to find a podcast topic that resonates with your audience.

HOW BRANDS ARE USING DIGITAL STORYTELLING IN PODCASTS: PODCASTS AS A DEMOCRATIC VOICE

Importantly, podcasts are also key in providing an alternative viewpoint for many audiences, as they seek different news and information sources to traditional ones. As we see more democratic media under threat from the shrinking of independent sources, podcasts offer a way for 'public discussions' to 'bypass large, commercially driven media monopolies' (Rogers and Herbert, 2019). Not for profits and social justice brands may benefit most from this as the goal is to communicate diversity and public debate on critical issues. This is seen in *The Conversation*'s (Canada) podcast, *Don't Call Me Resilient*, a podcast aimed at tackling systemic racism. For brands, this is a way to tap into relevance and resonance and strategically align with the collective narrative. Rather than a direct brand approach, the focus is on building a sustainable relationship with an audience over time; to encourage listeners to come back again and again. The building of trust and authenticity is perhaps one of the greatest benefits of using podcasts as a part of an overall brand strategy. This can also be extended to using sound more generally. In the following case study we discuss a use of sound, not an actual podcast, to develop the brand and brand association.

CASE STUDY
The power of audio - sonic branding

Alongside podcasts and on demand radio programmes, we've seen organisations and brands explore alternative options to capitalise on the intimate, personalised feel associated with audio-based content. For example, in 2021 communication agency Ogilvy worked with the Swedish-Dutch multinational furniture retailer Ikea to turn its annual catalogue from print and digital into an immersive audio version. Over 3 hours and 41 minutes, audiences could explore the 286 pages of the traditional print catalogue in a new and immersive format. Even though this new format does not appear to have been replicated for the following year(s), it illustrates that there are always new and novel storytelling approaches to be explored by creative communicators.

Another context in which audio is being explored is sonic branding. Some sounds are simply iconic and forever ingrained in our memory. If you had a Nokia phone, or a computer that started up with the Intel sound mark, you would know exactly how powerful sound can be over time. The impact and power of audio logos has increasingly been recognised as a crucial part of overall branding efforts; your unique sound becomes part of your brand story. An audio logo is essentially a sound bite, no more than a few seconds long, that may either accompany the visual logo or may even entirely replace it. Think of the McDonald's catchy 'ba da baba ba' whistle, the Netflix 'ta-dum' intro or – for movie lovers – the MGM lion roar. They immediately let us know what to expect and evoke a powerful, emotional connection – from 'yay, I really need a burger' to 'time for binge-watching', and a craving for movie nostalgia.

Brands are increasingly investing in audio – or sonic – branding, supported by specialised audio consultants, to create a more immersive, engaging and subtle brand storytelling experience. Audio branding supports a deeper level of brand recognition and recall. For example, faced with the challenge that electric vehicles no longer come with the traditional engine noises that many consumers associate with driving pleasure, car manufacturers have been prompted to rethink the driving experience they want to create. BMW prides itself on the fact that the sound of its combustion engine had always been recognisable to fans and experts of the German car. Something as simple as an engine sound can elicit deep emotional reactions, from safety and comfort, to adventure and family time. So how do you translate these deep emotions to a supposedly silent, electronically powered vehicle? BMW partnered with composer, music producer and Academy Award winner Hans Zimmer (think *Lion King*, *Gladiator* and *Pirates of the Caribbean*) to develop special drive sounds for its new electric vehicles, with the aim to reflect the character of different BMW models. Rather than replicate traditional engine noises, the new electric drive sounds extend and deepen the connection with the brand, based on an interactive soundscape with catchy melodies and a strong recognition value.

The idea of sonic branding adds yet another layer to digital storytelling and signals a new future where all elements discussed in this book, when used, can enrich the storytelling world to one that is immersive, audio, visceral and dynamic. It's not one element of digital storytelling, but all the elements working together at different levels that will deliver the real storytelling of the future.

KEY PODCAST TERMINOLOGY USING STANDARD PODCASTING PLATFORMS

There are many platforms available to record podcasts, some of which may be quite expensive. There are a few platforms you can use that don't require you to spend much money (or any) at all to produce professional sounding podcasts. If you use a Mac computer you can use GarageBand; this comes free with the Mac platform.

Podcast creators can download an open-source program called Audacity (www.audacityteam.org/) which is an 'easy-to-use, multi-track audio editor and recorder for Windows, macOS, GNU/Linux and other operating systems' (Audacity, 2019). This program allows you to produce and post-produce your podcasts including music, voice and sound. Other platforms, like e.g. Zencastr, enable you to record podcasts with multiple contributors based in different locations.

Some very basic terms that you may come across in podcasting include (but are not limited to):

- **Condenser microphone**: A sensitive microphone with a lightweight diaphragm, which is suspended by a fixed plate and designed to pick up delicate sounds. These are particularly useful in a studio setup.
- **Dynamic microphone**: A microphone that converts sound into an electronic signal by means of electromagnetism. Think of the types of microphones that are being used at a live performance, where there is a loud sound source. These are less sensitive and are used by most podcasters.
- **Mixer**: Hardware device that allows you to plug in different microphones and adjust levels while recording (can also be done in most software platforms).
- **Interface**: Hardware that is the link between the microphone and the software. If you plug a microphone directly into a computer (i.e. USB), you won't need this hardware.
- **Pop filter**: A noise protection shield placed between the microphone and your mouth that reduces the popping sound of Ps and Bs.

These terms are specific to podcasting software:

- **Mute**: Cuts off the sound/ microphone.
- **Solo**: Isolates one or more individual tracks.
- **Gain**: Magnification of the signal – similar to volume.
- **Pan**: Sends a (stereo) signal to left or right speakers.
- **Expand/collapse**: Makes tracks vertically smaller or larger.
- **Playback speed**: Increases or decreases audio playback speed.
- **Fit project to width**: Fits your tracks into the width of the screen.
- **Undo/redo**: Typical function, as used in other contexts, i.e. reversing a previous action.
- **Intro music**: Music that starts gentle and then climaxes at about 4 seconds (length: ~5 secs).
- **Podcast theme music**: Music that is distinct to a particular podcast and is hence recognisable, conveys the feeling of your podcast (length: ~10 secs).
- **Cut music**: Conveys the end of something and beginning of something new (length: 2–3 secs).
- **Emotive music**: Moving and poignant music, emphasises the impact of the interview (length: ~10 secs).

PODCAST STRUCTURE AND INTERVIEW TECHNIQUE

(Brand) podcasts generally use standard narrative techniques (either fiction or non-fiction) to signal key turning points, tension build up and how to keep the audience interested. They often follow a typical three-part dramatic arc (see Chapter 4) that highlights exposition (background), rising action (with climax) and resolution (wrapping up). *This American Life* typically follows this structure in all their podcasts in which they call it Act 1, Act 2 and Act 3. The first segment needs to create a 'hook' or angle to get the listener interested. This is really an outline of your XY statement (with the focus on the Y). Tell the audience why the story is interesting, without giving them the answer. The following parts or acts will funnel down into more information, each time giving a little more insight to keep the listener interested. Small details are important and powerful in podcasting – they combine to tell the larger narrative.

In developing a podcast there are three key stages: pre-production, production and post-production. **Pre-production** involves the planning stage where you map out the overall narrative, devise each episode's theme and decide on the host and format. At this stage you may use storyboards to map out the narrative for each episode to create a clear picture. This stage should also include any known scripting including intro, outro, interview questions, monologues and segues so the production is professional. While some discussions between co-hosts and interviewees may be unscripted (and are authentic to include), a pre-production guide will ensure a smooth podcast.

Production is the physical recording when you bring your interviewee(s) and contributor(s) in to record the segment. If you are producing a fictional podcast, you may include voice actors and sound to produce an authentic recording. Many podcasts are not live or recorded in one take, so there's no pressure for accuracy and you can re-record elements that don't work. In some cases, regular podcasts are now filmed as well as being recorded. In this case more accuracy and attention to detail are needed.

Post-production is when you can edit your recording in your chosen podcast software. You will include your intro and outro, sound effects (if relevant), interval music, advertising (if applicable) and much more. This is one of the most time-consuming parts of the podcasting process. This will also include graphics for the cover art and a synopsis of each episode, which you will then upload to your chosen platforms. For accessibility reasons you should also include a full transcript with each episode.

Writing for the ear

Writing for the ear is more akin to writing a speech than writing a media release, or a book! You need to use natural language and you need to read out what you've written so you can hear the cadence and tone. Podcasts should allow for the personality of the hosts. Further, silence is a powerful element – you don't always need to fill it. If you listen to some well-known podcasts, you'll notice that many commence by setting the scene (background). Given the lack of a visual aid, telling the listener what environment the story is set in is crucial as it helps them picture it. As the ear can tire, it also helps to tell the listener what you are going to tell them, as an enticer for what is to come. Although podcasts are considered long-form digital content, the language should be concise, again so as not to tire the ear. A way to break the narrative up for the listener is to include reflective moments, where the host or narrator pauses the journey of the narrative and inserts their own opinions. Here we have a breakdown that outlines some key elements of how you might structure a podcast:

- **Prologue**: Interesting discussion, sound bite or noise from your recording to create intrigue among the audience.
- **Intro**: Podcast name and topic, host name and background, what the podcast is about (synopsis) and your call to action.
- **Music jingle**: Same music at the beginning of each episode to help the audience easily identify the podcast.
- **Topic 1**: Key theme, and discuss a point, topic or segment in detail.
- **Interlude**: Same music used at each interval point. May have advertising.
- **Topic 2**: Discuss one point, topic or segment in detail.
- **Interlude**: Music break or sponsor ad.
- **Topic 3**: Discuss one point, topic or segment in detail.
- **Outro**: Summarise theme, recap on discussion with conclusion.
- **Closing remarks**: Thank audience, thank guests, talk about the next episode, and final call to action.
- **Closing music jingle**: Repeat music jingle to help listeners identify the jingle with the podcast.

Metadata to include in your podcast

1. Podcast name.
2. Episode number – important to use these in chronological order.
3. Episode title – a creative title is good but it should represent the content of the show.
4. Music or sound effects – try using original music where you can and insert interesting noises that help set the scene.
5. Hosts' names – audiences should be able to look them up, but also discuss who they are as part of your podcasts.
6. Podcast tagline/explanation – important in the marketing phase; if your audience wants to find a podcast on corporate storytelling, you need that included in the tagline.

7. Summary/introduction – tell the audience what you are going to tell them in the podcast.

8. Media outlet – if your podcast is produced by a media outlet, state it.

9. Recorded date.

10. Sponsors – you may have included their advertisements but you should also mention them at the end.

11. Disclaimer – if you need to include one (e.g. content reflects solely the views of the individuals involved, trigger warnings, copyright, liability limitations), do so.

Key points to consider when preparing a podcast

Podcasting is a little formulaic, and primarily creative; understanding the dance between the formula and creativity can help you produce an effective podcast. Here are a few tips to ensure you remain authentic, yet structured:

- Always consider how you might deliver background information – it's important but do it in an interesting way.
- Set the scene and talk through important details – what the room or a person looks like, use the sounds of the environment (i.e. a busy coffee shop, train station, water running/birds tweeting, etc.).
- Have a list of questions when interviewing, but allow for time to 'go down the rabbit hole' if the interviewee starts talking about something interesting (but related to the podcast).
- Focus on micro stories that highlight great narratives.
- Podcasting needs a build-up to get to the conclusion.
- You might have a three-part structure, but you don't have to follow a chronological story structure: you can start the story in the middle, or at the end, and then unravel the story.
- Every 45 seconds to a minute, something new should be happening – this progresses the story.
- Edit interviews and make them punchy – you don't need to include everything.

Mapping out an interview and creating a narrative

Interviewing is an art form, but the more you practise and learn techniques, the better and more confident you will become. A good interviewer has the ability to ask the right questions at the right time. A good interviewee is considered 'good talent', and this means it's not always the most senior person, or the 'expert', but someone who is authentic and has the ability to speak in layperson's terms. Their discussion will be engaging – just ensure it is accurate. To find a good interviewee, look for the storytellers in an organisation; the best ones may not be the official media spokespeople.

Before you interview someone, you should do your research on them, find out what they are interested in, and if you have any commonalities. You may want to share a personal story first that is related to the topic. This is called modelling and can encourage your interviewee to talk more freely. When a person feels relaxed, they will often speak more honestly. It's important to have questions prepared, but don't be afraid to go off script and explore interesting elements. When the interview is complete, go back, listen and look for the story arc. Note timestamps for key content, so when you edit you have a clear idea of what information you will include in each act. You can think about turning points and rising action to really ensure you structure your podcast well. Include any compelling parts early in the podcast to gain intrigue from your audiences.

During the podcast you should indicate where you are going, and comment on where you have been along the way, i.e. include clear signposts. This not only helps break up the narrative but reminds the listener of the trajectory of the story. If you feel more clarity or context is needed, you can paraphrase in interviews to help the audience understand what the interviewee is saying. You might do this by saying 'in other words...' but remember to keep it concise and allow the interviewee to agree with you.

CASE STUDY
General Electric and *The Message*

The Message is not your usual brand digital storytelling podcast, and it is for this reason that we discuss it in this chapter. Similar to the Burberry case study (Chapter 1), although the podcast launched in 2015, it presented a truly ground-breaking approach for a corporate brand and still provides many relevant learnings today in terms of digital storytelling and podcasting. Also similar to Burberry, General Electric (GE) echoed the sentiment that they were a content creator in the digital space, just as much as they were a multinational conglomerate in healthcare, aviation, power, renewable energy, digital industry and manufacturing. Previously, corporations may have rarely thought about undertaking a fictional podcast for their brand. GE had this in mind when they produced *The Message*, an eight-episode podcast produced by GE Podcast Theater, its advertising agency BBDO New York and podcast network Panoply, as they believed it was a key means to differentiate the brand. The premise of the fictional podcast was a story narrated by Nicky Tomalin, who worked with a team of cryptologists to decipher an alien message. The podcast is frequently listed online in rankings of the Best Fiction Podcasts and won a Webby Award in 2016 for best use of native advertising. Native advertising is a form of instream advertising - delivered in a way more like editorial than advertising. In other words, rather than sponsor a hit podcast, GE created their own, inspired by the success of *Serial* (Walker, 2016). Andy Goldberg, GE's global creative director at the time said, 'It flipped a switch for us that podcasting was no longer going to be informational pieces but could be entertainment'

(Toonkel, 2015). Similar to the *Serial* podcast, *The Message* had a *War of the Worlds*-like feel, and followed a traditional dramatic structure narrative with key characters. The initial aim of the podcast was a branding exercise to raise the GE profile among a younger audience (Toonkel, 2015) and build a connection. As Goldberg pointed out, 'It's a science fiction story to connect listeners with what the GE brand is about, without selling the GE brand' (Hazard Owen, 2015). GE understood a key element of modern branding in the digital storytelling world, i.e. that branded content shouldn't be about your brand if you want to truly connect and engage. This style of digital storytelling and branding is more about who the organisation is on a deeper level; in this case, GE is positioning itself as a leader in podcasting, and also storytelling. It's a subtle way to build goodwill for an organisation or brand, based on the fact that audiences will come back and seek you out over and over again for similarly effective and engaging storytelling.

Another key element of the GE podcast was the ability to build an emotional connection with a younger audience that might not be familiar with the brand. Building emotion through digital storytelling is a sustainable approach to branding, one that is likely to create a deep and long-lasting relationship with the brand. GE, similar to Burberry, have followed a brand model that puts the customer/audience at the heart of their brand and hence 'implementing customer emotions at the centre of a company's business strategy can strengthen relationships and provide innovative digital channel experiences' (Straker and Wrigley, 2016).

The success of *The Message* was illustrated when fan groups started to organically emerge online on platforms like Reddit (Walker, 2016). In a nod to the collective narrative, GE were ahead of the game in that they understood the podcast was less about direct sales, and more about inserting itself, 'however obliquely, into broader cultural conversations' and 'for doing something the best advertising always strives for: "capitalizing on the zeitgeist"'(Walker, 2016).

CHAPTER SUMMARY

This chapter discusses podcasts and how they have been used innovatively by brands to create a deep, sustainable relationship with audiences. The importance of podcasts in their role to create powerful visuals is discussed, as well as the crucial role of honesty and emotion.

The 2014 podcast *Serial* is discussed as a historically significant production, leading to the increase in popularity of podcasts, and making brands become aware of their potential. Podcasts use elements of narrative and also participatory culture to build a fan base and engage listeners on a deeper level than traditional branding.

The XY formula is used as a guide to create a strong story that is of interest to an audience, prompting you to summarise: *'I'm doing a story about X. And what's interesting about it is Y'.*

Podcasts are increasing in popularity across the world and their use for branding has become commonplace with audio strategy now being included in most marketing plans. The role of podcasts as a democratic voice is also considered in delivering alternative formats to the standard media approach.

The outline of a podcast and interview techniques are discussed along with key terminology to learn more about how to structure a podcast. Finally, the case study of GE's *The Message* is discussed as a best-practice use of a fictional podcast for brand storytelling.

DISCUSSION QUESTIONS

1. Choose a podcast from This American Life, The Dave Ramsey Show, Gimlet Media etc. and reverse engineer it. This involves breaking down the structure of the narrative. Consider the following elements:
   a. Linear/chronological, dramatic arc, fractured, framed, circular
   b. Exposition, introduction, build-up, complication, rising action, tension, setting, characters, problem, solution, timeline, narrative style, audience, emotion, falling action, climax, resolution (narrative structure)
2. For your brand/client define your story using the formula: I'm doing a story about 'X' and it's interesting because of 'Y'.
3. Write down a list of 'micro stories' derived from your big narrative.
4. Take a look at the two following podcasts (listen to the first episodes only) and discuss if you think they are effective for the organisation.
   BMW, Hypnopolis - www.bmw.com/en/innovation/hypnopolis-podcast.html
   Ford, Bring Back Bronco - https://youtu.be/NYWbsrIL4mc
   Discuss and consider:
   a. Do they use a storytelling approach?
   b. Who is the likely audience for each podcast?
   c. Compare and contrast the different approaches of BMW and Ford, two car manufacturers - one is traditional storytelling, the other is brand storytelling - which is more effective?
   d. Is there scope for other podcasts for each of the organisations? What might they be? Draft a brief concept proposal.

READINGS

Rogers, D., Herbert, M., Whitzman, C., McCann, E., Maginn, P.J., Watts, B., Alam, A., Pill, M., Keil, R., Dreher, T., Novacevski, M., Byrne, J., Osborne, N., Büdenbender, M., Alizadeh, T., Murray, K., Dombroski, K., Prasad, D., Connolly, C. and Kass, A. (2020). The city under COVID-19: Podcasting as digital methodology. *Tijdschrift voor economische en sociale geografie*, 111(3), 434–450. doi:10.1111/tesg.12426.

This article discusses podcasting and reflects on an international podcast project about cities during COVID-19. It discusses the role of the podcast as a democratic voice and also a historical journal.

Blumberg, A. (2022). Power Your Podcast with Storytelling with Alex Blumberg. [online] CreativeLive. Available at: https://www.creativelive.com/class/power-your-podcast-storytelling-alex-blumberg.

This is an extension and paid class you can take to learn more about podcasting. The website mentions 'Join Alex Blumberg, award-winning reporter and producer for This American Life and co-host of NPR's Planet Money, for Power Your Podcast with Storytelling, and learn podcast tips on how to tell powerful, memorable stories through audio.'

REFERENCES

Abel, J. (2016). Grab your audience's attention with the XY story formula. [online] *Jessica Abel*. Available at: https://jessicaabel.com/xy-story-formula/ [Accessed 23 November 2022].

Abel, J. and Broadway Books (2015). *Out on the Wire: The Storytelling Secrets of the New Masters of Radio*. New York: B/D/W/Y/Broadway Books.

Audacity (2019). *Audacity | Free, open source, cross-platform audio software for multi-track recording and editing*. [online] Available at: www.audacityteam.org/ [Accessed 23 November 2022].

Blumberg, A. (2022). Power your podcast with storytelling with Alex Blumberg. [online] *CreativeLive*. Available at: www.creativelive.com/class/power-your-podcast-storytelling-alex-blumberg [Accessed 24 November 2022].

Edison Research (2022). The infinite dial 2022 Australia. [online] *Edison Research*. Available at: www.edisonresearch.com/the-infinite-dial-2022-australia/ [Accessed 23 November 2022].

Hardey, M. and James, S.J. (2022). Digital seriality and narrative branching: The podcast *Serial*, season one. *Communication and Critical/Cultural Studies*, 19(1), 1–17. doi: 10.1080/14791420.2022.2029513.

Hazard Owen, L. (2015). How did the GE-branded podcast *The Message* hit No. 1 on iTunes? In part, by sounding nothing like an ad. [online] *Nieman Lab*. Available at: www.niemanlab.org/2015/11/how-did-the-ge-branded-podcast-the-message-hit-no-1-on-itunes-in-part-by-sounding-nothing-like-an-ad/ [Accessed 23 November 2022].

Jenkins, H. (2006). Confronting the challenges of participatory culture: Media education for the 21st century (part one). [online] *Henry Jenkins*. Available at: http://henry jenkins.org/blog/2006/10/confronting_the_challenges_of.html [Accessed 19 October 2022].

McCracken, E. (ed.) (2017). *The 'Serial' Podcast and Storytelling in the Digital Age*. Abingdon: Routledge.

Rogers, D. and Herbert, M. (2019). Podcasts and cities: 'You're always commenting on power'. [online] *The Conversation*. Available at: https://theconversation.com/podcasts-and-cities-youre-always-commenting-on-power-114176 [Accessed 24 November 2022].

Rogers, D., Herbert, M., Whitzman, C., McCann, E., Maginn, P.J., Watts, B., Alam, A., Pill, M., Keil, R., Dreher, T., Novacevski, M., Byrne, J., Osborne, N., Büdenbender, M., Alizadeh, T., Murray, K., Dombroski, K., Prasad, D., Connolly, C. and Kass, A. (2020). The city under COVID-19: Podcasting as digital methodology. *Tijdschrift voor economische en sociale geografie*, 111(3), 434–450. doi:10.1111/tesg.12426.

Stevenson, N. (2022). Establishing a culture of storytelling. [online] *IDEO U*. Available at: www.ideou.com/blogs/inspiration/establishing-a-culture-of-storytelling [Accessed 22 November 2022].

Straker, K. and Wrigley, C. (2016). Emotionally engaging customers in the digital age: The case study of 'Burberry love'. *Journal of Fashion Marketing and Management: An International Journal*, 20(3), 276–299. doi:10.1108/jfmm-10-2015-0077.

Toonkel, J. (2015). General Electric producing science fiction podcast series. [online] *Reuters, GMA News Online*. Available at: www.gmanetwork.com/news/scitech/science/539341/general-electric-producing-science-fiction-podcast-series/story/ [Accessed 24 November 2022].

Walker, R. (2016). Forget filling ad breaks: Some marketers make the podcasts. [online] *The New York Times*, 20 November. Available at: www.nytimes.com/2016/11/21/business/media/marketers-make-the-podcasts.html [Accessed 24 November 2022].

Wikipedia (2019). *The War of the Worlds (1938 Radio Drama)*. [online] Available at: https://en.wikipedia.org/wiki/The_War_of_the_Worlds_(1938_radio_drama) [Accessed 24 November 2022].

10

BRAND STORYTELLING AND REPUTATION MANAGEMENT

OBJECTIVES

1. Explore reputation management and stakeholder theory
2. Understand how brand storytelling, trust and reputation are linked
3. Learn how to manage online criticism, and how to appropriately respond in times of crisis

In a crisis the world turns to social media, and so do journalists. When time is of the essence, online commentary and insights provide convenient and swift context. This might be located on your own channels, such as a blog or a website, if recognised as a valuable information source. However, in the absence of timely, honest organisational insights, the media – and other stakeholders – may be more inclined to seek out third-party accounts. This chapter provides an overview of key reputation management principles. It outlines how digital storytelling affects online reputation and how brands can protect themselves through listening and appropriate responding. The chapter outlines current reputational management and stakeholder theory and how their management has changed since the advent of digital. Trust and authenticity are key concepts that are discussed, including how they are linked to building, maintaining and repairing a reputation.

WHY DOES REPUTATION MATTER?

The most important thing to understand about reputation is that you do not own it. Indeed, reputation is often confused with an organisation's identity or image (Cornelissen, 2017). An organisational identity reflects the values communicated by an organisation via symbols, logos, its communication style and indeed the types of stories that it is choosing to share. This leads to the 'image', i.e. an immediate set of associations an individual may have in response to one or more signals or messages from an organisation. For example, we may perceive some organisations as risk averse or reliable, and others as adventurous, outspoken advocates on particular issues, or even deliberately contentious (for example: Irish low-cost airline Ryanair). In contrast, reputation reflects an individual's collective representation of past interactions with an organisation, which is formed through their encounters with the organisation, related brands and their communication over time. You may want to think of reputation as a psychological contract between brands, customers and employees (Hartley, 2019). It can also act as a shortcut, enabling a stakeholder who may not know much about an organisation to decide whether to trust it or not, based on others' perceptions. You can shape your reputation based on your behaviour and stakeholder engagement strategies, but you can never own it! Indeed, it's not yours to own. In the words of SenateSHJ (2020), an Australasian communication consultancy specialising in reputation and risk management:

> [Reputation] is not what you think you are; it is how others perceive you. It is the connections your employees have with your customers and stakeholders, how they behave and how engaged they are with your organisation. It is about reacting in the right way, when things go wrong.

Unfortunately, many organisations don't consider reputation management as a priority when things go well. Often, business as usual and other urgent activities are prioritised, which means reputation-related considerations only really come to the forefront once a crisis strikes. Realistically, by that time, it's too late. Remember, your reputation reflects your stakeholders' engagement with you and your brand over time. This experience will shape how they will judge you during times of crisis. Importantly, keep in mind that you can't protect a reputation if you haven't built it in the first place! Ironically, leaving your reputation management until the very last minute, ultimately requiring you to rebuild a reputation post-crisis, tends to be far more expensive than investing in reputation management up front.

Marketers and communication professionals are best placed to look after and advise on an organisation's reputation, as they are expected to not only be the eyes and ears of the organisation, but also its ethical guardian. In order to do their work successfully, they need to have a holistic understanding of the organisation and its various business units and will therefore be well positioned to manage its image and brand(s). In addition, a key responsibility of their role is to understand different stakeholder perspectives and to anticipate emerging issues. Communication professionals are trained in how to build, manage and protect a reputation. The increased move into a digital world has made organisations and their behaviour more visible. The resulting 24-hour news cycle and visibility of many different – supporting and sometimes hostile – voices have increased the challenges associated with managing a reputation. However, keep in mind that a reputation is not built overnight. Instead, you can curate a reputation over time, by carefully planning how to engage with your different audiences, strategically planning ahead how and for what you want to be known. The entrepreneur Warren Buffett's infamous quote states that it takes 20 years to build a reputation, but only five minutes to ruin it (Schwantes, 2021). While this can be true, strategic investment in your reputation over time may equally enable you to weather the storm and indeed bounce back quicker in difficult times, especially if an issue or crisis is not a result of your own doing. If your stakeholders know you as a responsible organisation that cares about its staff, the community and customers, an organisation that has done the right things by them on multiple previous occasions, then they are more likely to speak up on your behalf and forgive missteps as human error. Most importantly, they will trust you to rectify the error that led to the issue or crisis in the first place.

In a communication context we refer to this phenomenon as a bucket or bank of goodwill. Imagine you have a bucket or a piggy bank, which you continuously

Figure 10.1 Goodwill keeps the balance growing much like a piggy bank, Photo by Sasun Bughdaryan on Unsplash

fill by doing the right things by your various stakeholders. Your goodwill balance keeps on growing, which means when a crisis hits, your balance may be reduced, but there are likely still some 'goodwill' funds left that help you to recover and rebuild. In contrast, if you have not been investing in your reputation, if you have been taking shortcuts, failed to listen to your stakeholders, are known to side-line staff, or have experienced a number of issues previously, well, then your balance is most likely already limited and your reputation is more likely to take a bigger hit. In some cases, this may mean recovering your reputation after a major crisis will take a long time – or may even signal the end of an oganisation or brand.

Traditionally, reputation has been regarded as an intangible asset, i.e. a non-monetary asset without physical substance. However, thinking in this space is increasingly shifting towards recognising reputation as a tangible, measurable factor that reflects an organisation's performance, behaviour and communication, multiplied by the authenticity of its actions (Doorley and Garcia, 2020). Indeed, according to research by SenateSHJ (2020), corporate reputation is recognised by the vast majority of Australian (95%) and New Zealand based (97%) organisations as a primary asset. A similar study by the global communication network Weber Shandwick (2020) found that on average global executives attribute 63% of their company's market value to reputation.

Notably, a reputation can't be built and managed by a single person, like a dedicated 'Reputation Manager', or department, as it is constantly shifting and more importantly 'omnidriven', i.e. it is influenced by a variety of factors (Weber Shandwick, 2020). Just think about which organisations and brands you regard highly. We are influenced by the quality of products or services, the quality of interactions with employees representing the organisation, their customer service, the level of innovation, ethics and values, corporate culture, the quality of the CEO or other spokespeople, the organisation's engagement with the community, their reputation as an employer and much, much more. A reputation is a collective representation of an organisation's actions and behaviours over time, as perceived and experienced by its stakeholders. Hence how an organisation engages online, i.e. decides to engage with audiences, responds to criticism or even general feedback and commentary, makes all the difference as it shapes stakeholders' perception. However, reputation is rarely considered in isolation, but frequently within the context of the wider market or its direct competitors; think for example of Coca Cola vs Pepsi, or Adidas vs Nike.

The drive to be seen as a purpose-driven business is one of the current key trends in global reputation management (Langham, 2019; Weber Shandwick, 2020; RepTrak, 2021). This shift is further emphasised by a global move towards ESG (environment, sustainability, governance) reporting requirements (PricewaterhouseCoopers, 2022). As global citizens, we are increasingly focusing on more than just the quality of products and services, and indeed their price, when we determine who we trust and who we choose to do business with, work for or invest in. Although this may be a very personal decision, audiences are increasingly prepared to speak up and share their views – in support of or with criticism of organisations and brands. Traditionally, these opinions and perceptions were largely shared at a local level, with immediate friends and acquaintances; however, with the emergence of social and digital media these conversations are increasingly taking place online, influencing global audiences' perceptions and in turn brands' reputations. Ask yourself: what kind of information shapes your understanding of organisations and brands? Is it what an organisation says about itself and its credential via its formal channels? Or is it indeed what other people share about the organisation, their interactions with it and critical analysis of its performance? In a world in which we are increasingly overloaded and overwhelmed by the sheer volume of information available, we tend to carefully select who we trust and listen to, and that's typically people like us, rather than polished corporate statements.

AUTHENTICITY AND REPUTATION

As we have discussed previously in this book, the focus on purpose-driven business strategies and cause-related marketing can be a double-edged sword, as it needs to be perceived as authentic and aligned with existing business values. Audiences are ready to publicly call out businesses and communication efforts which are perceived to be solely self-serving, under the disguise of supporting the greater good. Authenticity is increasingly recognised as a core determinant of success. Earlier, we mentioned Doorley and Garcia's (2020) reputation formula or equation, which over the years has been developed to now recognise authenticity as a multiplying factor. The idea of the formula is that "Reputation = (Performance + Behaviour + Communication) x Authenticity Factor" (Doorley & Garcia, 2020, p. 13).

Your business performance may be excellent, as well as your behaviour (e.g. as an employer, corporate citizen), and your communication efforts (e.g. you may create the most amazing digital storylines), however, if your actions and words are not perceived as authentic, i.e. if your authenticity-based multiplying factor is close to 0, then all the amazing work done by the various departments and individuals involved amounts to a very limited reputation.

Research, e.g. the annual Trust Barometer by the global communication consultancy Edelman (2022), clearly indicates that consumers want brands and their CEOs to take a stand on socio-political issues. However, if cause-related marketing efforts are perceived to be driven by the desire to tap into the zeitgeist purely to exploit societal concerns for personal gain, then they may face public criticism of woke (or cause) washing, i.e. the appropriation of ethical and progressive values by a corporation, institution or individual purely for promotional purposes, as opposed to a genuine commitment to change. A classic example in this space is the over-saturation of claims made in support of International Women's Day (IWD). Organisations are increasingly being called out for 'pinkwashing', as they advocate for women in ads and other promotional messages to mark IWD, purely to drive sales. Further, organisations have been caught out for making IWD statements that do not align with their day-to-day commitment to gender equality. The question audiences are increasingly asking is: if you are a true champion of equality and women's rights, why do we only hear about this in an #IWD-branded promotional message? Likewise, 'rainbow-washing' or 'rainbow capitalism' has increasingly emerged as a phenomenon, as organisations wield rainbow symbolism without actually bringing about any meaningful change for the LGBTQ+ community. For example, the British retailer Marks & Spencer experienced public criticism for its LGBT sandwich, a version of its traditional BLT (Beacon, Lettuce, Tomato) sandwich with guacamole added to justify the labelling and rainbow-coloured packaging. On the other hand, given its existing commitment to value-based brand activism and support of the LGBTQ+ community, ice-cream brand Ben & Jerry's renaming of its chocolate chip cookie dough flavour to 'I Dough, I Dough', in commemoration of the United States Supreme Court's ruling in favour of marriage equality in 2015, was received very differently, resulting in online engagement (notably: not all positive, which arguably added to the perception of authenticity) and strengthened brand value alignment.

If done well, purpose-driven brands are found to perform better than their competitors; indeed, a study by communication agency Kantar (2018) found they were growing at more than twice the rate.

TRUST

Keith Weed, former head of marketing at Unilever, captured why authenticity is so crucial when he stated, 'without trust a brand is just a product and its advertising is just noise' (Lepitak, 2020). Today's audiences are savvy. They want to engage with organisations and brands that align with their personal values. That means we no longer want to be simply entertained by great brand narratives and award-winning advertising campaigns; instead we want to be able to trust in an organisation's ability to deliver on the expectations set in their communication.

As audiences have increasingly lost trust in traditional information sources, like news media, governments and NGOs (see e.g. the Edelman Trust Barometer, Edelman, 2022), employers have emerged as a key source of information, in particular during the global COVID-19 pandemic. The Edelman Trust Barometer has been measuring attitudes about the state of trust in business, government, NGOs and media across 28 countries since 2001 and provides a great yearly synopsis of how our understanding of and attitude towards 'trust' have shifted over time. Over the years we have, for example, seen the rise of influencers as a trusted 'person like me', followed by their decline, as audiences are becoming increasingly cynical. According to the Barometer's 2022 summary, 'societal leadership is now a core function of business', as audiences increasingly expect CEOs to shape conversations and policies on societal issues, including global issues like climate change (Edelman, 2022). As consumers, investors and employees, we no longer judge organisations by the products and services they provide, their profit or working conditions alone; instead, we want to see organisations who perform an active role in shaping our future and who take their role as corporate citizens seriously. An interesting example of this is a shift from traditional boycotts, i.e. deliberately punishing a business by refusing to buy products or services of brands that may be perceived to have broken their social licence to operate, towards 'buycotts', the deliberate purchase of a company's product or services in support of their policies and behaviour, often at a higher price.

REPUTATION AND DIGITAL STORYTELLING

Digital platforms have made organisations and their behaviour more visible. As a result, reputational risk is omnipresent, as any action or indeed customer experience can be shared and scrutinised within seconds, in front of a global audience. As traditional barriers have been removed, everyone is now a publisher and in control of the narrative they'd like to share. Stories – carefully crafted but also those accidentally shared or inadvertently created – are no longer contained and can go global within seconds. More importantly, they don't have a shelf-life, as anything shared can be captured and reproduced. Digital audiences have a long memory, which means native stories may re-emerge at critical times.

However, digital enables proactive organisations and brands to engage with audiences in a positive way and – most importantly – to listen. Traditionally, organisations have relied on formal feedback surveys and sales figures to gain an understanding of audience sentiment. However, just because you can't hear something being said about you, your staff, products or a particular customer experience doesn't mean that these conversations aren't taking place. Digital has provided audiences with a greater share of voice, but it has also enabled organisations to listen, respond and engage more effectively and in a more targeted way.

More than ever, listening has become vitally important to organisations to ensure their long-term success (Brunner, 2008). As mentioned earlier, public trust in institutions has been declining. All too often, audiences feel they are not being listened to, which in turn drives frustration. In the post-truth era, audiences seek facts – and potentially 'alternative' facts from other sources, if they don't feel heard. As a result of a two-year, three-continent study, Macnamara (2022) identified a crisis of listening in modern societies, driven by organisational investment in what he refers to as an 'architecture of speaking' – as opposed to an architecture of listening. The question emerges: why are organisations so focused on speaking, i.e. promotional campaigns and one-way communication, as opposed to genuine listening and stakeholder engagement? Why is it so tempting to turn a blind eye, close your ears and simply block out any criticism or unfavourable feedback? Arguably, this kind of behaviour is human, and further driven by KPIs that motivate communicators and marketers to present their own work in the most favourable light. However, this attitude is flawed and no longer sustainable in a digital society.

Organisations and brands that are prepared to listen will find that digital platforms can provide them with instant feedback on products, services and indeed any communication campaigns or proposed changes. No longer will they have to wait until the next formal review round or campaign evaluation; by then it is often too late to action any meaningful changes without a potential reputational – and financial – loss. Digital channels enable (potential) customers to reach out and engage in conversations, which is especially crucial when a query is time sensitive and/or traditional communication channels, such as phone lines, may be at capacity or unavailable. Any potential issue can be swiftly addressed or taken offline if necessary. More importantly, organisations can demonstrate to a broader audience that they are taking stakeholder engagement seriously. Further, proactive listening enables the identification of positive stories and experiences that customers and other stakeholders may have shared, providing additional opportunities to share, amplify and build relationships by proactively reaching out and thanking stakeholders for their feedback. Indeed, if empowered, digital enables the curation of a true participatory culture, no longer reliant on corporate messaging, but increasingly driven by advocates and a growing 'fan base'. As issues emerge or in times of a crisis, it is these advocates that a brand or organisation may be able to draw on as part of their reputation management and rebuilding efforts, as they are more likely to speak out in defence of the organisation and its actions based on their previous experience. As mentioned at the beginning of this chapter, trust, and hence reputation, is built over time. If you want to connect with your audiences and encourage them to be part of your story – helping you to define who you are, what you do and how you ultimately solve and respond to challenges – then you need to empower them over time.

CASE STUDY
LEGO, participatory culture and reputation

LEGO is a global household name. Most of the readers of this book will be very familiar with LEGO, as no doubt are your parents and even some of your grandparents. However, despite being repeatedly listed as one of the most reputable organisations in the world (see e.g. the annual global RepTrak report) the family-owned Danish toy manufacturer is not unfamiliar with controversy. In 2014 the company faced major criticism for its partnership with Royal Dutch Shell, predominantly on the back of a targeted Greenpeace campaign, which resulted in LEGO eventually withdrawing from the 50-year partnership. Indeed, a few years earlier, 70 years after its 1932 launch, LEGO almost went bankrupt on the back of a drive to innovate, diversify and invest in theme parks. Facing $800 million in debt, what they did next turned LEGO into one of the most powerful and recognised brands in the world. Essentially, LEGO went back to basics - or rather what it's known for: the brick. Rather than assume what their audience might want, the organisation has been heavily investing in listening and audience engagement, via ethnographic studies and an infrastructure that effectively creates a LEGO community in which children, but also adult fans, are encouraged to share their inventions and suggestions.

Many may have perceived the move towards digital as a challenge for a brick-based toy. However, LEGO has proactively embraced the so-called toys-to-life movement, remaining true to itself and the brick, whilst facilitating the interaction of physical action figures and landscapes in video games and via hybrid toys, such as its music video maker.

Today, the LEGO Group Way is all about play, employees, partners and local communities. Most importantly, on- and offline, LEGO remains about creativity and (content) creation. In line with audiences' demands for more sustainable business practices and an increased focus on ESG reporting, LEGO has heavily invested in a shift towards more sustainable packaging and material. To be honest, anyone who has ever stepped barefoot on a LEGO brick will appreciate that LEGO by definition is almost indestructible. Indeed, the longevity of its products has shaped programmes like LEGO Replay, which enable the donation of used, in good condition bricks to children in need (of play), thereby creating a circular economy. This initiative exists in addition to other, existing donation programmes, via the LEGO Foundation. In addition, over the past several years the organisation has heavily invested in sustainable materials, resulting in the ambition to make all LEGO bricks from sustainable resources by 2030 without compromising its infamous quality or safety. In 2018 the company began to make elements of its products from bio-polyethylene, a durable and flexible plastic derived from Brazilian sugarcane. Rather than innovate in the background or locked away in labs, current efforts to for example test bricks made from recycled plastic bottles are shared with the LEGO fan community via the corporate website and other owned channels, effectively involving interested stakeholders in LEGO's journey towards a more sustainable future.

Focused on its key stakeholders, LEGO positions play as a fundamental right, unlocking essential skills, like creativity and problem solving, boosting wellbeing, resilience and a love of learning that last a lifetime. In doing so it promotes environmental stewardship, modelling a commitment to 'the builders of tomorrow' and the world they are to inherit, and it further proactively advocates on behalf of children and their rights via the LEGO Foundation.

Through its actions LEGO has fostered an active, engaged and passionate brand or fan community, building relationships well beyond the purchase and indeed its original customer base. Social media afforded engagement via dedicated hashtags, tagging features and a co-creation process drive user-generated content, increase brand visibility and provide first-hand insight into customer behaviour, trends and emerging issues.

What this case study illustrates is that a move away from a fixation on tight brand management and message control can create valuable opportunities. In engaging with audiences and inviting them to play (literally) an active part in the brand story and its future narrative, LEGO has effectively embraced technology that many would have perceived to be at odds with its original product and has reinvented itself.

THE ROLE OF STAKEHOLDERS IN REPUTATION

Throughout this book we have referred to stakeholders on a regular basis, but who or what are stakeholders? As mentioned, reputation does not exist in isolation; instead, it is created by a large group of constituents, or stakeholders. Essentially, a stakeholder is any person, group or organisation who can place a claim on an organisation's attention, resources or output, or – in turn – is affected by the organisation's actions, policies, practices and decisions (Harrison, 2020). As the name suggests: they hold a 'stake' in your organisation, either because they choose to do so (e.g. a customer, an employee or investor), or in some cases without having any choice (e.g. the local community, impacted by a new factory expansion). It is important to acknowledge that an organisation can have multiple reputations, or indeed different reputations with several audiences at the same time (Langham, 2019). You may be recognised as an excellent employer, providing plenty of advancement opportunities and employment benefits, but your engagement with, e.g. relevant First Nations groups may be less than desirable, due to a lack of engagement or desire to actively listen to their concerns. Likewise, different brands owned by the same organisation may be differently positioned, targeted and hence have dissimilar reputations; think e.g. Dove and Lynx, or Streets and Ben and Jerry's, which are all Unilever brands. Hence, different units or stakeholder groups may require different communication responses or indeed levels of engagement. You may hear the term 'stakeholder management' from time to time. But don't be fooled: you can't 'manage' stakeholders; you can only manage your relationship with them!

Much of the foundational work in stakeholder theory in organisational communication focused on legitimacy, power and urgency (e.g. Mitchell, Agle and Wood, 1997) to identify key stakeholder groups and determine the appropriate response or level of engagement. Indeed, economist and statistician Milton Friedman, who is often cited as a – or even 'the' – pioneer of stakeholder theory, is known for stating that 'an entity's greatest responsibility lies in the satisfaction of the shareholders' (Friedman, 1970). Note that what is known as the 'Friedman Doctrine' refers to shareholders, i.e. investors, as a particular group of stakeholders. Despite its success (at the time), the doctrine has faced its fair share of criticism. Indeed, it can be argued that it no longer applies in an increasingly socially conscious, digitally driven society. Some stakeholder groups may be more important than others to a particular business or brand at a distinct moment in time, however a single stakeholder focus effectively ignores the omni-driven nature of reputation. Shareholders may be the financial engine of a business, but even investors are increasingly recognising their responsibility to society at large. An example of this could be observed when the global mining giant Rio Tinto in May 2020 decided to destroy 46,000-year-old rock shelters at Juukan Gorge in remote Western Australia to access remaining iron ore reserves, without taking traditional owners' concerns relating to the site's significant cultural value into account (Rio Tinto, 2020). Its actions may have been legal, based on local legislation and approval processes, but they resulted in a global outcry and condemnation. However, arguably it was public condemnation by major shareholders like the Australian Council of Superannuation Investors that have placed pressure on the entire mining industry to (re-)consider their role in society beyond those economic drivers that were traditionally the primary (if not sole) focus of shareholders. Prolonged, public condemnation of Rio Tinto's action across digital platforms and channels has no doubt contributed to these public statements of condemnation. Emphasising the multi-faceted nature of reputation: beyond investment decisions and community criticism, the miner's actions will no doubt have an impact on its talent retention and attraction efforts.

At any given time, an organisation faces many – often competing – demands from stakeholders (Ackerman and Eden, 2011). So how do you identify stakeholders? Typically, you may want to begin by drawing up a list, asking yourself:

- What groups and individuals are affected by your organisation or brand – positively or negatively?
- Who else may have a stake or interest in your organisation or brand?
- How far do these groups' values and expectations align with your organisation's purpose and values?
- How robust is your relationship with these groups and individuals? – indeed, have you already got an established relationship?
- What type of relationship do these individuals and groups expect to have with you? What kind of information may they need? And how would they like to receive this or be engaged with?
- How are these groups and individuals connected? Who is influencing their opinions about your organisation and related issues? (Note: you may have to further expand your list of stakeholders to include secondary ones.)
- What is their potential to influence your organisation or brand – positively or negatively?

Your stakeholder list will continuously change and grow as you gain a better understanding of your organisation and its current challenges and opportunities. Most importantly, it will only ever be a starting point as you cannot engage with everyone. Lengthy lists of stakeholders become unhelpful. Hence, next you will need to prioritise your stakeholders. Note that the most vocal stakeholders may not necessarily represent the majority or automatically warrant being a primary focus of attention. Digital channels tend to amplify some voices more than may be warranted. However, we would never advise entirely ignoring any public criticism, irrespective of how insignificant the author may appear to your organisation at that particular point in time. If in doubt, offer to take the conversation offline.

Realistically, even though all stakeholders matter, some matter more than others. Weber Shandwick's (2020) *State of Corporate Reputation* report identifies customers, investors and employees as the most important stakeholder groups, followed by suppliers and partners, people in the local community, and government officials and regulators. Note that according to this study 'the media' (i.e. traditional media) only ranks seventh in terms of perceived importance, as judged by executives across a variety of industries.

There are a number of stakeholder classification systems, although the power-interest (or attention) matrix or grid remains one of the most frequently referenced ones (e.g. Johnson et al., 2017; Ackerman and Eden, 2011).

Stakeholder power-interest grid

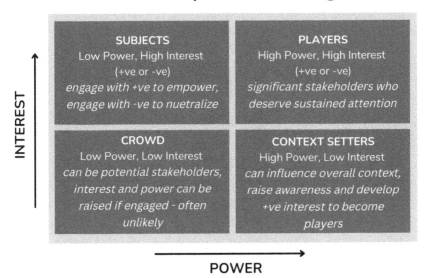

Figure 10.2   Stakeholder power-interest grid, Source: Based on Johnson et al. (2017); Ackerman and Eden (2011)

Power is the ability of individuals or groups to persuade, induce or coerce others into following certain causes or actions. This may be formal power, obtained by access to resources or particular skills, but also informal power, i.e. an individual may be particularly charismatic.

Stakeholders vary in the attention they pay to an organisation and particular actions within it. For example, major shareholders may not care about a particular (e.g. promotional) campaign. Issues often emerge as a result of expectation violations, i.e. a gap between an organisation's behaviour and its stakeholders' expectations. As the power-interest matrix indicates, even if a stakeholder may not be particularly interested in your actions at a given point in time, their interest could be quickly raised, hence it is valuable to make information available, or at least easily accessible via your owned channels.

Employees

In recent years we have seen a power shift from employers to employees, as organisations increasingly compete for the attraction and retention of talent. Further, more attention is being paid to work conditions and culture (Reptrak, 2021). Employees are no longer replaceable, but employers increasingly are. Organisations and brands progressively recognise that employees are not only central in the creation of (corporate) reputation, but essential in the prevention of a reduction in or loss of reputation. Hence, it is important that employees understand and become committed to an organisation's dominant intrinsic identity, as in difficult times this will determine how they will act, and what they will do. For example, if employees feel valued, they will advocate on behalf of the organisation and hence become the greatest asset during a crisis or emerging issue. Think about a time when an employee shaped your perception of an organisation or a brand. Our advice: treat your employees as an asset, or they may become a liability.

RESPONDING TO ONLINE CRITICISM

Social media can be a very useful (and powerful) tool in a crisis and many emergency service organisations currently use it for this purpose. However, there's a downside to using social media as people can immediately criticise you and you may not have sufficient time to respond – especially during a time of already stretched resources. However, we encourage you to embrace online feedback as an opportunity – an opportunity to gain first-hand insight into the conversations that are taking place about you, your organisation, your operating environment, your brand and stakeholders' interactions with it. Traditionally, you may not have been able to hear these conversations – and to many organisations it may appear tempting to shut them down and drown them out – but keep in mind that just because you can't hear something doesn't mean it is not happening in the first place. Sometimes, social media is the only avenue for stakeholders to be heard, if organisations are preoccupied with talking rather than listening. If you take your responsibility as a guardian of reputation seriously, then you engage with both positive and negative feedback. Online criticism provides you with an opportunity to get to the bottom of issues that you may not have been aware of in the first place and rectify them, or to clarify any misunderstanding. Conversations can always be taken offline or into a direct message exchange if required.

CASE STUDY
Boeing

Reputation is frequently referred to within the context of a crisis. A crisis can undermine and effectively destroy years of investment in an organisation's reputation. Likewise, if handled well, a crisis can assist in building and further strengthening an organisation's - and associated individuals' - reputation.

The argument has been made that in some cases, i.e. if you have sufficient power, compete on price or provide a niche service, reputation doesn't matter as there will always be someone to do business with you, regardless of your reputation. This case study explores one of those cases: Boeing is a leading global aerospace company, that together with its European competitor Airbus has been enjoying a duopoly in the international large jet airliner market since the 1990s. Indeed, until relatively recently, Boeing was the largest aerospace company by revenue. The reasons for recent operating losses and the grounding of the Boeing 737 Max fleet are the focus of this section, in which we argue that reputation does matter, irrespective of power, market size and how niche your offering may be.

Poor communication or a slow response can quickly escalate an issue to a crisis - and escalate an existing issue even further. A crisis creates the need for timely and relevant information, including regular updates. Even if you don't have all the answers at hand (yet) or have not had the time to get to the bottom of an issue, it is important to acknowledge that something has happened and that you are committed to keeping relevant stakeholders up to date as new information emerges. Essentially, in a digital age there is a need for speed, as otherwise any information vacuum will be quickly filled by other - often critical - voices and rumours.

A need for speed

The 'golden hour' of crisis response (see e.g. Doorley and Garcia, 2020), which in the digital age no longer reflects exactly 60 minutes, is a long-held principle which refers to those early phases when the opportunity to influence the outcome of a major issue or emerging crisis is the greatest. On- and offline responses are nowadays very much blurred as you are expected to monitor and communicate across different channels. Digital technologies have made issues even more visible, which means the golden hour - and fast action - have become even more crucial.

Ideally, an organisation will exercise its first-mover advantage. A swift response is key in any crisis. Don't wait for rumours to emerge. The ability to respond quickly is even more important if your crisis has an online component (and to be honest: are there really any crises nowadays that manage to remain purely offline?). Essentially, with the emergence of digital and in particular social media, the speed at which you need to respond has increased.

It's well known in crisis communication that it is better to break your own bad news to the media, than have someone else do it for you.

Doorley and Garcia (2020) refer to the rule of 45 minutes, 6 hours, 3 days and 2 weeks: the first 45 minutes provide you with the maximum ability to shape your stakeholder interactions and to set the tone. Honesty is key. Realistically, especially for large organisations and government departments with multi-layer approval processes in place, it may take longer to issue a public announcement. Within the first six hours your organisation or brand will suffer reputational distress due to greater visibility, but there is still an opportunity to let your stakeholders know that you are aware of the issue, promising to provide answers as soon as possible.

Three days may sound like a long time, but don't be surprised how many - often large and well-known - organisations take at least this long to comment on a crisis, frequently in the apparent hope that the issue will blow over. In a digital world, resulting in increased visibility and scrutiny, this is increasingly less viable, as the case study illustrates. Doorley and Garcia (2020) argue further that if you cannot control the story during the first three days, then you can expect at least two weeks of negative coverage. In the case of Boeing, due to poor communication choices and emerging internal issues, the organisation is yet to recover.

When Ethiopian Airlines flight ET302 crashed outside Addis Ababa shortly after take-off on 10 March 2019, killing all 157 passengers on board, Boeing, the manufacturer of the 737 Max plane at the centre of the crash, remained tight-lipped. The international aircraft manufacturer issued two statements, largely focused on defending the airworthiness of the 737 Max, despite a similar crash of a Lion Airplane in late 2018, which killed all 189 people on board in Indonesia. Indeed, Boeing's Chief Executive Dennis A. Muilenburg stayed out of sight for more than a week following the second incident, until increasing international pressure arguably forced him to make an appearance. In a crisis where there is a loss of life it is important to be compassionate and empathetic. Instead, Boeing's focus remained on assuring the global community that there was no issue with the safety of its planes, at a time where images of the crash clearly told a very different story. The company continued to refuse to make itself available to answer any questions by the media. Country after country grounded the aircraft, whilst Boeing maintained its planes were safe. Boeing eventually went one step further, pointing a finger at the pilots involved in both crashes, suggesting they weren't sufficiently trained. It's important to keep in mind that audiences do not trust institutions - they trust individuals (Hartley, 2019). Hence, make sure you choose your spokespeople wisely - it does not always have to be the CEO, but make sure you put a name to your statements to make them more credible and authentic.

Boeing's response to the crisis was too defensive and most importantly too slow. It lacked openness and accountability, effectively creating an opportunity for others to comment and speculate, rather than take control of the crisis and recovery narrative. As mentioned, a crisis creates an urgent need for timely information. Any vacuum is quickly filled by other, often critical voices. The longer the organisation at the centre of the crisis waits to communicate, the more likely that void will be filled by critics, in this case aviation experts, the media, lawyers, airplane safety advocates, employees and family members of victims. Silence is passive and suggests that an organisation is neither in control nor trying to take control of a situation. Boeing's silence has allowed others to frame the issues and control the narrative. As a result, Boeing has found itself having to defend a storyline that suggests the company was more interested in profits than people in the rush to produce an aircraft that accounts for about a third of its revenue.

What could Boeing have done?

Boeing could have adopted a proactive approach, such as taking the initiative to ground its own planes, pending further investigation, rather than simply watch on as this decision was essentially taken out of its hands. The aircraft manufacturer hesitated, appeared to hope for the conversation to move on, and failed to accept any responsibility for what had happened, leaving it to airlines, countries and regulators to ground the 737 Max, a decision which impacts the organisation's reputation well beyond a single aircraft type. The statements issued by Boeing were full of platitudes, lacking meaningful information, instead repeating that safety is one of its core values – thereby creating a disconnect between values and first-hand accounts.

When a crisis results in serious injury or – as in this case – death, crisis management should include stress and trauma counselling for employees and (other) victims. Safety should be your number one priority – expressed not based on corporate messaging, but in actions. You want to express empathy and utilise all available communication channels. This includes providing regular updates to ensure stakeholders, including employees, understand what is happening.

The cascading crisis has disrupted the global aviation industry, as airlines review their existing and future orders, and it eventually resulted in the departure of Boeing's CEO. However, the organisation's failure to take responsibility and shape its own narrative has resulted in a continued, steady drip of bad news and embarrassing revelations, culminating in revelations that a key contributing factor was Boeing's culture, highlighting senior employees' lack of regard for regulators, customers and co-workers. Whistleblowers have since highlighted a culture of concealment, a focus on profits and speed of delivery over quality, safety concerns and overall poor morale.

Reputation always matters

Together with Airbus, Boeing controls 85–90% of the so-called large jets market. It's not an end-user facing organisation. Instead, its target audience are representatives of major airlines, like United and Southwest Airlines, Ryanair and Emirates. Given the limited competition, one may assume that the reputation paradox applies: at the end of the day there is limited choice and airline customers typically book their travel based on individual airlines' prices, safety records and convenience, rather than aircraft preference. However, given the visibility of the two catastrophic incidents, combined with Boeing's lacklustre public response and lack of reassurances to address underlying safety concerns, airlines have been forced to review their purchase decisions in an attempt to protect their own reputation. For example, soon after the Ethiopian Airlines crash, Indonesia's flagship airline, Garuda, cancelled a $5 billion order for 49 Max jets, citing loss of trust and confidence in the plane by its passengers. Insights into Boeing's corporate culture will no doubt have a further impact not only on employee retention but talent acquisition.

As this case study illustrates, even if you are operating in a very specialised market with effectively guaranteed demand, your actions continue to have major implications for your reputation, stakeholder response, talent retention and acquisition and effectively your licence to operate.

CHAPTER SUMMARY

The shift to an increasingly digital communication landscape has made organisations and brands – and their behaviours – more visible. This increased visibility intensifies the need for accountability and a genuine commitment to stakeholder engagement, as any 'window dressing' is quickly exposed and called out. However, the digital landscape also provides organisations that are committed to authentic communication with additional opportunities to build brand communities and a group of passionate advocates, who are likely to speak out on your organisation's behalf if things go wrong. The most important fact about reputation to remember is that you don't own it – your stakeholders do. You can't manage your reputation, but only your stakeholder relations. If you are committed to doing the right thing by your stakeholders, you will continuously build the balance in your 'bank of goodwill', effectively creating a reputation 'buffer' for when issues emerge and threaten your organisation or brand.

Traditionally regarded as an intangible asset, reputation is increasingly being recognised as an omni-driven indicator of an organisation's success, which can be tracked and measured. Authenticity in your communication and the way you engage with your stakeholders is key. Indeed, it has been recognised as a core factor, without which performance, behaviour and your communication are devalued. Today's audiences expect organisations and brands to take a stance on issues close to their hearts; they are critical and expect more of organisations than simply to provide products and services. Whilst woke washing is frowned upon, authentic engagement is highly regarded, further building support for your brand and organisation when things do not go to plan.

Our understanding of stakeholders has advanced over the past several decades, recognising the need to prioritise your communication efforts, but also to think well beyond pleasing investors and customers. For example, employees have emerged as a key stakeholder group that requires attention – but also one that will step up and advocate on behalf of your organisation or brand if they feel valued, empowered and connected.

Reputation should be regarded as an investment that limits damage to your organisation or brand in times of crisis and/or uncertainty. If a crisis should unexpectedly hit, it is crucial that you respond quickly, own it and communicate to your various stakeholders that you continue your commitment to open, honest, empathetic and authentic communication. Most importantly, it is important for brand to respond quickly and communicate to their stakeholders and the public. If a brand doesn't respond, other voices, often critical, will fill the void. Digital media have provided organisations and brands with additional and novel opportunities to build and guard their reputation. Be the source of truth, and stakeholders will turn to you for up-to-date information and updates – now, and into the future.

DISCUSSION QUESTIONS

1. What are the types of online reputational risks for a brand/organisation (chosen by instructor)? Create a list/typology.
2. Identify a brand that has recently faced a reputational challenge. What audiences and stakeholder groups did the brand engage with and how? Create a stakeholder map. Were there any audiences that could have been engaged with more successfully?
3. Using the Boeing case study, write a plan on what they can do to restore their international reputation in relation to safety. How can digital storytelling form a key part of this?

READINGS

Fombrun, C.J. (1996). *Reputation: Realizing Value from the Corporate Image*. Boston, MA: Harvard Business School Press.

One of the original books on reputation from a brand perspective, this book analyses how the internet has made corporate reputation more valuable in terms of how branding issues propagate faster across traditional and social media.

Seitel, F.P. and Doorley, J. (2012). *Rethinking Reputation: How PR Trumps Marketing and Advertising in the New Media World*. New York: Palgrave Macmillan.

Reptrak states (2021): 'PR experts Seitel and Doorley discuss everything from the Lewinsky scandal to the launch of an online slipper company to show that, at its root, corporate reputation is about building relationships, and that any good relationship is built on trust'.

Coombs, T. (2022). *Crisis Communication Blog by Timothy Coombs*. [online] Available at: https://coombscrisiscommunication.wordpress.com/ [Accessed 10 November 2022].

This blog is written by a leading researcher and consultant on crisis communication. It's a bridge between theory and practice and offers a range of articles that can be used in class readings on timely topics, for example the reputation management issue Spotify faced with misinformation.

International Air Transport Association (IATA) (2022). *Guidelines – Crisis Communications in the Digital Age*. [online] Available at: www.iata.org/en/publications/crisis-communications-guidelines/ [Accessed 10 November 2022].

This website contains useful readings to get an understanding of crisis communication in practice within an industry – the airline industry. This set of guidelines discusses best practice on how to manage a serious crisis.

REFERENCES

Ackermann, F. and Eden, C. (2011). Strategic management of stakeholders: Theory and practice. *Long Range Planning*, 44(3), 179–196. doi:10.1016/j.lrp.2010.08.001.

Brunner, B.R. (2008). Listening, communication & trust: Practitioners' perspectives of business/organizational relationships. *International Journal of Listening*, 22(1), 73–82. doi:10.1080/10904010701808482.

Cornelissen, J. (2017). *Corporate Communication: A Guide to Theory and Practice* (5th edn). London: SAGE Publications Ltd.

Doorley, J. and Garcia, H.F. (2020). *Reputation Management: The Key to Successful Public Relations and Corporate Communication* (4th edn). New York: Routledge.

Edelman (2022). *Edelman Trust Barometer*. [online] Available at: www.edelman.com/trust/trust-barometer [Accessed 2 November 2022].

Friedman, M. (1970). A Friedman doctrine: The social responsibility of business is to increase its profits. *The New York Times Magazine*, 13, 32–33.

Harrison, K. (2020). Reputation and stakeholder relations: Stakeholder relations. [online] *Cutting Edge PR Insights*. Available at: https://cuttingedgepr.com/stakeholder-relations-management-key-skill/ [Accessed 2 November 2022].

Hartley, K. (2019). *Communicate in a Crisis: Understand, Engage and Influence Consumer Behaviour to Maximize Brand Trust*. London: Kogan Page.

Johnson, G., Whittington, R., Scholes, K., Angwin, D. and Regnér, P. (2017). *Exploring Strategy: Text and Cases* (11th edn). Harlow: Pearson Education.

Kantar (2018). *Purpose 2020*. [online] Available at: www.kantar.com/Inspiration/Brands/The-Journey-Towards-Purpose-Led-Growth [Accessed 2 November 2022].

Langham, T. (2019). *Reputation Management: The Future of Corporate Communications and Public Relations*. Bingley: Emerald Publishing.

Lepitak, S. (2020). Keith Weed: 'Without trust a brand is just a product and its advertising is just noise'. [online] *The Drum*. Available at: www.thedrum.com/news/2020/01/02/keith-weed-without-trust-brand-just-product-and-its-advertising-just-noise [Accessed 10 November 2022].

Macnamara, J. (2022). *Organizational Listening in Public Communication: Emerging Theory and Practice*. [online] Available at: https://opus.lib.uts.edu.au/handle/10453/158330 [Accessed 10 November 2022].

Mitchell, R.K., Agle, B.R. and Wood, D.J. (1997). Toward a theory of stakeholder identification and salience: Defining the principle of who and what really counts. *Academy of Management Review*, 22(4), 853–886.

PricewaterhouseCoopers (2022). *ESG – An Opportunity for Companies to Build Greater Trust*. [online] Available at: www.pwc.com.au/assurance/esg-reporting.html [Accessed 10 November 2022].

RepTrak (2021). *2021 Global RepTrak® 100*. [online] Available at: www.reptrak.com/rankings/ [Accessed 10 November 2022].

Rio Tinto (2020). *Inquiry into Juukan Gorge*. [online] Available at: www.riotinto.com/en/news/inquiry-into-juukan-gorge [Accessed 10 November 2022].

Schwantes, M. (2021). Warren Buffett says you can ruin your life in 5 minutes by making this critical mistake. [online] *Inc.com*. Available at: www.inc.com/marcel-schwantes/warren-buffett-says-you-can-ruin-your-life-in-5-minutes-by-making-1-critical-mistake.html [Accessed 10 November 2022].

SenateSHJ (2020). Reputation reality 2020. [online] *SenateSHJ – Perspectives*. Available at: https://senateshj.com/perspective/reputationreality/ [Accessed 10 November 2022].

Weber Shandwick (2020). *The State of Corporate Reputation in 2020: Everything Matters Now*. [online] Available at: www.webershandwick.com/news/corporate-reputation-2020-everything-matters-now/ [Accessed 10 November 2022].

11

OUTRAGE, MIS- AND DISINFORMATION IN THE DIGITAL WORLD

OBJECTIVES

1. Analyse the digital media environment to understand key terms, including mis- and disinformation
2. Understand how to critically evaluate the credibility of news and fact checking
3. Understand how misleading news is impacting digital storytelling

Misinformation is increasingly becoming an issue for digital storytellers. This chapter discusses how to manage mis- and disinformation, which is often driven by – or circulated for the purpose of causing – outrage. Key terms are defined and best practice in dealing with both types of information is discussed, using ideas from around the world. Advice on dealing with mis- and disinformation will be reviewed, with a focus on the UK Government RESIST Counter Disinformation Toolkit. The chapter also discusses how to manage outrage in a digital world, as well as the role of automated machines (bots) and algorithms that help spread incorrect information.

The fake news subject has become so prevalent that the Commons Culture, Media and Sport Committee is currently investigating concerns about the public being swayed by propaganda and untruths. The curation of high-quality journalism is also at stake, since an increasing proportion of adults are getting their news from social media and fictional stories are presented in such a way that it can be very difficult to tell them apart from what is authentic. (Figueira and Oliveira, 2017, p. 819)

DEFINING MIS- AND DISINFORMATION

Mis- and disinformation are often confused or used interchangeably. However, despite their related nature, it is important to distinguish between the two.

'Disinformation' is 'the deliberate creation and sharing of false and/or manipu-lated information that is intended to deceive and mislead audiences, either for the purposes of causing harm, or for political, personal or financial gain. (Digital, Culture, Media and Sport Committee, 2018, p. 2)

In contrast:

'Misinformation' refers to the inadvertent sharing of false information. (Digital, Culture, Media and Sport Committee, 2018, p. 2)

Note the emphasis on a deliberate intention to deceive within the context of disinformation.

In a society characterised by information overload, individuals may see a post or link to an article that resonates with them, creating a desire to quickly pass the information on without double-checking its merit and authenticity. They may also pass on half-truths shared by individuals they trust, and therefore end up inadvert-ently contributing to the circulation of incorrect information.

In recent years you may have also heard the terms 'alternative facts' and 'fake news'. Whilst not new terms, both came into popular use following the election of Donald Trump as President of the United States of America (Allcott and Gentzkow, 2017). It is worth noting that governments around the world are moving away from the use of both terms. As the UNESCO noted in 2018 in its *Journalism, 'Fake News' & Disinformation* handbook (UNESCO, 2019), the purveyors of disinforma-tion typically prey on the vulnerability of potential recipients who they seek to use as amplifiers and multipliers of their messages. They often do so by using emo-tionally charged words, which provoke outrage. A particular danger of this type of 'news' is that it is typically free, meaning that people who cannot afford to pay for quality journalism, or who lack access to independent public news media, are particularly vulnerable. Therefore, it has been argued that the term 'fake news' in itself equals misinformation.

Misinformation may appear as the following (Farte and Obada, 2018):

- Clickbait
- Satire or parody
- Imposter content
- Misleading content
- False connection
- False context
- Manipulated content
- Fabricated content

Social distortion may contribute to misinformation in that attention can be influenced by the way in which some social media platforms 'reward' emotional or attention attracting messages that are liked, disliked or easily shared, thereby further amplifying expressions of moral outrage (Albright, 2017). Indeed, studies of online networks show that text spreads more virally when it contains a high degree of 'moral emotion' (Brady et al., 2017), often contributing to a sense of urgency and a reduced desire to check the reliability and accuracy of the information. McLoughlin, Brady and Crockett (2021) confirmed that 'misinformation news links were consistently associated with more moral outrage evocation than factual, accurate URLs'.

The role of outrage

Misinformation frequently attaches itself to existing outrage. For example, when in 2020 the death of George Floyd sparked outrage first across North America and then the world, resulting in the emergence of the Black Lives Matter (BLM) protest movement, multiple articles detailing the misappropriation of the #BLM hashtag and associated donations emerged. By tapping into the existing familiarity with the movement and associated outrage, these types of stories provided a different angle and often reached millions of people before they were identified as false. By that time, of course, it becomes very difficult to convince original consumers of these messages of their misleading nature as audiences may have already moved on to the next 'news' item. Macnamara (2020) argues that professionalised communication industries of advertising, PR, political and government communication, and even journalism, driven by a desire for click-throughs and likes, aided by a lack of critical media literacy, have systematically contributed to disinformation, deception and manipulation.

The backfire effect

What makes combatting mis- and disinformation increasingly difficult is our heightened propensity to dismiss facts, even if evidence is presented that should motivate us to assess our original beliefs. This occurs due to a cognitive bias known as the *backfire effect*.

The backfire effect is important for communicators to understand, as it not only impacts our ability to change other people's opinions, but also shapes our own ability to rationally assess information and its validity.

The backfire effect is a cognitive bias that causes people who encounter evidence that challenges their beliefs to not only swiftly reject that evidence, but to further strengthen their support of their original stance. Essentially, the backfire effect means that showing people evidence which proves that they are wrong is often ineffective, as it can literally end up backfiring by causing the other side to support their original stance even more strongly than they previously did.

The backfire effect has been observed in a number of scientific studies, relating to voting preferences (Redlawsk, 2002), misconceptions as part of politically charged topics (Nyhan and Reifler, 2010), and in particular in relation to vaccinations – both for children (Nyhan et al., 2014) and against the flu (Nyhan and Reifler, 2015). When a person is presented with information that suggests their pre-existing beliefs are wrong, they feel threatened, which in turn causes them to experience a variety of negative emotions. Essentially, information that challenges our beliefs also challenges our sense of self. To make us feel better, we feel tempted to dismiss anything that challenges our identity and self-esteem, thereby discounting and dismissing information that is incongruent with existing perspectives.

Hence, the reason for people to dismiss corrective information is not an indication of their intelligence or ability to comprehend a counter-argument. However, in order to reject corrective information, they will seek to recall their pre-existing knowledge to justify their stance. This process in itself may result in that knowledge being further reinforced, not only because it makes them feel better about themselves, but also because it is now front of mind.

What this demonstrates is that it is increasingly difficult to change people's opinions. The last thing you want to do is to call people out, to challenge them or cause them to feel threatened. If mocked or challenged, the other person is likely to adopt a defensive mindset.

The backfire bias is closely related to the *confirmation bias*, which results in us undervaluing evidence that contradicts our beliefs, whilst overvaluing any evidence that supports existing opinions. As humans we tend to filter out any inconvenient truths. This is why echo chambers can feel so comforting, as they literally confirm our existing perspective and preferences. However, this provides a false sense of security. We encourage every single one of our readers to regularly challenge their own views and to make conscious efforts to escape their echo chambers and filter bubbles to improve their ability to connect with audiences from all walks of life.

Misinfographics

Mis- and disinformation are not limited to traditional texts, and there has been a noted rise of 'misinfographics'. Further, images and videos are easily altered thanks to advances in technology, adding a powerful, sometimes amusing, but frequently misleading narrative. Irregularities in light and shadow are typically the easiest way to identify an altered image. However, with technological advances, including deepfake technology, it will become increasingly difficult to identify unauthentic, often highly misleading visual content. The prediction is that audiences will increasingly rely on websites like snopes.com that help them identify altered content. The best defence against mis- and disinformation is to stop fake content by simply not sharing it further (on social media). Also, learn to trust your intuition.

Responding to misinformation

For an organisation or brand impacted by mis- and disinformation, the challenge becomes much bigger than a decision not to distribute misleading information any further. The circulation of misinformation in this context may not only damage an organisation's bottom line and stakeholder trust, it may have far more severe consequences, for example within the context of public health information. Indeed, the thinking in this space has shifted dramatically over the past few years. Traditionally, the advice was to debunk any false assertions step by step, by repeating the incorrect information, followed by the corrected claims. The problem with this approach is that it further confirms and engrains any false statements, effectively making them more memorable and easier to recall. Hence, the advice is now for organisations not to repeat any false statements, but instead to purely focus on the sharing of desired, correct statements in a user friendly, easily digestible and effortless to recall format. The World Health Organization has been working with researchers on a number of creative solutions to what they refer to as an 'infomedic' (World Health Organization, 2021), the overabundance of information – some accurate, some not – that spreads alongside a disease outbreak, including toolkits, information campaigns and educational games.

Not a new, but a useful theory in this space is inoculation theory (McGuire, 1961), which is a model for building resistance to persuasion attempts. Rooted in psychology, inoculation theory argues that individuals are able to build up resistance against false or misleading information by being presented with a weakened version of a misleading argument before being exposed to the 'real' information, thereby seeking to build public resilience or immunity. One such example is GoViral! (see goviralgame.com), a game that was developed by scientists exposing users to the most common ways in which false and misleading information about COVID-19 is being spread, thereby effectively improving people's ability to identify misinformation – in an interactive and enjoyable way. The main objective of GoViral! is to reach audiences vulnerable to misinformation and expose them to information in an engaging gamified format to direct them to credible sources of information. Operating literally like a traditional, medical 'vaccine' against misleading information, the assumption is that if exposed to smaller doses of false and misleading information, you are able to demystify claims and resist the (initial) temptation to engage in or share false statements.

FIGHTING MISINFORMATION WITH TRUST

A useful resource in the fight against mis- and disinformation is the Trust Project (see thetrustproject.org), an international consortium of approximately 120 news organisations, seeking to work towards greater transparency and accountability in the global news industry. Out of an initial set of 37 indicators, the Trust Project has settled on a core of eight 'trust indicators', designed to assist audiences in the assessment of the quality of news items. These indicators encourage audiences to ask themselves a series of questions, such as:

- **Best practices**: Do you know the organisation behind these news items? What rules and ethical standards do they uphold?
- **Author expertise**: Who is the journalist behind this news item? As we typically rely on a reporter's interpretation of events, what do you know about them and the (ethical) standards they uphold?
- **Type of work**: Is this news item impartial or deliberately biased? Stories should be clearly labelled if they are designed to persuade (e.g. 'Opinion Piece').
- **Citations and references**: What information sources did the journalist behind this story rely on? Eyewitness accounts? Other documents? How reliable are they? Can we check them out ourselves?
- **Methods**: What (research) methods did the journalist use for their story? This will indicate how well-researched or impartial the story may be.
- **Local**: Does the story draw on local knowledge to ensure accuracy and sensitivity, either because the journalist knows or lives in the community or because he/she draws on local knowledge?
- **Diverse voices**: Are certain voices missing from the story? Or do we get a full picture that includes less commonly heard voices?
- **Feedback**: Does the news site invite and listen to feedback?

(The Trust Project, 2017)

As a content creator you can contribute to the fight against mis- and disinformation by demonstrating a commitment to transparency and honesty, clearly labelling where information has come from and how you've ensured its integrity – essentially complying with the eight quality indicators outlined above.

Personal influence and authenticity are key drivers of how people consume 'news'. The Edelman Trust Barometer (Edelman, 2022) has been documenting a decline in trust in traditional media sources. Whilst this is a concerning trend, it highlights a return to local connections and communities, i.e. a focus on people we actually know and trust; those who belong to our 'tribe'. To counter misinformation and distorted narratives, experts recommend the identification of 'tribe' representatives to lead any discussions about facts, thereby driving a narrative correction.

Likewise, the UK's Government Communication Service's (GCS) RESIST Counter Disinformation Toolkit (Pamment, 2021) promotes the role of a collective approach by social media platforms, technology companies, government and the media to stop the spread of misinformation. The toolkit differentiates between a high, medium and low need for intervention to address misinformation. For example, if a rumour emerges that is only being circulated by fringe groups and runs counter to current mainstream debates, an organisational response should be prepared, but the focus should remain on monitoring, enabling the identification of any sudden changes and/or an emerging need for intervention. In contrast, if the disinformation has the potential to affect national security and has a high likelihood to make headlines, senior staff need to be aware and an immediate response prepared and distributed to relevant stakeholders.

Keep in mind that the GCS toolkit has been prepared with a focus on government or public communication. The nature of the organisation and/or sector you are representing will shape your mis- and disinformation response.

There are ways to empower individuals to evaluate the credibility of news.

- **Fact checking websites** – e.g. PolitiFact and Snopes in the US and ABC FactCheck in Australia
- **Lists of fake websites** – https://en.wikipedia.org/wiki/ List_of_fake_news_websites
- **Education and support** – www.internetmatters.org/issues/ fake-news-and-misinformation-advice-hub/
- **Online structural change** – to prevent exposure to fake news in the first place including:
  - ○ More robust fact checking for accuracy (Facebook/Instagram)
  - ○ Algorithms to help review reported breaches of policies (Twitter)
  - ○ Investment in the news media to support independent reporting (Google)

MANAGING OUTRAGE

In this book we have discussed the value of stakeholder engagement, participatory culture and user-generated content – but what if audiences turn against you?

The good news is that research has indicated that customers do not trust polished, 'too good to be true' reviews of products and services. Likewise, we have learned to cast a critical eye over negative (online) reviews. Today's stakeholders are savvy; they read between the lines (Zhuang, Cui and Peng, 2018). At the same time, customers expect organisations to balance organisational responses with a respect for user-owned spaces. Brands need to know what they stand for and who their audience is and will have to accept that they won't be able to please everyone. Or in the words of Aesop: 'if you try to please all, you please none'. Just think of Nike and their decision to endorse civil rights activist and football quarterback Colin Kaepernick. The advertisements and related communication around this campaign combined with the organisation's stance on #BlackLivesMatter attracted controversy, criticism and multiple versions of individuals filming themselves whilst burning their Nike socks and/or shoes. However, a year later the effects of the now iconic campaign were positive, resulting in a high net promoter score and Nike being recognised as one of the most well-regarded and healthiest brands around the globe. Sometimes you have to trust your brand positioning and the fact that you may alienate some – sometimes highly outspoken – individuals.

However, in some cases audiences may have a valid reason to voice their dissatisfaction with a brand online. It helps to understand why some people may take to social media to vent their frustrations. Hartley (2019) explains:

> We feel outrage when something hits at our core beliefs or values – religious, political, moral, ethical or nationalistic. And it's happening more and more. We're living in a world where outrage is political currency. Our political leaders use it to galvanize us into voting for them. Our world is becoming more polarised between left and right. (p. 39)

Passion brands

Some brands are particularly good at inspiring passion. We invest in them because we want to be associated with them. This association provides us with a sense of social security. Indeed, our investment in the brand has become a part of our identity. However, at the same time we know that loyalty to everyday brands is declining; they are increasingly becoming a means to an end. Passion brands, on the other hand, are the ones that make us feel loyalty beyond reason and stand for something bigger than the product or service they are offering. They are particularly good at creating connections with their audiences; think for example of Apple, Google, Ben & Jerry's, Jeep, Red Bull or Nike. They invite us to enter a psychological contract with them. However, because we feel so connected, if passion brands betray us – or indeed the psychological contract we have with them – then passion can quickly turn to anger, which is frequently shared online. As emotions, love and hate or resentment are closely positioned to each other, as they relate to the same region of our brain.

As human beings, we are hardwired to crave a sense of belonging. We seek endorsement and approval. We share things that make us feel so strongly that we have a physiological response to them, i.e. we want to do something about them. This could be a positive response, encouraging us to publicly provide support, or a negative response, which may motivate audiences to turn on a brand or a spokesperson for doing something that has violated the existing psychological contract. Hence, shutting down negative conversations about a brand on social media will only fuel the fire further. If you increase someone's sense of powerlessness by deleting their posts or shutting the conversation down, you will increase their motivation to speak out again, further fuelling their frustration about simply not being heard (Hartley, 2019). More than ever, today's (online) audiences want to be heard. You don't have to agree, but it's important to acknowledge that by undermining core beliefs, values or ethical standards a brand's behaviour can have a negative impact on an individual's identity. For example, think about Volkswagen drivers feeling cheated after news of the emissions scandal broke (D'Orazio, 2015). Or supporters and followers of the former elite cyclist Lance Armstrong, when he was stripped of his seven consecutive Tour de France titles due to a history of taking performance-enhancing drugs. Keep in mind that you can always take conversations offline or onto a direct message platform to discuss individual issues or manage expectations away from the public eye. Further, ensure that you have clear conduct rules in place for all your communication channels.

Trolls

Voicing online criticism and dissatisfaction should not be confused with trolling. A troll is someone who posts unkind or offensive messages on social media sites, often motivated by the desire to start an argument with other users. Rather than being motivated by passion for a particular brand or organisation, seeking the resolution of issues or a (perceived) breached psychological contract, trolls revel in chaos. Hartley (2019) defines trolls as 'people who deliberately and maliciously act to bring people down, just for the fun of it' (p. 13). They enjoy the opportunity to antagonise others by posting inflammatory, often irrelevant and offensive comments. Social media has provided trolls with multiple platforms to gain attention. Indeed, it is the attention that trolls crave, a little bit like an unruly toddler. Advice on deterring trolls very much focuses on the need for strong online communities that can draw on advocates that indicate to any emerging trolls that they are not welcome. Often, strong brand communities will address trolls and unreasonable behaviour before the brand or organisation behind the platform even becomes aware of the issue. Having clear, transparent and well-established community rules for all your social media platforms and digital channels is crucial. Reward good behaviour by involving your brand community, which in turn fosters a strong participatory culture.

Blocking people may not always prevent them from coming back, but it can be a necessary first step. Make sure you take control of your own platforms.

If necessary you can close posts to comments or delete abusive posts. However, make sure you don't confuse free speech and genuine criticism with abusive comments, i.e. differentiate between someone who is trolling and someone who is frustrated following a poor experience with your brand and deserves your attention. Don't write off your most passionate advocates as trolls because they may have strong opinions. Instead, listen, as they may have indeed identified an important issue, and collectively embrace their close attachment to your brand.

CHANGING THE NARRATIVE

While mis- and disinformation are elements of the online world that are not going to go away overnight, there are things brands can do to change the narrative, if the brand story being told isn't the one you want. Albright (2017) emphasises that 'people need to be exposed to the facts before the narrative can be strategically distorted' (p. 89), however as discussed recent research has pointed out that even when faced with the truth, people are unlikely to change their opinions. Instead experts call for an approach that identifies people to see others as 'their tribe' and then have the discussion on the facts.

An approach on how to do this is using fans to spread the correct or desirable narrative. Using fans to correct the narrative can be more powerful than brands doing this themselves. Individuals can minimise the role they play in spreading incorrect information by:

- Refraining from sharing news (particularly on social media) that you can't verify (sharing is part of the problem).
- Understanding facts as observable – if you can't observe it, it may not be true.
- Understanding that journalistic truth relies on context – isolated information cannot be trusted.
- Understanding that not all evidence is equal. Direct evidence is more trustworthy than indirect evidence (i.e. word of mouth).
- Asking yourself does this seem true? What don't I know? Go to sites that fact check and confirm the accuracy of this news item.

CASE STUDY
Alex Jones' InfoWars and the pro-gun lobby

In 1999, just prior to the new millennium, Alex Jones, the co-winner of the 'Best Austin Talk Radio Host', started his own broadcasting show from his home with just an ISDN connection

(Leon, 2019). From this early beginning, Jones gradually built a broadcasting empire that just two years later saw his shows syndicated across approximately 100 stations. Following the 9/11 terrorist attack against four sites in the US, Jones' polarising views became sought after, attracting millions of listeners each week, who were soaking up perspectives that were different - often contrary - to the reporting in the mainstream media. Jones effectively tapped into the collective outrage, driven by feelings of powerlessness, triggered by one of the most visible terrorist attacks the world has seen. He also tapped into the rhetoric around guns and gun ownership, narratives that have endured for hundreds of years across the US. These narratives include that guns are 'tools (the importance of guns in the foundation of the US as a nation), that guns are wonders (gun collecting is a part of identity) and guns are quintessentially American (they are central to what it means to be American)' (Ott and Dickinson, 2022). These narratives were important to how Jones connected with his audience; however, far from being a harmless conspiracy theorist, Jones arguably played 'a role in propagating the misinformation and confusion that is permeating America' (This American Life, 2019).

Today, Jones' opinions are widely considered far-right conspiracy theories. His views came into the spotlight during his persistent pursuit of parents whose children died in the 2012 Sandy Hook Elementary School shooting, the focus of this case study. The mass-shooting incident occurred on 14 December 2012 in Connecticut, US, when 20-year-old Adam Lanza entered the primary school and shot dead 26 people, including 20 children. At the time this was the deadliest mass shooting at an elementary school in US history. The gunman also killed his mother and then shot himself. News of the massacre travelled around the world. The images were incredibly confronting, eliciting tearful reactions from national leaders and community members alike. Then President Barack Obama described the 14 December as the worst day of his presidency.

However, amidst the confronting scenes and outpourings of grief, Alex Jones denied the Sandy Hook massacre ever happened, or at least that anyone died as a result of the shooting. His repeated public denial of the events resulted in a drawn out legal battle, as a defamation lawsuit was filed against him and his broadcasting platform, InfoWars (Murdock, 2019). Some commentators (see Holpuch, 2013; Harmon, 2019) argued that Jones is a 'raving lunatic', implying that he should not be taken seriously. However, to dismiss the broadcaster's power and influence over his audience would be a misstep for any communication professional in terms of understanding how misinformation spreads, and how pervasive views can affect campaigns. Reports in 2017 stated that the InfoWars website received approximately 10 million monthly visits (Quantcast, 2017), signifying a greater reach than some established mainstream websites, such as *The Economist* or *Newsweek*. Alex Jones' commentary became increasingly popular as the alt-right radio show host effectively built a small media empire. Jones has been a vocal gun rights advocate and his platform InfoWars has dogmatically pursued his conspiracy beliefs in an activist-style fashion to ensure incidents like Sandy Hook did not undermine his - and by extension the powerful US gun lobby's - position on gun ownership. In 2021 Alex Jones lost the defamation lawsuit from Sandy Hook Parents and was found liable for damages. 2022 saw him appeal this decision only to lose again in trying to reduce the damages to be paid (Queen, 2022). In total Jones was ordered to pay $1.44bn in damages and he has since admitted that the attack in which 20 children and six adults were killed on 14 December 2012 was "100% real'" (BBC News, 2022).

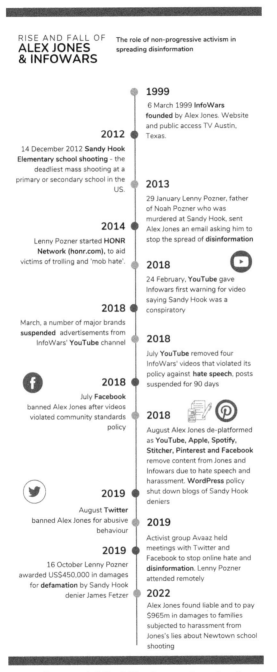

RISE AND FALL OF
**ALEX JONES
& INFOWARS**

The role of non-progressive activism in
spreading disinformation

1999
6 March 1999 **InfoWars
founded** by Alex Jones. Website
and public access TV Austin,
Texas.

2012
14 December 2012 **Sandy Hook
Elementary school shooting** - the
deadliest mass shooting at a
primary or secondary school in the
US.

2013
29 January Lenny Pozner, father
of Noah Pozner who was
murdered at Sandy Hook, sent
Alex Jones an email asking him to
stop the spread of **disinformation**

2014
Lenny Pozner started **HONR
Network (honr.com),** to aid
victims of trolling and 'mob hate'.

2018
24 February, **YouTube** gave
Infowars first warning for video
saying Sandy Hook was a
conspiratory

2018
March, a number of major brands
suspended advertisements from
InfoWars' **YouTube** channel

2018
July **YouTube** removed four
InfoWars' videos that violated its
policy against **hate speech**, posts
suspended for 90 days

2018
July **Facebook**
banned Alex Jones after videos
violated community standards
policy

2018
August Alex Jones de-platformed
as **YouTube, Apple, Spotify,
Stitcher, Pinterest and Facebook**
remove content from Jones and
Infowars due to hate speech and
harassment. **WordPress** policy
shut down blogs of Sandy Hook
deniers

2019
August **Twitter**
banned Alex Jones for abusive
behaviour

2019
Activist group Avaaz held
meetings with Twitter and
Facebook to stop online hate and
disinformation. Lenny Pozner
attended remotely

2019
16 October Lenny Pozner
awarded US$450,000 in damages
for **defamation** by Sandy Hook
denier James Fetzer

2022
Alex Jones found liable and to pay
$965m in damages to families
subjected to harassment from
Jones's lies about Newtown school
shooting

Figure 11.1   Timeline of rise and fall of Alex Jones, the role of non-progressive
activism in spreading disinformation

Disinformation and non-progressive activism

The rise of dis- and misinformation is increasing the significance of non-progressive activism for communication professionals and the brands and organisations they represent. The 2019 Institute for Public Relations Disinformation in Society Report (McCorkindale, 2019) noted an increasing concern, among both practitioners and the general public, about disinformation – particularly in the political sphere and in relation to its ability to affect both political campaigns and policy. As outlined earlier in this chapter, disinformation is defined as 'the deliberate creation and sharing of false and/or manipulated information that is intended to deceive and mislead audiences, either for the purposes of causing harm, or for political, personal, or financial gain' (Digital, Culture, Media and Sport Committee, 2019, p. 2). This is not the same as misinformation, which is defined as 'the inadvertent sharing of false information' (Digital, Culture, Media and Sport Committee, 2019).

Mis- and disinformation is evidently not limited to non-progressive movements or activist groups. However, as Bennett and Livingston (2018) point out, disinformation is frequently 'associated with the efforts of movements and parties on the radical right to mobilize supporters against centre parties and the mainstream press that carries their messages' (p. 122). The authors cite the Brexit campaign in the UK and the election of Donald Trump in the US as 'prominent examples of disinformation campaigns' (p. 122). Originally disregarded as a marginal figure, Alex Jones gradually shifted closer to the mainstream to eventually see himself and his platform endorsed by the future and then elected US President Donald Trump. Dismissed as racist and sensationalist by some, Jones' power in proactively shaping and re-shaping the narrative of events like Sandy Hook cannot be underestimated, which was a key argument during the legal case against him.

The role of the fan in non-progressive activism and disinformation

The role of the fan played a critical role in how Alex Jones and InfoWars were able to amass an engaged audience of millions. Stanfill (2019) highlights that fan studies traditionally frame 'fandom as fundamentally progressive' (p. 2), and not usually positioned within a political context. Arguably, this is how a fan is being positioned differently compared to an activist; fans are assumed to have no political motivation, whereas an activist ultimately seeks to influence policy (positive or negative). Applying Jenkins' (2009) model of participatory culture, Jones used most of the five key elements with his audience and, as a result, was able to build a strong fan base that aided in growing his power and influence, but also in sharing disinformation. Of the five elements, two elements emerged as most prominent: Jones ensured his fans felt their involvement mattered, praising and encouraging their contributions, plus there was a low barrier to engagement. Indeed, Jones is a master in building communities and a strong participatory culture, which were the core drivers for his gradually increasing media empire. Empowered, Alex Jones' fans constructed their own narrative that was replicated, shared and re-shared, thereby intensifying his power and the influence of his narrative.

Understanding the role platforms had to play in building Jones' fan base is important for digital storytellers in dealing with mis- and disinformation. If Jones' power is largely derived from his fans, does he still have a voice when his platforms are removed? If he does still have a voice, does it remain as effective or powerful? The role of social media in forming fans or non-progressive activists cannot be dissociated from the power and influence the platforms have, as fans' contributions are amplified by both the algorithm but also other fans and/or like-minded individuals.

De-platforming the trolls

Stanfill (2019) argues 'if fans are rebellious and subversive and challenge social power, we must ask, which kinds' (p. 4). Alex Jones challenged a version of history, and while he is not the first conspiracy theorist to deny a historical event, previous attempts have arguably not had the social reach he has had. Is power derived from the platform or from the narrative? *The New York Times* reported that when Alex Jones was de-platformed his audience was effectively cut in half, falling from a daily average of 1.4 million visits (website, YouTube and Facebook) to approximately 715,000 visits (Nicas, 2018). Whilst it did not stop him spreading disinformation, it did severely limit it. The European Commission report into disinformation (European Commission, 2018) notes online platforms are stepping up their response to the spread of disinformation. In late October 2019 Twitter announced a ban on all political advertising on its platform from 22 November 2019, and while this may be a step in the right direction, it is limited to paid advertising, hence will be unable to ensure the accuracy of all political commentary, including content similar to that shared by Alex Jones. Previously, Twitter has admitted a bias in its algorithms for right-wing politicians and news outlets across geographical areas (Milmo, 2021), effectively highlighting the role social media platforms play in fuelling outrage and driving mis- and disinformation.

The power and influence of the platform in the context of this case study cannot be separated from the narrative, as it is the platform that in-part enables the message and how it is spread. Hence non-progressive activists like Alex Jones are perhaps not the only ones to blame for the spread of misinformation. As Lenny Pozner, father of Noah Pozner, who was killed at Sandy Hook, states, 'the crazies are not running the asylums, it's the platforms who are allowing this to go on' (This American Life, 2019).

As access to technology increases, the believability of some of the disinformation being produced will make it harder for communication professionals to 'win the battle' against compelling content that works against politicians, corporate business and individuals. The USC 2019 Global Communications Report (USC Annenberg Center for Public Relations, 2019) highlighted that by 2024 the average person will not be able to distinguish between paid, earned and owned media and, more importantly, they will not care. Audiences' focus is increasingly driven by entertainment factors and information overload. This has significant implications for governments, organisations and brands in their battle against mis- and disinformation.

Albright (2017) argued that objectivity and trust in news sites is not enough to combat disinformation as facts only play a partial role in framing their narrative. In this way, de-platforming may indeed have a role to play in the case of extremist content, but if it does, what are the implications for freedom of speech? Who is to decide whose views are extreme? When does hate-speech constitute danger vs opinion?

Legal intervention

Alex Jones is not new to litigation. On the back of his multiple conspiracy theories he has for example been sued by a pizza restaurant and the yoghurt company Chobani. However, his continuously amplified claim that 'no one died' in the Sandy Hook school shooting, which he argued was a staged, manufactured hoax, coordinated by gun control advocates, has effectively resulted in a ruling that has de-platformed InfoWars. In mid-2022 the conspiracy theorist was ordered to pay a combined total of $49.3 million, including $45.2 million in punitive damages. This amount may be considerably less than the $150 million sought by the parents of one Jesse Lewis, one of the 26 victims, but it marks a clear departure from earlier court cases in which Jones largely relied on apologies and retractions of earlier claims. Punitive damages are meant to punish defendants for particularly egregious conduct, beyond the monetary compensation awarded to the plaintiffs. The large amount awarded in this case has been interpreted as the jurors wanting to send an important message to society at large, deterring others from similar conduct. In two further cases, Alex Jones was ordered to pay a further $473 million in punitive damages on top of a nearly $1 billion verdict handed down for his defamatory claims about the 2012 Sandy Hook mass shooting. InfoWar's parent company, Free Speech Systems, which is also liable for the verdicts, filed for bankruptcy in July 2022. Sandy Hook families have intervened and urged judges to freeze any assets over concerns that the company has been burdened with 'fabricated' debt, amidst earlier reports of attempts to hide assets. Jones' actual wealth remains unclear, but he remains defiant.

At the time of writing it remains unclear how much of the fines will be recoverable from Jones and his companies. This case study highlights the potential wide-reaching appeal and power of disinformation, which often overshadows the influence of individuals and fact-checking organisations. It thereby highlights the need for an increasingly proactive role to be played by (social media) platforms and legislative systems in limiting the spread of mis- and disinformation, therefore protecting those who may get caught up in the attractiveness of conspiracy theories, lacking the skills or desire to fact check, and so effectively society at large.

CHAPTER SUMMARY

Mis- and disinformation is not new, but its impact and reach has been amplified via digital media and social media algorithms, which reportedly favour divisive, outrage-generating content over more balanced reporting. The circulation of incorrect information – either distributed deliberately (disinformation) or unintentionally (misinformation) – presents a major challenge for governments, organisations, brands and indeed society itself.

In this chapter we discuss a number of tools and guidelines, as well as relevant theories (e.g. inoculation theory) and novel approaches to increase awareness of manipulated information (e.g. gamification). However, we also encourage a critical debate about responsibility, at a personal level, as well as the need for higher-level interventions at a platform and judicial level. Through a critical lens it may be argued that different voices, however polarising, add to the multitude of ideas circulating in a given society. However, does disinformation really add a new perspective, or does it build on our fears, concerns and increased tendency to be outraged as we struggle to make sense of the ever-increasing volume of information available to us at any given point in time?

Outrage in itself is not a negative emotion by definition. It indicates the breach of a psychological contract and in the case of passionate advocates outrage can indicate a serious breach of trust or values that warrants organisations and brands to investigate and address. However, professional communicators have to become increasingly skilled not only at fact checking and the dissemination of clear, accurate and easily memorable messaging; they also have to become increasingly accomplished in distinguishing between trolls, unwarranted outrage and actionable concerns.

DISCUSSION QUESTIONS

1. Prepare an infographic on how to spot a fake photo or video. Keep the tips simple; then, write a list of all the tools that can help identify mis- and disinformation.
2. A lot of misinformation has bias at its core. Look at the examples and discuss if you think there is bias in the article:
   a. A blog written by the Head of the National Medical Association about the impact of the chemicals used in fracking on human health.
   c. The President of Plains Exploration and Production Company (producers of natural gas) writes a letter to the editor of a national newspaper about the number of people his company hires to work in hydraulic fracturing.
   d. Professor of Geology at a national university and member of the board of the Plains Exploration and Production Company publishes an article in the newsletter of Australia's Gas Alliance summarising studies denying a link between hydraulic fracturing and groundwater contamination.
3. Split the class in two and hold a debate on the topic: 'Does de-platforming known trolls and people who spread mis- and disinformation stop the issue?' Have a yes and a no team. Investigate the issues surrounding this.
4. Read The Trust Project's Trust Indicator (https://thetrustproject.org) and outline what news site you believe does a good job of meeting all eight of these criteria. Expand on each criterion and state why they are doing this (give examples).
   a. *Best practices*: Do you know the organisation behind these news items? What rules and ethical standards do they uphold?

b. *Author expertise*: Who is the journalist behind this news item? As we typically rely on the reporter's interpretation of events, what do you know about them and the (ethical) standards they uphold?

c. *Type of work*: Is this news item impartial or deliberately biased? Stories should be clearly labelled if they are designed to persuade.

d. *Citations and references*: What information sources did the journalist behind this story rely on? Eye witness accounts? Other documents? How reliable are they? Can we check them out ourselves?

e. *Methods*: What (research) methods did the journalist use for their story? This will indicate how well-researched or impartial the story may be.

f. *Local*: Does the story draw on local knowledge to ensure accuracy and sensitivity, either because the journalist knows or lives in the community or because he/she draws on local knowledge?

g. *Diverse voices*: Are certain voices missing from the story? Or do we get a full picture that includes less commonly heard voices?

h. *Feedback*: Does the news site invite and listen to feedback?

(The Trust Project, 2017)

READINGS

Click, M.A. (2019). *Anti-Fandom: Dislike and Hate in the Digital Age.* New York: New York University Press.

This book discusses the role of the anti-fan and publishes 15 different articles from academics. An interesting read in a world of growing disinformation and how to understand the anti-fan in a culture of outrage.

Newlin, K. (2009). *Passion Brands: Why Some Brands Are Just Gotta Have, Drive All Night For, and Tell All Your Friends About.* Buffalo, NY: Prometheus Books.

This book discusses the power of some brands to build long-lasting loyalty and enthusiasm. In the age of mis- and disinformation, building a passion brand is one key way to fight online outrage and trolls.

Vaccari, C. and Chadwick, A. (2020). Deepfakes and disinformation: Exploring the impact of synthetic political video on deception, uncertainty, and trust in news. *Social Media + Society*, 6(1). doi:10.1177/2056305120903408.

This article discusses the role of visual communication in disseminating disinformation. Studying 'deepfakes' or synthetic media (videos that are made to look real), the study identifies new challenges to democratic society.

Keith, W. (2018). Denialism: What drives people to reject the truth. [online] *The Guardian*, 3 September. Available at: www.theguardian.com/news/audio/2018/sep/03/denialism-what-drives-people-to-reject-the-truth-podcast [Accessed 22 November 2022].

This podcast discusses what drives people to reject the truth. It highlights the role of denialism and asks why we have failed to understand its role in society.

REFERENCES

Albright, J. (2017). Welcome to the era of fake news. *Media and Communication*, 5(2), 87. doi:10.17645/mac.v5i2.977.

Allcott, H. and Gentzkow, M. (2017). Social media and fake news in the 2016 election. *Journal of Economic Perspectives*, 31(2), 211–236. doi:10.1257/jep.31.2.211.

BBC News (2022). Alex Jones to pay extra $473m damages over 'fake Sandy Hook' claim. BBC News. [online] 10 Nov. Available at: https://www.bbc.com/news/world-us-canada-63592386.

Bennett, W.L. and Livingston, S. (2018). The disinformation order: Disruptive communication and the decline of democratic institutions. *European Journal of Communication*, 33(2), 122–139. doi:10.1177/0267323118760317.

Brady, W.J., Wills, J.A., Jost, J.T., Tucker, J.A. and Van Bavel, J.J. (2017). Emotion shapes the diffusion of moralized content in social networks. *Proceedings of the National Academy of Sciences*, 114(28), 7313–7318. doi:10.1073/pnas.1618923114.

Digital, Culture, Media and Sport Committee (2018). *Fifth Report of Session 2017–19, Disinformation and 'Fake News': Interim Report.* London: Parliament UK.

Digital, Culture, Media and Sport Committee (2019). *Disinformation and 'Fake News': Final Report Eighth Report of Session 2017–19 Report, Together with Formal Minutes Relating to the Report.* [online] Available at: https://publications.parliament.uk/pa/cm201719/cmselect/cmcumeds/1791/1791.pdf [Accessed 2 November 2022].

D'Orazio, D. (2015). Volkswagen apologizes for emissions scandal with full-page ad in dozens of papers. [online] *The Verge.* Available at: www.theverge.com/transportation/2015/11/15/9739960/volkswagen-apologizes-with-full-page-ad-in-dozens-of-newspapers [Accessed 2 November 2022].

Edelman (2022). *Edelman Trust Barometer.* [online] Available at: www.edelman.com/trust/trust-barometer [Accessed 2 November 2022].

European Commission (2018). Online disinformation | Shaping Europe's digital future. [online] digital-strategy.ec.europa.eu. Available at: https://digital-strategy.ec.europa.eu/en/policies/online-disinformation.

Farte, G.I. and Obada, D.R. (2018). Reactive public relations strategies for managing fake news in the online environment. *Postmodern Openings*, 9(2), 26–44. doi:10.18662/po/16.

Figueira, Á. and Oliveira, L. (2017). The current state of fake news: Challenges and opportunities. *Procedia Computer Science*, 121, 817–825. doi:10.1016/j.procs.2017.11.106.

Harmon, L. (2019). The Alex Jones origin story: On Austin Public Access TV, his act was never an act. [online] *Observer.* Available at: https://observer.com/2019/04/alex-jones-austin-public-access-tv-origin-story/ [Accessed 8 November 2022].

Hartley, K. (2019). *Communicate in a Crisis: Understand, Engage and Influence Consumer Behaviour to Maximize Brand Trust.* London: Kogan Page.

Holpuch, A. (2013). Alex Jones: Fierce gun advocate doubles as prolific conspiracy theorist. [online] *The Guardian.* Available at: www.theguardian.com/world/2013/jan/08/alex-jones-piers-morgan-profile [Accessed 8 November 2022].

Jenkins, H. (2009). *Confronting the Challenges of Participatory Culture: Media Education for the 21st Century.* Cambridge, MA: MIT Press.

Leon, H. (2019). The Alex Jones Origin Story: On Austin Public Access TV, His Act Was Never an Act. [online] Observer. Available at: https://observer.com/2019/04/alex-jones-austin-public-access-tv-origin-story [Accessed 13 Feb. 2023].

Macnamara, J. (2020). *Beyond Post-Communication.* New York: Peter Lang Incorporated, International Academic Publishers.

McCorkindale, T. (2019). *2019 IPR Disinformation in Society Report: How Americans Perceive Intentionally Misleading News or Information.* [online] Available at: https://instituteforpr.org/ipr-disinformation-study/ [Accessed 2 November 2022].

McGuire, W.J. (1961). The effectiveness of supportive and refutational defenses in immunizing and restoring beliefs against persuasion. *Sociometry*, 24, 184–197.

McLoughlin, K.L., Brady, W.J. and Crockett, M.J. (2021). The role of moral outrage in the spread of misinformation. *Technology, Mind & Society 2021 Conference Proceedings.* APA Open. doi:10.1037/tms0000136.

Milmo, D. (2021). Twitter admits bias in algorithm for rightwing politicians and news outlets. [online] *The Guardian.* Available at: www.theguardian.com/technology/2021/oct/22/twitter-admits-bias-in-algorithm-for-rightwing-politicians-and-news-outlets [Accessed 2 November 2022].

Murdock, S. (2019). Alex Jones loses another legal battle in Sandy Hook defamation case. [online] *HuffPost.* Available at: www.huffingtonpost.com.au/entry/alex-jones-loses-another-legal-battle-in-sandy-hook-defamation-case_n_5d6fc811e4b0110804582c59?ri18n=true [Accessed 8 November 2022].

Nicas, J. (2018). Alex Jones said bans would strengthen him: He was wrong. [online] *The New York Times*, 4 September. Available at: www.nytimes.com/2018/09/04/technology/alex-jones-infowars-bans-traffic.html [Accessed 8 November 2022].

Nyhan, B. and Reifler, J. (2010). When corrections fail: The persistence of political misperceptions. *Political Behavior*, 32(2), 303–330.

Nyhan, B. and Reifler, J. (2015). Does correcting myths about the flu vaccine work? An experimental evaluation of the effects of corrective information. *Vaccine*, 33(3), 459–464.

Nyhan, B., Reifler, J., Richey, S. and Freed, G.L. (2014). Effective messages in vaccine promotion: A randomized trial. *Pediatrics*, 133(4), e835–e842.

Ott, B.L. and Dickinson, G. (2022). Look at 3 enduring stories Americans tell about guns to understand the debate over them. [online] *The Conversation.* Available at: https://theconversation.com/look-at-3-enduring-stories-americans-tell-about-guns-to-understand-the-debate-over-them-184597 [Accessed 8 November 2022].

Pamment, J. (2021). *RESIST 2 Counter Disinformation Toolkit.* [online] Available at: https://gcs.civilservice.gov.uk/publications/resist-2-counter-disinformation-toolkit/ [Accessed 8 November 2022].

Quantcast (2017). *Infowars.com Audience Insights*. [online] Available at: http://quantcast.com [Accessed 9 December 2017].

Queen, J. (2022). Alex Jones loses bid to slash $50 million Sandy Hook defamation verdict. Reuters. [online] 23 Nov. Available at: https://www.reuters.com/legal/alex-jones-loses-bid-slash-50-million-sandy-hook-defamation-verdict-2022-11-22/ [Accessed 13 Feb. 2023].

Redlawsk, D.P. (2002). Hot cognition or cool consideration? Testing the effects of motivated reasoning on political decision making. *Journal of Politics*, 64(4), 1021–1044.

Stanfill, M. (2019). Introduction: The reactionary in the fan and the fan in the reactionary. *Television & New Media*, 21(2). doi:10.1177/1527476419879912.

The Trust Project (2017). *Frontpage*. [online] Available at: https://thetrustproject.org/ [Accessed 8 November 2022].

This American Life (2019). Beware the Jabberwock. [online] *This American Life*. Available at: www.thisamericanlife.org/670/beware-the-jabberwock [Accessed 8 November 2022].

UNESCO (2019). *Journalism, 'Fake News' and Disinformation: A Handbook for Journalism Education and Training*. [online] Available at: https://en.unesco.org/fightfakenews [Accessed 8 November 2022].

USC Annenberg Center for Public Relations (2019). *PR: Tech, The Future of Technology in Communication*. [online] Available at: https://assets.uscannenberg.org/docs/2019-global-communications-report.pdf [Accessed 8 November 2022].

World Health Organization (2021). Fighting misinformation in the time of COVID-19, one click at a time. [online] *WHO*. Available at: www.who.int/news-room/feature-stories/detail/fighting-misinformation-in-the-time-of-covid-19-one-click-at-a-time [Accessed 8 November 2022].

Zhuang, M., Cui, G. and Peng, L. (2018). Manufactured opinions: The effect of manipulating online product reviews. *Journal of Business Research*, 87, 24–35. doi:10.1016/j.jbusres.2018.02.016.

12

ARTIFICIAL INTELLIGENCE, VIRTUAL REALITY AND THE FUTURE OF STORYTELLING

OBJECTIVES

1. Understand the definitions of artificial intelligence, virtual reality and augmented reality
2. Explore how new technologies are being used in digital storytelling
3. Consider the future of storytelling, including ethical considerations

In this final chapter we engage in some future gazing, by discussing how emerging technologies like artificial intelligence, virtual reality, augmented reality and bots may shape the future of storytelling. However, despite the opportunities that they may present, these technologies will also pose some challenges; hence, we will also take a look at associated pitfalls. We'll explore the different types of opportunities presented by these technologies and how they can be used for digital storytelling in marketing and communication campaigns and programmes.

DEFINING ARTIFICIAL INTELLIGENCE, VIRTUAL REALITY AND AUGMENTED REALITY

Artificial intelligence

The term artificial intelligence (AI) was first coined in 1956 by John McCarthy in reference to the idea of 'thinking machines' (Wright, 1984). The idea of a 'thinking machine' isn't far removed from how AI is used today; AI scholars explore how machines can imitate human intelligence. Essentially, AI is a computer system that is able to perform tasks that ordinarily require human intelligence. Many AI systems are powered by machine learning. In daily life, we use many AI applications including Amazon (machine-learning systems), Google, Netflix, ChatGPT and also Facebook. AI is now used in anything from spam filters, automated transcriptions (think e.g. Otter.ai) and television show recommendations on Netflix, to smart assistants ('Hey, Siri'), automated media monitoring (think brand mentions and the ability to quickly respond), as well as interactive maps. AI is built to do specific things, so it isn't a general sentient force, but instead uses existing data to undertake a task. Even if we are not consciously aware of it, AI is all around us: it has become a crucial part of our lives and is increasingly venturing into the creative space. For example, you can write a blog post with AI, giving it certain parameters like 'write a blog about digital storytelling in the voice of Russell Brand', and the software will undertake the task. Also, AI image generators that convert text to images using AI algorithms are increasingly being used, blurring the line between creative input and questions of copyright. The idea is that these images complement your ideas and concepts by turning them into visual representations within seconds, based on an existing database of images and the ability to learn how to generate new ones. A key think to keep in mind with AI is that it relies on existing data and ideas. It may be able to cleverly summarise large amounts of data, e.g. for literature review purposes, however, it is not able to think independently or to create new, novel ideas – at least not for the time being. Because of the reliance on existing data, there is also always a time lag, i.e. AI won't be able to provide any insights into live or even very recent events.

Here are just a few of the ways in which AI is being used in branding and communication (Peterson, 2019):

- Data-driven campaigns: Automation and machine learning can aid in the creation of new campaigns while simultaneously eliminating the guesswork.
- Automation of mundane tasks and responsibilities: Tasks like scheduling calendars, structuring meeting notes, setting due dates, creating Gantt charts and sending out follow-ups can now be completed by an emerging technology practice called 'robotic process automation', a form of AI that enables business professionals to automate rules-based processes.

- Sentiment analysis and crisis management: AI is now used in sentiment analysis, which utilises natural language processing to differentiate vocabulary use, tone and language context. The real-time insight that AI provides allows companies to respond quickly and effectively to any issues that may arise regardless of sentiment.

CASE STUDY

How Charity:Water uses AI to tell their story

Charity:Water has a simple mission as a charity – they want to provide clean, safe water for everyone, and across the years they have funded 111,795 water projects in 29 countries (Charity:Water, 2022). A key premise for the charity is that 100% of their donations fund clean water, and in making this promise the organisation needed to provide a way to showcase the story of where donations go. As the charity writes on their website:

> Transparency is one of our core values, so along with using every penny you donate to fund clean water projects, we also prove each project with photos and GPS coordinates. (Charity:Water, 2022)

First a charity, second a technology company, Charity:Water sought out the best data-driven approaches to ensure they could show transparency in relation to every single dollar that came into the charity. This also allowed them to build a deep story that can pinpoint exact locations and the number of people served by their water projects.

To show the location, each water project is tagged with a GPS monitor and linked to Google maps – this allows donors to see where their money is going. Further, information regarding the project costs and details of local partners are included, supported by photos that document the realisation of the new water project (Bertoni, 2013). To this end, Charity:Water is using their own data to help build a narrative of transparency, thereby addressing a common criticism across the not-for-profit sector, i.e. donors querying where their money has gone and if it has been invested responsibly.

In addition to this, Charity:Water has used AI, through the use of the platform Persado, to gain a better understanding of how the language and images used in Facebook advertisements resonate with their existing audiences (and potential donors) (O'Brien, 2019). This illustrates a clever use of AI to sharpen the brand story, provide visual reference points, and ensure it is sufficiently emotive to encourage your audience to take the call to action and make a donation. Persado states:

> Charity:Water used Persado to machine-generate 16 Facebook ads across 1,024 permutations spanning different emotional sentiments, imagery, and narratives. This approach allowed them to pinpoint precisely which stories and imagery were most powerful for different age segments and genders. (Persado, 2019)

Understanding the principles of storytelling is important to ensure your story will reso-nate; using the data and AI to identify which stories create the most emotion, and develop similar stories in future, ensures your stories are more likely to get your audience to act. 'The lines between creativity and data keep blurring, and the effects are mostly positive, especially when it comes to uncovering a campaign's most effective ads' (O'Brien, 2019).

Virtual reality

The original idea of virtual reality (VR) can be traced back to the mid-1960s 'when Ivan Sutherland in a pivotal manuscript attempted to describe VR as a window through which a user perceives the virtual world as if it looked, felt, sounded real and in which the user could act realistically' (Cipresso et al., 2018, p. 2). There are many definitions of VR but for the purpose of digital storytelling, perhaps this one covers the key elements that are relevant to the field, in that 'virtual reality refers to immersive, interactive, multi-sensory, viewer-centered, 3D computer generated environments and the combination of technologies required for building environ-ments' (Cruz-Neira, 1993). VR environments allow people to see, feel, hear and 'touch' a world other than their own. For the digital storyteller, this allows a fully immersive experience of a brand, product or service, which has the ability to build a deep and lasting connection.

CASE STUDY
A Walk Through Dementia, Alzheimer's Research UK

www.awalkthroughdementia.org/
   Some of the most innovative uses of new technology are by charity groups as they seek to tell their story from a first-person perspective. Alzheimer's Research in the UK uses VR to enable their audience to 'walk in the shoes' of an Alzheimer's sufferer or a carer. Using VR, they simulate symptoms people experience beyond memory loss, many that the ordinary/average person doesn't know about. This can help not only with the diag-nosis of new patients, but also in educating carers further about the disease. In the general audience it builds emotion and support for the charity, which may lead to donations. The VR experience is focused on building empathy and provides an immersive way of digital storytelling for a charity aimed at providing the public with information on the disease.
   On the website the charity states:

   A Walk Through Dementia is a virtual reality app for Android smartphones which allows you to look at everyday life through a new lens. The experience, which can also be viewed via the app or on YouTube, uses a combination of computer gen-erated environments and 360 degree video sequences to illustrate in powerful detail how even the most everyday task of making a cup of tea can become a challenge for someone with dementia. This app was developed by Alzheimer's Research UK, guided by people living with different forms of dementia. They were all keen to help you understand what everyday life can be like for them. (Alzheimer's Research UK, 2022)

Possibly one of the biggest challenges for charities in the past has been building an emotional connection with their potential donors. People are most likely to give money to charities they know or they feel an emotional connection to, and VR opens many doors to facilitate a greater level of immersion and connection by engaging stakeholders in a 'day in the life' scenario.

Virtual influencers

Blurring the lines further is the emergence of virtual influencers. These are fictional computer-generated characters with life-like characteristics, features and personalities of humans. Given that collaboration with real-life influencers can present a number of challenges and potential risks, many high-profile brands have turned towards virtual influencers like Lil Miquela (@lilmiquela), who was created in 2016 based on the idea of a 19-year-old Brazilian-American model. Virtual influencers engage in the same type of storytelling as human influencers do – they dance, they release songs, they shop, they have their own style and indicate empathy for social causes. Miquela has collaborated with brands like Prada, Chanel and Samsung – but she has also illustrated that even virtual influencers don't come without an element of risk, as at the end of the day virtual influencers are created by humans – and humans, and human-created storylines – can be fallible. For example, in 2016 Lil Miquela released a vlog in which she discussed being sexually harassed in the back of a rideshare. An important topic, many may argue, but the blurring of lines between virtual and actual reality was widely criticised as ignorant and offensive, especially to those having experienced real trauma. In terms of mass appeal, Lil Miquela has since been overtaken by Lu Do Magalu (@magazineluiza), a Brazilian influencer, who was originally created as a virtual private shopping assistant, but now has twice the followers (approx. 6 million in November 2022) on Instagram alone. However, there are plenty of other examples of virtual influencers out there, see www.virtualhumans.org/ for an overview and annual ranking based on reach and popularity. Other brands have opted to create their own virtual characters and associate storylines, as opposed to collaborating with a third-party character like Lil Miquela or Lu Do Magalu, who based on their millions of Instagram followers may present an attractive promotional platform to others. For example, in 2019 the car manufacturer Renault launched its own virtual influencer, Liv, who has promised to take audiences on authentic driving experiences.

Metaverse

The metaverse may be considered a form of VR in that it can extend the physical world – using both augmented and virtual technologies. The metaverse can be defined as an idea of the internet as a single, universal and immersive virtual world – facilitated by the use of VR and AR (Wikipedia, 2020). While the futuristic version of the metaverse uses avatars and holograms, it could be argued there are versions of the metaverse in existence already, such as through Facebook and virtual games like *Fortnite* and *Roblox*. These worlds offer opportunities for co-creation of experiences and storytelling as they blend the real with the online. *Fortnite*, a multiplayer online game, has done this through virtual concerts that were watched by millions. In 2021 English band Easy Life used the game for a virtual concert where players were 'ushered into a virtual re-creation of The O2 Arena in London, where the band welcomes you via a gigantic screen' (Webster, 2021). The concert took a surreal turn when players were flushed down a gigantic toilet and went down a path where players would 'dance inside the corpse of a huge monster, ride a hoverboard across a twisted city straight out of Inception, and then float amid the stars' (Webster, 2021). This is an immersive way of building a fan base with audiences that may not be as accessible if you had asked them to a live concert. *Fortnite*, or more specifically its creator Epic Games, take a transmedia approach to storytelling and stream the game live on Twitch and YouTube so fans, not involved in the game, can also watch on and follow the storyline. This is an example of a true transmedia narrative and use of a virtual environment, spanning many platforms and real life.

However, the metaverse may also cater for more traditional audiences. For example, in 2022 Swedish pop group ABBA made headlines for its digitally altered residency concert series, featuring a live band, together with life-size 'ABBAtars', thereby stretching the audience's understanding of what the metaverse is and how it can be experienced, here, in traditional concert venues, with ABBAtars replacing the original musicians without the need for headsets or other technical equipment that's typically associated with AR or VR technology. Drawing on nostalgia and the in-person concert experience, concert attendees could (almost) persuade themselves that they were enjoying a real-life concert of their favourite band, taking them all the way back to the concert experiences of their youth in the 1970s – virtual, immersive storytelling at its best!

Augmented reality

Augmented reality (AR) is another 'new' technology that is deepening the way we as consumers interact with brands and charities. 'AR is technology that overlays information and virtual objects on real-world scenes in real-time' (Marr, 2018). The technology is often used in conjunction with VR to offer a truly immersive world.

If you've ever tried on a pair of sunglasses online, or perhaps even a sneaker without visiting the store, then you've experienced AR. Many platforms – like Instagram and Snapchat – now offer AR filters that allow you to change the look of your face, the colour of your hair, and much more. Serious applications of AR include the Gatwick Airport passenger app that allows users to navigate its terminals through a map on their phone. In healthcare AR is being used as a telehealth option that allows doctors to interact with patients and provide real-time information for the doctor to assist the patient. Home care services provider Silver Chain in Australia uses what they call 'enhanced medical mixed reality' where the doctor can see the patient and the patient can speak to a holographic doctor, despite not being in the same room – or even city (Lammens, 2017).

In the branding world, many companies use a form of AR to invite audiences to explore their digital story. Australian Wine label Howard Park did this in 2018 with the launch of their sparkling wine Petit Jeté NV. The label allowed buyers of the wine to scan a QR code on the bottle with their smartphone, which in turn provided them with access to behind-the-scenes footage of the wine-making process. It was this commitment to authentic storytelling and the creative approach to brand extension that saw the wine win Best Australian Sparkling at the prestigious Sparkling Wine World Championships in London (B&T Magazine, 2021).

CASE STUDY
Break Free to Fly, end sexual exploitation of children

End Child Prostitution and Trafficking (ECPAT) used both AR and VR to launch an innovative immersive digital campaign. The Break Free to Fly campaign launched in 2022 and partnered with Meta and three international NGOs – International Justice Mission (IJM), Agape International Missions (AIM) and A21. The campaign reached nearly 10 million people (IJM, 2022). IJM, a key driver of the initiative, stated on its website (2022):

> The campaign, which was launched in August 2022 to 14 markets on Instagram, Facebook and Horizon Worlds, transports the audience into a re-enactment of a space where victims were once confined. The user hears the voices of survivors in their native languages and then watches as they break free like butterflies into a space that represents hope, transformation, freedom and the joy to live again. 'Break Free to Fly' is now Meta's first case study for using augmented and virtual reality for non-profits and was produced over eight months by a team at Meta and an external agency.

Online sexual exploitation of children is a sinister topic and unfortunately is one of the world's fastest-growing crimes (IJM, 2022). Due to the nature of the subject, people viewing awareness campaigns may be likely to turn away from' or 'scroll past' the content. To combat this, the campaign gained the attention of screen viewers with augmented butterflies flying across the screen, enticing the viewer to follow the butterflies. The use of AR and VR in this campaign is similar to Alzheimer's Research UK in that its initial aim is to build a positive connection with the viewer, followed by an opportunity for the viewer to create their own story as they explore the room the child was abused in, complemented by the child's own voice and insights into their experience. This is far more powerful and memorable than a static website and the offer of hope is given at the end with the story changing to show how the child was saved and has a new (safe) room. The release of butterflies at the end of the experience is a metaphor for innocence and freedom. IJM has deepened their mission to end sexual exploitation of children through their deep and immersive storytelling on many levels. This is seen in their podcast https://fightofmy.life/, which delivers a compelling and disturbing personal story of one girl's story into the sexual trafficking world. As a charity, IJM has found a creative way to encourage audiences to deeply immerse themselves in a storyline based on an issue that they might usually shy away from.

Deepfakes

Deepfakes are considered a type of AR, and in recent years have attracted a considerable amount of attention. Deepfake is a portmanteau of deep learning and fake. They are a type of synthetic media in which the original person or existing image is replaced with someone else's likeness. Concerns have been raised that deepfake technology can be used to create fake news and misleading content, as since they use deep learning AI they can be difficult to identify and hard to differentiate from an original video. Drawing on large sets of data, deep learning algorithms teach themselves how to replace faces in video and digital content. As computers become better at simulating reality, they may influence real-life events by providing us with the impression that someone has said or done something that they clearly haven't. Some deepfake examples are created to be both amusing and educational; for example, Chris Ume's TikTok Tom Cruise videos (@deeptomcruise) have attracted millions of viewers. Entertaining to some, these videos have caused alarm, because they highlight how dangerous this technology can be if it falls into the wrong hands (Corcoran and Henry, 2021). However, like any technology, deepfake videos can also be used in the public interest. For example, in 2022 Dutch police created a deepfake video of a murdered 13-year-old teen in an attempt to help solve the cold case. More than two decades after his death, the video resulted in dozens of new leads – not only because the existing information was presented in a new and easily shareable way, but also because the technology enabled Dutch police to tell the story of Sedar Soares.

For digital storytellers, deepfakes may open up opportunities (i.e. the Dutch police example) or challenges. The key is being aware they exist and developing strong communication approaches should they become an issue.

ETHICAL CONSIDERATIONS IN THE FUTURE OF STORYTELLING

Much of the literature and related industry reports on ethics in VR, AR and AI have predominantly focused on AI within the context of automation. Indeed, Galloway and Swiatek (2018) argued that automation-related concerns and their implications for future jobs have overshadowed the creative potential that these new technologies can offer. They emphasise that communication and marketing professionals do not need to become expert technologists, but they need to develop sufficient knowledge of AI's present and potential uses to ensure they can provide professional counsel to clients and internal audiences. Challenges will occur in areas like trust, bias, privacy, data security, safety and fake news in which these technologies can make it easier to deceive.

Many organisations are using AI for tasks such as monitoring social media and predicting media trends. Practitioners also employ widely available AI-based tools such as Buzzsumo, Trendkite and Hootsuite for social media analysis, and use the technology to automate and perform various tasks. These tasks include writing data-driven stories, organising and updating media lists, aiding in crisis management, converting and transcribing audio into text, following and predicting media (Panda, Upadhyay and Khandelwal, 2019).

AI will affect most industries and professions in the future (if it isn't already), and we are already seeing an impact in communication, advertising and marketing fields. Despite challenges, as illustrated with the earlier examples in this chapter, AI, VR, AR and related technologies can expand the digital storyteller's toolkit and provide new opportunities. As captured in the title of one of the Chartered Institute of Public Relations (CIPR) #AIinPR panel reports: 'Humans [will be] still needed' to make sense of data, apply critical thinking skills and make ethical judgements (Valin, 2018). Machines rely on data provided by humans. Hence, if unintended – or possibly even intended – human or organisational biases or flaws are embedded, then they will be replicated by the machine without any further questioning. This has been observed in a human resources context, where AI technology is increasingly used as part of recruitment processes. Although video and voice interview analysis via AI may speed up the process and remove the risk of interviewer bias, the algorithms rely on human programming skills, which have increasingly been called out for a lack of fairness and indeed discrimination against certain groups of people (Köchling and Wehner, 2020; Fernández-Martínez and Fernández, 2020). As Valin (2018) emphasises: 'It's not about the quality of the data, but the ethical factors we build into decision-making' (p. 4), as AI offers the potential to further amplify existing power inequalities. The #AIinPR panel (see www.cipr.co.uk/AI) directs communicators to the Global Alliance's Principles of Ethical Practice, which emphasise that communicators should make decisions that favour the public – as opposed to personal or organisational – interest(s) (Valin and Gregory, 2020).

However, research by the panel has further documented the industry-wide limited knowledge of AI and lack of confidence in using it, therefore accusing public relations and communication professionals of 'sleepwalking into artificial intelligence' (Gregory and Virmani, 2020), risking being left behind other professions (Virmani and Gregory, 2021).

The criticism is valid. Yes, new AI-powered technologies provide communicators with fantastic opportunities to streamline their work and insights into key audiences by drawing on social monitoring tools that flag emerging topics, track engagement and predict trends. AI can assist us with (meeting) transcriptions, minutes and language conversion, and makes even simple tasks like finding a new client's office easier, through easily available interactive maps. These may be convenient tools, but they fail to embrace the real potential of AI, VR and AR for storytelling purposes. Today's communication landscape provides talented storytellers with incredible opportunities to engage with audiences on a deeper, much more meaningful level, fostering long-term brand engagement that translates into active brand communities. Existing genres and traditional storytelling techniques will remain relevant, but new technologies will enable you to build and expand on these, making audience experiences not only more interactive, but also more relevant and personalised. This in turn will have implications for brand trust and reputation management in the long run.

Although new technologies may provide benefits to digital storytelling, with the potential of removing some of the more time-consuming processes, they can't replace creative thinking. Powerful stories shape identities – what does that communicate about the impact of AI, VR and AR in shaping who we are and how we understand our role in society? For example, for consumers, the real problem with friendly (chat) bots is that the human touch they offer is just an illusion. Bots use our trust to promote purchases, garner votes, build desires and so on (Donath, 2019). You think you're getting a truly personalised service, when you're simply getting cheaper service. There are many implications of the use of this type of technology – positive and negative. Let's look at a few issues that may arise:

- While storytelling might be more immersive and hence effective, how do we understand what is authentic and what has been fabricated when engaging with virtual characters in artificially created worlds?
- As AR filters become the norm, how do we allow people to interact with the technology if it is changing beauty norms? What are the implications for children and young adults in how they perceive their 'self'?
- As virtual influencers enter into social commentary space, can younger generations discern the difference between what is real and what is not?
- As AI writes more content, are we knowingly decreasing jobs in this space – is this a positive development in that it opens up other opportunities for creative exploration and strategic impact, or negative in that we are making ourselves and existing, human-based skills redundant?

These are just a few examples of the tricky questions we need to consider, but despite this, AI, VR and AR provide immense potential when it comes to increasing the richness and immersiveness of storytelling like we've never seen before.

CHAPTER SUMMARY

This chapter discusses the key definitions of artificial intelligence, virtual reality and augmented reality:

- AI is a computer system that is able to perform tasks that ordinarily require human intelligence.
- 'Virtual reality refers to immersive, interactive, multi-sensory, viewer-centered, 3D computer generated environments and the combination of technologies required building environments' (Cruz-Neira, 1993).
- 'AR is technology that overlays information and virtual objects on real-world scenes in real-time' (Marr, 2018).

The chapter discusses the case study of Charity:Water and its use of AI to deepen their story of building wells and making it a transparent process. This case study is the application of data to enrich its narrative, and also see what stories resonate best with their audiences, so they can better create narratives that will connect.

The case study of A Walk Through Dementia, Alzheimer's Research UK is discussed to highlight a unique use of VR, enabling viewers to experience what living with Alzheimer's is like. This has many benefits for the charity to build empathy and also provide public information.

The 2022 case study of Break Free to Fly, end sexual exploitation of children, is used to highlight the power of both AR and VR by placing the viewer in a room where a child was abused. Although a confronting subject, the campaign was done in such a way that enabled viewers to be drawn into the narrative via the use of 3D butterflies appearing to fly across the (computer) screen.

Virtual influencers, the metaverse and deepfakes are all discussed as uses of VR and AR respectively. This chapter discusses the ethical implications for digital storytellers. Despite their challenging nature and absence of a correct or definite answer, we encourage readers to engage with and reflect on the questions posed at the end of the chapter.

DISCUSSION QUESTIONS

1. **Are AR, AI and/or VR useful to digital storytelling? Why or why not? Can you think of some examples?**

2. Discuss the use of VR in a campaign. Bringing together all your knowledge of digital storytelling, discuss the campaign and analyse how it is using digital storytelling.
3. In groups, look at the different uses of VR, AI and AR in digital storytelling campaigns. Prepare a presentation to discuss your brand with the rest of the class.
4. Check your knowledge of AI blog writing. First write a four-paragraph blog post (200-300 words) on the future of digital storytelling and AI. Next, using https:// simplified.com/ or https://openai.com/blog/chatgpt/ or a similar program, have the AI create another version for you. Compare and contrast the language, noting tone, structure and persuasiveness - which one do you think is better, and why?

READINGS

Rizvic, S., Okanovic, V. and Boskovic, D. (2020). Digital storytelling. In: F. Liarokapis, A. Voulodimos, N. Doulamis and A. Doulamis (eds.), *Visual Computing for Cultural Heritage*. Cham: Springer, pp. 347–367. doi:10.1007/978-3-030-37191-3_18.

This reading provides an understanding of using VR and AR in virtual cultural heritage presentations – useful for museums and tourism. It discusses the challenge of using classical storytelling methods and adjusting them to virtual environments.

Alexander, B. (2017). *The New Digital Storytelling: Creating Narratives with New Media (Revised and Updated)*. Santa Barbara, CA: Praeger.

Chapters 11 and 12 of this book discuss 'Augmented Reality: Telling Stories on the Worldboard' and 'Storytelling through Virtual Reality' respectively. Both are relevant to further developing terminology and understanding of narrative storytelling in this space.

REFERENCES

Alzheimer's Research UK (2022). *A Walk Through Dementia*. [online] Available at: www.alzheimersresearchuk.org/campaigns/awtd/ [Accessed 29 November 2022].

B&T Magazine (2021). Howard Park Wines extends West Australian ballet partnership in new creative campaign. [online] *B&T Magazine*. Available at: www.bandt. com.au/howard-park-wines-extends-west-australian-ballet-partnership-in-new-creative-campaign/ [Accessed 30 November 2022].

Bertoni, S. (2013). How Charity:Water won over the tech world. [online] *Forbes*. Available at: www.forbes.com/sites/stevenbertoni/2013/12/19/how-charity-water-won-over-the-tech-world/?sh=7cf1f07d7328 [Accessed 29 November 2022].

Charity:Water (2022). *Clean Drinking Water for Developing Countries*. [online] Available at: www.charitywater.org/ [Accessed 29 November 2022].

Cipresso, P., Giglioli, I.A.C., Raya, M.A. and Riva, G. (2018). The past, present, and future of virtual and augmented reality research: A network and cluster analysis of the literature. *Frontiers in Psychology*, 9(9). doi:10.3389/fpsyg.2018.02086.

Corcoran, M. and Henry, M. (2021). The Tom Cruise deepfake that set off 'terror' in the heart of Washington DC. [online] *ABC News*, 28 June. www.abc.net.au/news/2021-06-24/tom-cruise-deepfake-chris-ume-security-washington-dc/100234772 [Accessed 29 November 2022].

Cruz-Neira C. (1993). Virtual reality overview. In: *SIGGRAPH 93 Course Notes 21st International Conference on Computer Graphics and Interactive Techniques, Orange County Convention Center*, Orlando, FL.

Donath J (2019) The robot dog fetches for whom? In: Papacharissi Z (ed.) A Networked Self and Human Augmentics, Artificial Intelligence, Sentience. London: Routledge, pp. 10–24.

Fernández-Martínez, C. and Fernández, A. (2020). AI and recruiting software: Ethical and legal implications. *Paladyn, Journal of Behavioral Robotics*, 11(1), 199–216.

Galloway, C. and Swiatek, L. (2018). Public relations and artificial intelligence: It's not (just) about robots. Public Relations Review, 44(5), pp.734–740. doi: https://doi.org/10.1016/j.pubrev.2018.10.008.

Gregory, A. and Virmani, S. (2020) *The Effects of Artificial Intelligence on the Professions: A Literature Repository*. [online] Available at: https://cipr.co.uk/CIPR/Our_work/Policy/CIPR_Artificial_Intelligence_in_PR_panel.aspx [Accessed 29 November 2022].

IJM (2022). Meta partners with IJM in immersive awareness campaign. [online] *IJM USA*. Available at: www.ijm.org/news/meta-partners-ijm-immersive-awareness-campaign [Accessed 29 November 2022].

Köchling, A. and Wehner, M.C. (2020). Discriminated by an algorithm: A systematic review of discrimination and fairness by algorithmic decision-making in the context of HR recruitment and HR development. *Business Research*, 13(3), 795–848.

Lammens, M. (2017). Silver Chain Group reveals the next big thing in the healthcare world. [online] *healthiAR+VR+MR+XR*. Available at: https://healthiar.com/silver-chain-group-reveals-the-next-big-thing-in-the-healthcare-world [Accessed 29 November 2022].

Marr, B. (2018). 9 powerful real-world applications of augmented reality (AR) today. [online] *Forbes*. Available at: www.forbes.com/sites/bernardmarr/2018/07/30/9-powerful-real-world-applications-of-augmented-reality-ar-today/#37c4c16e2fe [Accessed 29 November 2022].

O'Brien, K. (2019). How Persado's AI helped clean water charity take 'trial-and-error' out of Facebook ads. [online] *The Drum*. Available at: www.thedrum.com/news/2019/02/13/how-persados-ai-helped-clean-water-charity-take-trial-and-error-out-facebook-ads [Accessed 29 November 2022].

Panda, G., Upadhyay, A.K. and Khandelwal, K. (2019). Artificial intelligence: A strategic disruption in public relations. *Journal of Creative Communications*, 14(3), 196–213. doi:10.1177/0973258619866585.

Persado (2019). How charity: water Used AI to Find the Narrative Which Inspired the Most Engagement. [online] Persado. Available at: https://www.persado.com/wp-content/uploads/charity-water-Persado-Case-Study-May-2019-1.pdf [Accessed 2023].

Peterson, A. (2019). *The Past, Present & Future of Artificial Intelligence in PR*. [online] Available at: www.cision.com/2019/01/artificial-intelligence-PR/ [Accessed 29 November 2022].

Valin, J. (2018). *Humans Still Needed: An Analysis of Skills and Tools in Public Relations*. [online] Available at: https://newsroom.cipr.co.uk/humans-still-needed—research-project-reveals-impact-of-artificial-intelligence-on-public-relations/ [Accessed 29 November 2022].

Valin, J. and Gregory, A. (2020). *Ethics Guide to Artificial Intelligence in PR*. [online] Available at: www.cipr.co.uk/AI [Accessed 29 November 2022].

Virmani, S. and Gregory, A. (2021). *The AI and Big Data Readiness Report*. [online] Available at: https://newsroom.cipr.co.uk/new-research-finds-pr-practitioners-limited-in-ai-knowledge-but-aware-of-huge-potential/ [Accessed 29 November 2022].

Webster, A. (2021). Fortnite's new virtual concert might be its trippiest yet. [online] The Verge. Available at: https://www.theverge.com/2021/6/25/22550240/fortnite-easy-life-concert-o2-arena.

Wikipedia (2020). Metaverse. [online] *Wikipedia*. Available at: https://en.wikipedia.org/wiki/Metaverse [Accessed 29 November 2022].

Wright, R. (1984). Thinking machines. *The Wilson Quarterly*, 8(5), 72–83. www.jstor.org/stable/40257629

Appendix

DIGITAL STORYTELLING STRATEGY FOR PERTH OBSERVATORY

A Report by Samantha Roberts, Hadi Rahimi, Zachary Cheir, Eva Tadrous and Ngoc Phuong Trinh Le (Curtin University, Western Australia, 2022)

Note: This is an example of how a student might put together a digital storytelling strategy and illustrates the key points mentioned in the book.

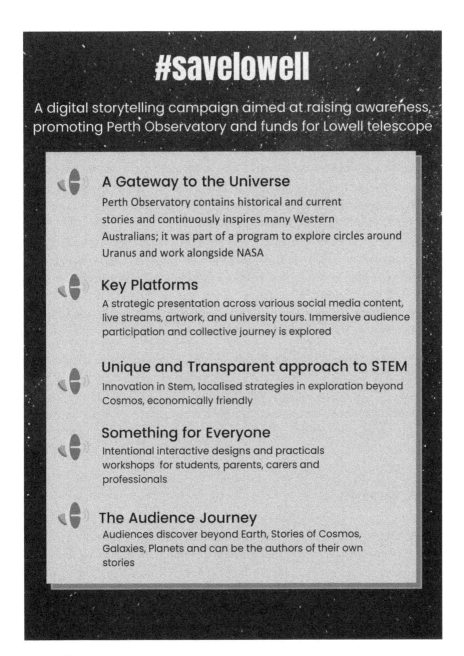

Figure 13.1

INTRODUCTION

Perth Observatory is one of Australia's most historical places in the science and technology world and it is the oldest observatory within Western Australia, serving over 120 years. As Perth Observatory continues to grow older, financial challenges to upkeep, refurbish and repair the observatory have become an increasing concern. Currently, Perth Observatory has a social media presence, although the Perth community lacks awareness of the importance and role of the observatory. We have offered four strategies and aim to run these campaigns for the fundraiser set on the 23 September 2023. This campaign seeks to raise awareness and promote Perth Observatory and the Lowell telescope with the main goal of raising AUD$500,000 for refurbishments and repairs of the Lowell telescope.

This report has been divided into three main sections:

1. The first section of this report consists of background research into the current state of the Perth Observatory. This section includes analyses of direct and indirect competitors to Perth Observatory, a social media and website audit and an in-depth PESTLE and SWOT analysis.
2. The second section of this report presents the key issues, goals, objectives, the key narrative and the three target audiences identified for this campaign.
3. The final section of this report outlines the four digital storytelling strategies in detail. The strategies presented are across various platforms such as social media content, livestreams, artwork and university tours. Lastly, the audience and collective journey are detailed.

Through our presented campaign we ensure Perth Observatory will address its key issues whilst achieving its main goal of raising awareness, promoting itself and most importantly obtaining the funds for the repair of the Lowell telescope. At the commencement of the campaign, we will provide a comprehensive evaluation. We look forward to bringing the Perth community back together with Perth Observatory.

BACKGROUND

Premier John Forrest originally submitted a proposal for an observatory for Perth to the State Parliament in 1891 but failed to obtain financial backing until funding was finally approved in 1895. The Perth Observatory, the oldest observatory in Western Australia, is situated near Bickley, 35 kilometres to the east of Perth. The Perth Observatory first opened its doors to the public in 1900, and before moving to its current location in Bickley in 1965, it was situated on Mount Eliza (Kaarta Garup), a part of King's Park (Hall, 2022). It was initially established for the Western Australian Government Astronomer to maintain Standard Time. The Observatory has been providing services to WA for more than 120 years and continues to be actively engaged in the service of public education via Day Tours for schools and Night Sky Tours for the general public. The Observatory was added to the state's Heritage Register in 2005 in recognition of its importance in science, culture and history. The Perth Observatory Volunteer Group has been managing the Observatory on behalf of the Western Australian government as of 1 July 2015. Important studies that have been done at the Observatory include the following: co-discovering the ring system around Uranus; publishing many Meridian Catalogues throughout its existence; participating in the NASA International Planetary Patrol in collaboration with the Lowell Observatory; 10% of all ground-based locations for Halley's Comet were generated by our astronomical observatory; 30 supernovas have been found by its automated supernova search; between 1970 and 1999, 29 minor planets were found. The Observatory also aided in the discovery of the super-Earth exoplanet OGLE-2005-BLG-390lb (Perth Observatory, 2022).

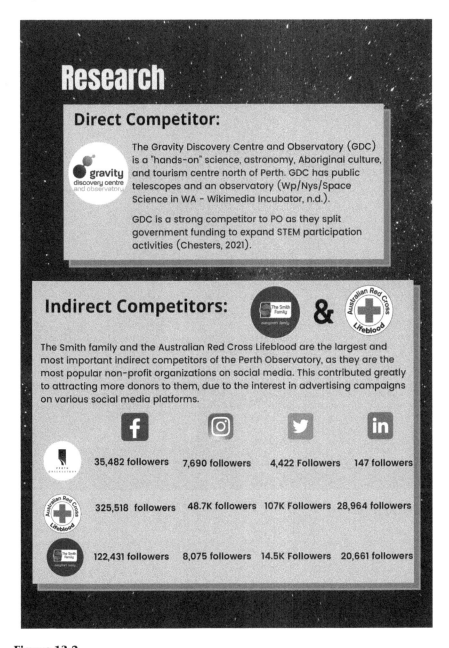

Figure 13.2

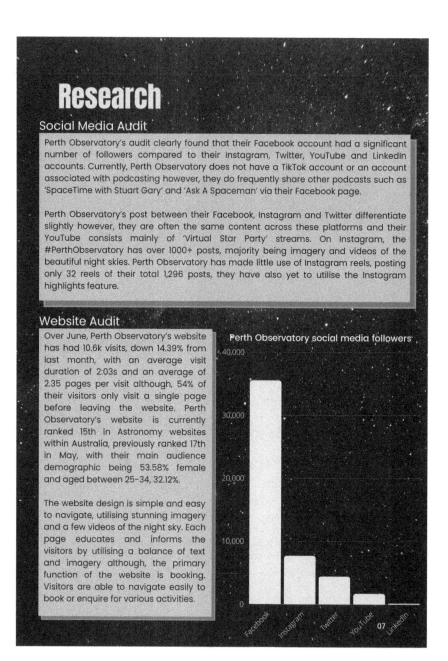

Research

Social Media Audit

Perth Observatory's audit clearly found that their Facebook account had a significant number of followers compared to their Instagram, Twitter, YouTube and LinkedIn accounts. Currently, Perth Observatory does not have a TikTok account or an account associated with podcasting however, they do frequently share other podcasts such as 'SpaceTime with Stuart Gary' and 'Ask A Spaceman' via their Facebook page.

Perth Observatory's post between their Facebook, Instagram and Twitter differentiate slightly however, they are often the same content across these platforms and their YouTube consists mainly of 'Virtual Star Party' streams. On Instagram, the #PerthObservatory has over 1000+ posts, majority being imagery and videos of the beautiful night skies. Perth Observatory has made little use of Instagram reels, posting only 32 reels of their total 1,296 posts, they have also yet to utilise the Instagram highlights feature.

Website Audit

Over June, Perth Observatory's website has had 10.6k visits, down 14.39% from last month, with an average visit duration of 2:03s and an average of 2.35 pages per visit although, 54% of their visitors only visit a single page before leaving the website. Perth Observatory's website is currently ranked 15th in Astronomy websites within Australia, previously ranked 17th in May, with their main audience demographic being 53.58% female and aged between 25–34, 32.12%.

The website design is simple and easy to navigate, utilising stunning imagery and a few videos of the night sky. Each page educates and informs the visitors by utilising a balance of text and imagery although, the primary function of the website is booking. Visitors are able to navigate easily to book or enquire for various activities.

Perth Observatory social media followers

Figure 13.3

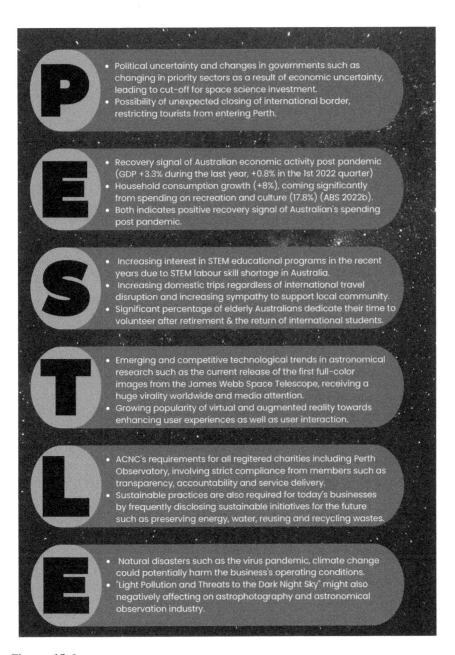

Figure 13.4

SWOT

Strengths

- Location within the Perth metropolitan area in a natural setting: Unique local experience for tourism thanks to the ability to monitor the skies in the southern hemisphere.
- Valuable history: The Observatory has provided services to the state of WA for more than 125 years and is still actively involved in providing services for public education.
- Perth Observatory building and Perth Lowell telescope are valuable heritage of WA.
- Worl Wangkiny (Noongar for Sky Stories), unique to WA for educating visitors on the cultural and practical significance astronomy played in Aboriginal life.

Weaknesses

- Lack of government financial support.
- Unstable financial condition due to limited income sources.
- Strong reliance on volunteers.
- Aging dome and telescopes that requires constant maintenance.
- Lack of investment to acquire advanced technologies to meet the growing demand of comprehensive education and night sky tour experience.
- Lack of visitors' centre: The Observatory was not intended for use by the general public, and the deteriorating historic infrastructure cannot completely accommodate the present needs of research, tourism and teaching.
- Lack of engagement in social media (few comments for event booking, only 147 LinkedIn followers, only 1 YT short, 1.68K YT followers, inactive status on Twitter, LinkedIn, YT).

Opportunities

- Growing demand for STEM education due to STEM shortage labour force in Australia is an opportunity for Perth Observatory to promote their role in astronomical education and research.
- Return of high tourist numbers is a chance to promote the Observatory's local tourist experience utilising strong cultural and historical identity.
- The increasing advocacy of social-conscious activities to support the local community. Potential donors are willing to support but might not have heard of Perth Observatory.
- Potential chance to diversify volunteer demographics to include young students, especially international students who are interested in seeking internship/voluntary opportunities.

Threats

- The vulnerability of depending strongly on volunteers.
- Intense competition for local fundraising (both direct and indirect competitors from different sectors).
- Natural disasters such as COVID-19 that could impact on human resources, business operating conditions and growth.
- Changing policy from the governments in priorities or funding.
- Lack of interest from the general public towards protecting and preserving historic sites such as Perth Observatory and the Lowell telescope.

KEY ISSUES

Through analysis of the Perth Observatory's social media and thorough situational analysis (SWOT and PESTLE), we have identified three key issues to be addressed.

1. The Perth community lacks awareness of Perth Observatory's significant roles in astronomical education, tourism and research. There is little to no knowledge within the community of the significance and the importance of Perth Observatory and the Lowell telescope.
2. The lack of knowledge also inhibits fundraising efforts; without knowing the significance of Perth Observatory and Lowell, the population will be less willing to donate as they do not see the impacts of giving for Lowell.
3. Finally, the scarcity of volunteers and experts to help run the observatory. Without a strong connection with volunteer groups and a continuous source of reliable volunteers, it will become increasingly challenging to keep up with demand.

GOALS

Correlating directly to the key issues above, the goals of this campaign are as follows:

1. Raise awareness of the Perth Observatory and the Lowell telescope and their importance to the Western Australian community.
2. Promote the observatory amongst community and volunteer groups to aid in the development of a more substantial, more extensive and reliable volunteer group who will be able to help with the upswing in activities, visitors and requirements of the Observatory.
3. Finally, the most significant goal of this campaign is to raise AUD$500,000 for the refurbishment and repair of the Lowell telescope.

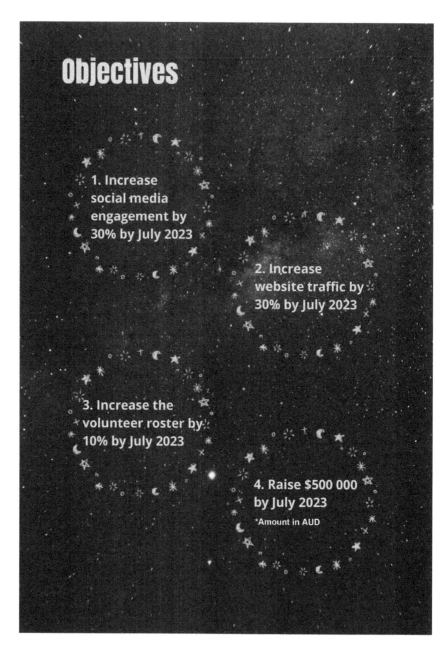

Figure 13.5

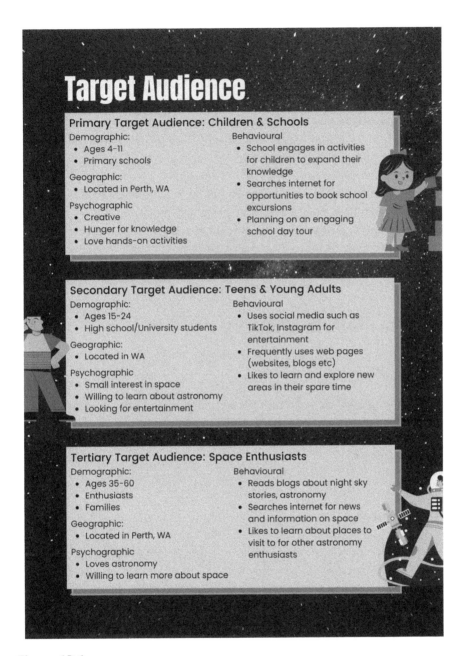

Target Audience

Primary Target Audience: Children & Schools

Demographic:
- Ages 4-11
- Primary schools

Geographic:
- Located in Perth, WA

Psychographic
- Creative
- Hunger for knowledge
- Love hands-on activities

Behavioural
- School engages in activities for children to expand their knowledge
- Searches internet for opportunities to book school excursions
- Planning on an engaging school day tour

Secondary Target Audience: Teens & Young Adults

Demographic:
- Ages 15-24
- High school/University students

Geographic:
- Located in WA

Psychographic
- Small interest in space
- Willing to learn about astronomy
- Looking for entertainment

Behavioural
- Uses social media such as TikTok, Instagram for entertainment
- Frequently uses web pages (websites, blogs etc)
- Likes to learn and explore new areas in their spare time

Tertiary Target Audience: Space Enthusiasts

Demographic:
- Ages 35-60
- Enthusiasts
- Families

Geographic:
- Located in Perth, WA

Psychographic
- Loves astronomy
- Willing to learn more about space

Behavioural
- Reads blogs about night sky stories, astronomy
- Searches internet for news and information on space
- Likes to learn about places to visit to for other astronomy enthusiasts

Figure 13.6

THE KEY NARRATIVE

The key narrative of this journey is to help #savelowell – the importance of both the Lowell telescope and Perth Observatory in the Perth community and the scientific community and the much-needed repairs for the Lowell telescope.

The main message is awareness and education; the digital storytelling strategies one, two and three focus on the education of the public, adults, hobbyists, enthusiasts and, most importantly, schools and children. The message aims to raise awareness of the Perth Observatory and its contributions to astronomy and science, making the public more likely to donate and fundraise for the overall #savelowell narrative and to achieve objectives one, two and four. The main message is broken down into separate digital storylines for different audiences, primarily adults and children, with strategies one and two focused on adults and three focused on children.

The secondary message is the importance of the volunteers involved in the Perth Observatory and the need for more; strategy four will focus on this message. Finally, the message aims to increase the roster of volunteers and participants within the Perth Observatory community to serve the expected increase of interest better once the digital storytelling strategies have been implemented; this will achieve objective three.

STRATEGY ONE: AWARENESS

Goals

1. To achieve 30,000 views for the releasing video of the Lowell telescope from all social media platforms by the end of 2022.
2. To reach at least 500 university students from the Lowell's university tour by October 2022.

Key message

- Perth Observatory is the oldest observatory in Western Australia, being a valuable historical site for not only tourists, but also for local travel experience.
- Let's wander around your hometown someday, visit Perth Observatory, experience the night sky and especially meet with Lowell – the historic Perth telescope.

Key tactics

1. Run a social media campaign to raise audiences' awareness of Perth Observatory and the Lowell telescope.
2. Set up an advertising booth and organise workshops at universities to approach young audiences, and also to promote the fundraising campaign.

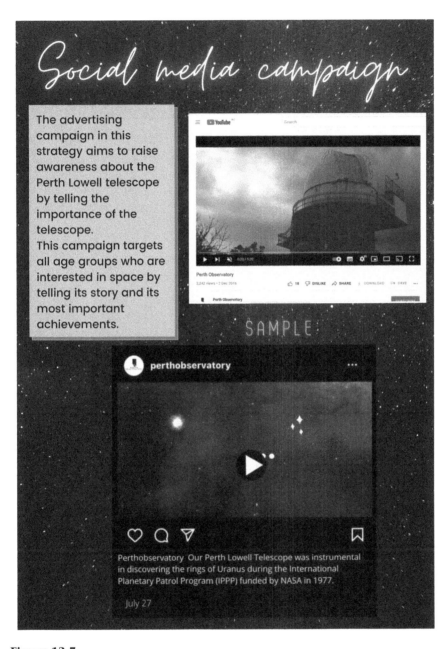

The advertising campaign in this strategy aims to raise awareness about the Perth Lowell telescope by telling the importance of the telescope.
This campaign targets all age groups who are interested in space by telling its story and its most important achievements.

Perth Observatory
2,842 views • 7 Dec 2016

Perth Observatory

SAMPLE

perthobservatory

Perthobservatory Our Perth Lowell Telescope was instrumental in discovering the rings of Uranus during the International Planetary Patrol Program (IPPP) funded by NASA in 1977.

July 27

Figure 13.7

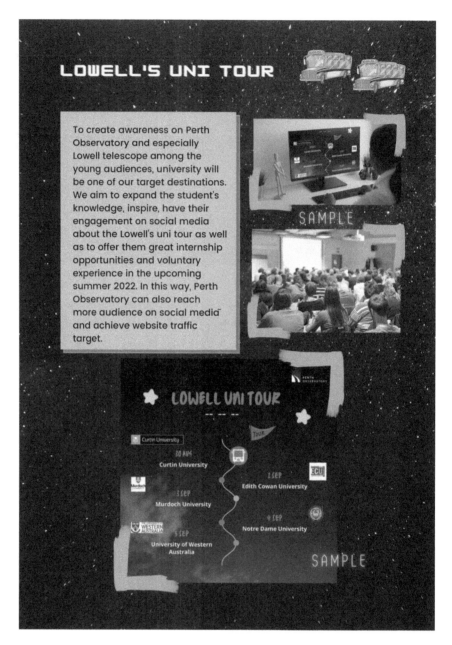

Figure 13.8

STRATEGY TWO: ENGAGEMENT

Goals

1. To increase website traffic by 10% by the end of 2022.
2. To achieve 50,000 views of Facebook Live videos by September 2022.
3. To achieve 2,000 QR code scans within two months by September 2022.

Key message

Lowell represents Australia and WA in the global astronomical research battle. Having Perth's DNA, we feel proud of Lowell for his achievements and contribution in the southern hemisphere observatory and the discovery of Uranus' rings. Hence, supporting and protecting Lowell means we are doing amazing things for our own hometown.

Key tactics

1. Create weekly Facebook live content to provide a virtual tour experience and build trust with audiences. One of the most popular blockers for fundraising is due to the lack of trust in charities (Australian Communities, 2017).
2. Feature WA's night sky and Perth Lowell Observatory artwork in Perth CBD to engage with Perth residents. By engaging with the artwork, they might also establish a personal connection with Perth Observatory which leads to funding possibilities (Australian Communities, 2017).

Figure 13.9

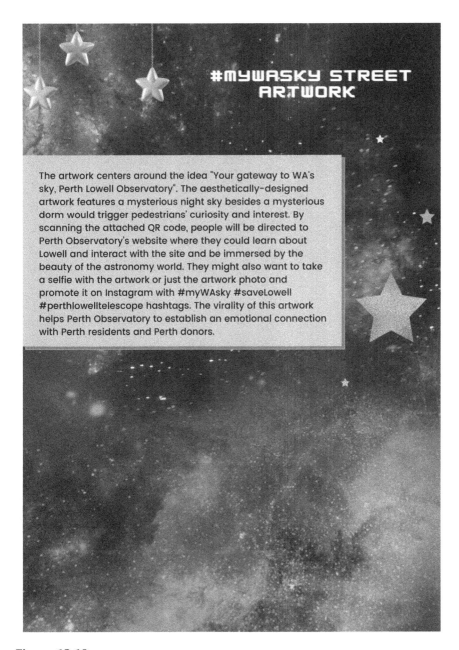

#MYWASKY STREET ARTWORK

The artwork centers around the idea "Your gateway to WA's sky, Perth Lowell Observatory". The aesthetically-designed artwork features a mysterious night sky besides a mysterious dorm would trigger pedestrians' curiosity and interest. By scanning the attached QR code, people will be directed to Perth Observatory's website where they could learn about Lowell and interact with the site and be immersed by the beauty of the astronomy world. They might also want to take a selfie with the artwork or just the artwork photo and promote it on Instagram with #myWAsky #saveLowell #perthlowelltelescope hashtags. The virality of this artwork helps Perth Observatory to establish an emotional connection with Perth residents and Perth donors.

Figure 13.10

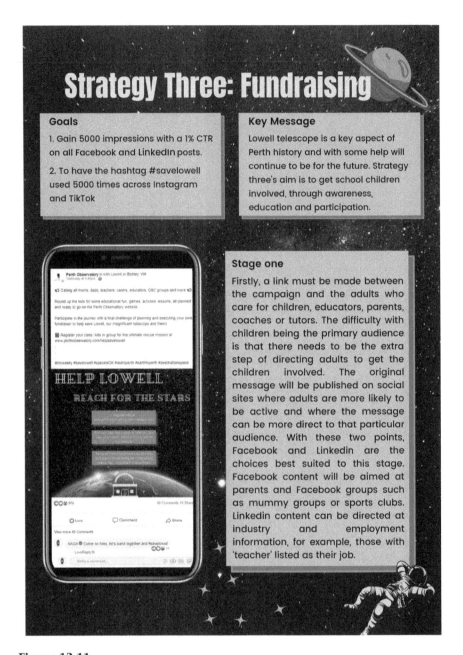

Figure 13.11

Stage two

The second stage of this campaign is introducing content aimed at children; as children are not expected to have access to social media such as Instagram, Twitter and TikTok, the content will primarily be posted on YouTube. The content will be both full-length videos and shorts, which can be shown to children in class or at home, and children can access them through YouTube Kids.

The initial touchpoint when children are introduced to Lowell in a YouTube video adds a level of emotion to the story, allowing the children to connect on a deeper level with the story. Lowell is not just a telescope; he is a friend. Following this, children are directed to the Perth Observatory website, which the teacher or parent facilitates. The website boasts many informative videos, activities and games to learn and explore. Each week a new video is released on YouTube, covering educational topics and encouraging children to get involved in the greatest adventure-rescue mission to #savelowell.

Stage three

Once the story of Lowell is established, children and classrooms are encouraged to form groups to create their fundraisers to help #savelowell. As these fundraisers begin to take place, user-generated content can be shared by parents, teachers and other adults on social media sites such as Instagram and TikTok with the hashtags #savelowell #mywasky #spaceisOK #astroperth #destinationspace. The message can reach a larger audience and encourage more people to get involved. Perth Observatory will also re-post some of the user-generated content onto their owned media to continue the story. Alongside the fundraisers, a cartoon version of Lowell will update on the progress of the fundraising; this will be posted to YouTube shorts so that children can view it.

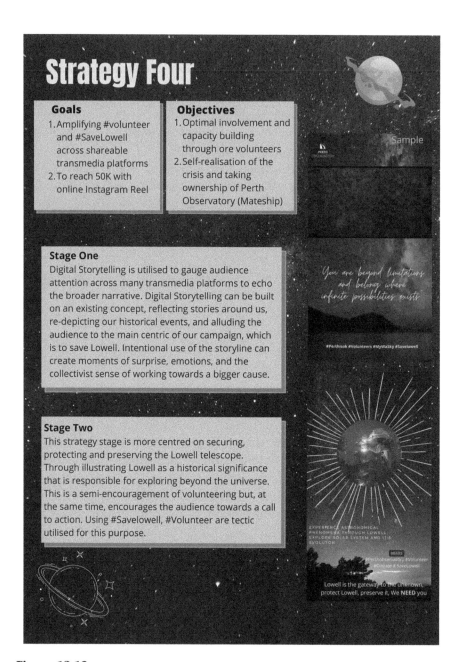

Figure 13.12

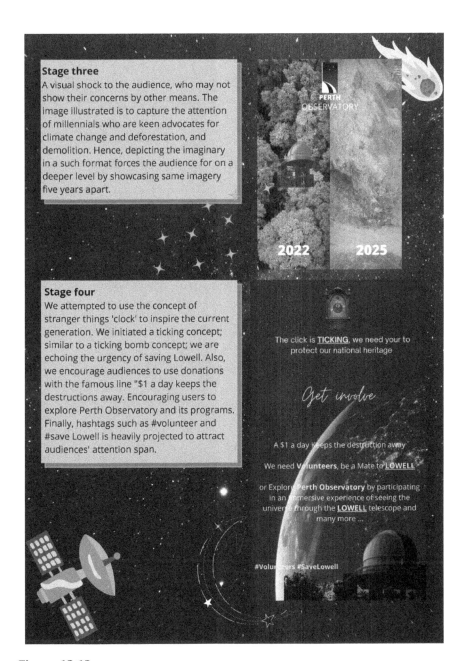

Stage three
A visual shock to the audience, who may not show their concerns by other means. The image illustrated is to capture the attention of millennials who are keen advocates for climate change and deforestation, and demolition. Hence, depicting the imaginary in a such format forces the audience for on a deeper level by showcasing same imagery five years apart.

PERTH OBSERVATORY

2022   2025

Stage four
We attempted to use the concept of stranger things 'clock' to inspire the current generation. We initiated a ticking concept; similar to a ticking bomb concept; we are echoing the urgency of saving Lowell. Also, we encourage audiences to use donations with the famous line "$1 a day keeps the destructions away. Encouraging users to explore Perth Observatory and its programs. Finally, hashtags such as #volunteer and #save Lowell is heavily projected to attract audiences' attention span.

The click is **TICKING**, we need your to protect our national heritage

Get involve

A $1 a day keeps the destruction away

We need **Volunteers**, be a Mate to **LOWELL**

or Explore **Perth Observatory** by participating in an immersive experience of seeing the universe through the **LOWELL** telescope and many more ...

#Volunteers #SaveLowell

Figure 13.13

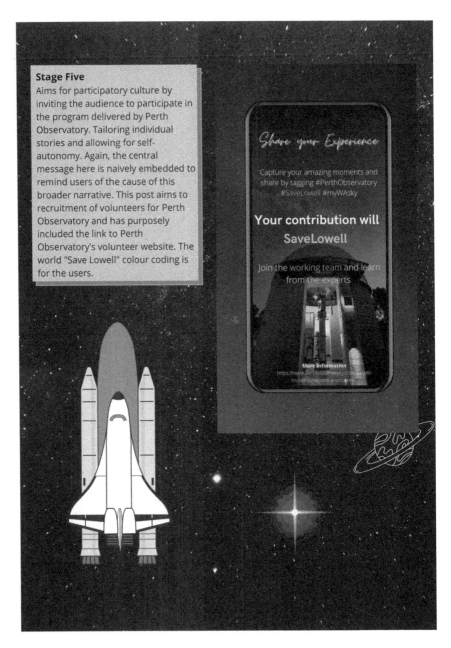

Figure 13.14

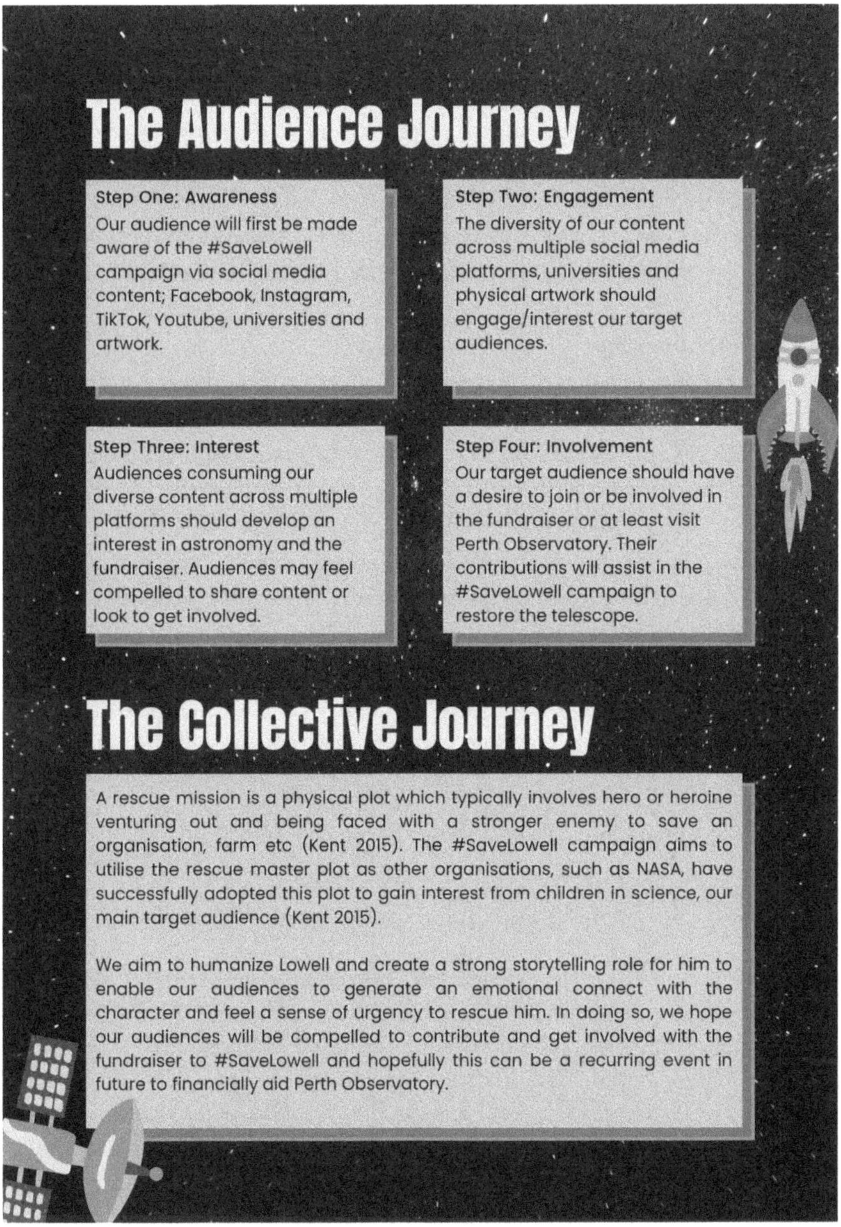

The Audience Journey

Step One: Awareness
Our audience will first be made aware of the #SaveLowell campaign via social media content; Facebook, Instagram, TikTok, Youtube, universities and artwork.

Step Two: Engagement
The diversity of our content across multiple social media platforms, universities and physical artwork should engage/interest our target audiences.

Step Three: Interest
Audiences consuming our diverse content across multiple platforms should develop an interest in astronomy and the fundraiser. Audiences may feel compelled to share content or look to get involved.

Step Four: Involvement
Our target audience should have a desire to join or be involved in the fundraiser or at least visit Perth Observatory. Their contributions will assist in the #SaveLowell campaign to restore the telescope.

The Collective Journey

A rescue mission is a physical plot which typically involves hero or heroine venturing out and being faced with a stronger enemy to save an organisation, farm etc (Kent 2015). The #SaveLowell campaign aims to utilise the rescue master plot as other organisations, such as NASA, have successfully adopted this plot to gain interest from children in science, our main target audience (Kent 2015).

We aim to humanize Lowell and create a strong storytelling role for him to enable our audiences to generate an emotional connect with the character and feel a sense of urgency to rescue him. In doing so, we hope our audiences will be compelled to contribute and get involved with the fundraiser to #SaveLowell and hopefully this can be a recurring event in future to financially aid Perth Observatory.

Figure 13.15

CONCLUSION

Perth Observatory is a scientific and technological hub serving the needs of Australia and international communities. Despite structural, economic and environmental challenges, Perth Observatory continues to provide some of the latest scientific developments. Perth Observatory has online interactions across multiple transmedia platforms, and our attempt to amplify awareness and the role of Perth Observatory has been detailed in this report. Perth Observatory's campaign objective of raising awareness, promoting and preserving the Lowell telescope is the central theme of this report.

This report has illustrated multiple uses of tools to showcase strategies and background research to meet the ongoing objectives of Perth Observatory. Website auditing and SWOT/PESTLE analysis clearly outline more significant strengths and ways of moving forward with Perth Observatory. The campaign has heavily utilised strategic digital storytelling to raise awareness and save the Lowell telescope. This campaign aims to bring the Australian communities towards shared ownership and responsibility for our historical legacy. The campaign aimed at raising AUD$500,000 and saving Lowell will hopefully be successful. We encourage the state government to be the leading body in investing in the innovation and technology space. We have new galaxy spaces yet to be explored, and with the help of the Lowell telescope, we could be a leading research body in the international community.

BIBLIOGRAPHY

Apollo.io (2022). *Perth Observatory – Leisure, Travel & Tourism – Overview, Competitors, and Employees*. [online] Available at: www.apollo.io/companies/Perth-Observatory/56d6bafcf3e5bb62cb001a4b?chart=count [Accessed 13 December 2022].

Australian Bureau of Statistics (2022a). 12 things that happened in the Australian economy in March quarter 2022. [online] *Australian Bureau of Statistics*. Available at: www.abs.gov.au/articles/12-things-happened-australian-economy-march-quarter-2022 [Accessed 13 December 2022].

Australian Bureau of Statistics (2022b). Monthly household spending indicator, July 2022. [online] *Australian Bureau of Statistics*. Available at: www.abs.gov.au/statistics/economy/finance/monthly-household-spending-indicator/jul-2022 [Accessed 13 December 2022].

Australian Charities and Not-for-Profits Commission (2022). Obligations to state and territory agencies. [online] *ACNC*. Available at: www.acnc.gov.au/for-charities/manage-your-charity/other-regulators/state-and-territory-regulators [Accessed 13 December 2022].

Australian Communities (2017). *Australian Community Trends Report*. [online] Available at: https://mccrindle.com.au/article/australian-community-trends-report/ [Accessed 13 December 2022].

Chesters, J. (2021). Funds for inspirational observatory. [online] *Perth Observatory*. Available at: www.perthobservatory.com.au/observatoryvolunteering/funds-for-inspirational-observatory [Accessed 13 December 2022].

Hall, S. (2022). Perth Observatory: What you need to know. [online] *Perth Is OK!* Available at: https://perthisok.com/explore/perth-observatory/ [Accessed 13 December 2022].

Kent, M.L. (2015). The power of storytelling in public relations: Introducing the 20 master plots. *Public Relations Review*, 41(4), 480–489. doi:10.1016/j.pubrev.2015.05.011.

Perth Observatory (2022). *Home*. [online] Available at: www.perthobservatory.com.au/wpcontent/uploads/strategic-plan-2020-30.pdf [Accessed 13 December 2022].

Index